The Made and the Found

Essays, Prose and Poetry in Honour of Michael Sheringham

LEGENDA

LEGENDA is the Modern Humanities Research Association's book imprint for new research in the Humanities. Founded in 1995 by Malcolm Bowie and others within the University of Oxford, Legenda has always been a collaborative publishing enterprise, directly governed by scholars. The Modern Humanities Research Association (MHRA) joined this collaboration in 1998, became half-owner in 2004, in partnership with Maney Publishing and then Routledge, and has since 2016 been sole owner. Titles range from medieval texts to contemporary cinema and form a widely comparative view of the modern humanities, including works on Arabic, Catalan, English, French, German, Greek, Italian, Portuguese, Russian, Spanish, and Yiddish literature. Editorial boards and committees of more than 60 leading academic specialists work in collaboration with bodies such as the Society for French Studies, the British Comparative Literature Association and the Association of Hispanists of Great Britain & Ireland.

The MHRA encourages and promotes advanced study and research in the field of the modern humanities, especially modern European languages and literature, including English, and also cinema. It aims to break down the barriers between scholars working in different disciplines and to maintain the unity of humanistic scholarship. The Association fulfils this purpose through the publication of journals, bibliographies, monographs, critical editions, and the MHRA Style Guide, and by making grants in support of research. Membership is open to all who work in the Humanities, whether independent or in a University post, and the participation of younger colleagues entering the field is especially welcomed.

ALSO PUBLISHED BY THE ASSOCIATION

Critical Texts
Tudor and Stuart Translations • *New Translations* • *European Translations*
MHRA Library of Medieval Welsh Literature

MHRA Bibliographies
Publications of the Modern Humanities Research Association

The Annual Bibliography of English Language & Literature
Austrian Studies
Modern Language Review
Portuguese Studies
The Slavonic and East European Review
Working Papers in the Humanities
The Yearbook of English Studies

www.mhra.org.uk
www.legendabooks.com

Micky Sheringham, by Bill Smock

The Made and the Found

Essays, Prose and Poetry in Honour of Michael Sheringham

Edited by
Patrick McGuinness and Emily McLaughlin

LEGENDA
Modern Humanities Research Association
2017

Published by Legenda
an imprint of the Modern Humanities Research Association
Salisbury House, Station Road, Cambridge CB1 2LA

ISBN 978-1-910887-17-2 (HB)
ISBN 978-1-78188-354-9 (PB)

First published 2017

Copy-Editor: Richard Correll

CONTENTS

PREFACE

This book of poems, prose and essays is a tribute to our friend and colleague Michael Sheringham. Micky himself had a large say in its conception, and from the beginning we discussed with him what form it might take. This is why it is the sort of book it is: a curious, border-crossing, genre-defying, analytical-creative homage *in kind* to someone who had all of those qualities in person and on the page. Micky was 'in on it' from the start, and we are glad that he was able to see a good portion of it before he died in January 2016.

What we have tried to present here is less a monument to Micky's scholarship (he made his own monuments, two of which — *Perpetual Motion* and *The Afterlives of Pierre Rivière: Foucault and the Archival Imaginary* — will appear in the coming year or so) than an expression of the very particular kind of thinker and critic he was. To do that, we had to think outside the parameters of *festschrifts* and 'Essays in honour of...', in order to take account of the friendships that Micky cultivated across the creative/critical divide. For him, of course, there is no divide, and this book arranges poems and prose pieces, critical essays and looser meditations in such a way as to reflect their fruitful coexistence.

Micky's career as an academic was unusual in that he combined the scholarly, the detailed and the rigorous with a happy tendency to go *off piste*: to allow himself to be drawn by what was accidental, unsystematic, eccentric and uncategorizable. As a writer, he was literary as well as scholarly: limpid writing and the pleasures of putting things well were not just felicities on the way to expressing ideas, but part of the point, part of the reason for doing it in the first place. Those of us who read *Devices and Desires* when it first came out (we were students then...), and those of us who read *Everyday Life* (by which time we were his colleagues), would have been struck by how Micky always gloried in the overspill of things, the way they leaked and mutated, the way one thing — a discipline, genre, a paradigm — segued into another, and the way he patiently parsed them and tracked them through their contortions in a prose that was both clear and full of enjoyment.

He was drawn to theories that cut between distinct areas of expertise (philosophy and urban planning, colour and subjectivity, zoology and ontology, fashion and freedom), to novels that were propelled by lengthy lists or encyclopedic citations, to poetic texts intercalated with photographs or scientific diagrams. He liked texts that, as they shifted between fiction and non-fiction, the visual and the verbal, prose and poetry, advertised the provisional nature of their organization, holding their form lightly or loosely, making us aware that the connections that we make between things continually expire and have to be continually recreated. The introductions to all his major projects stressed — whether he was writing on the self, the everyday, personal or collective memory — that his chosen subject was an indeterminate one, that he was trying to bring to consciousness the indistinct but omnipresent dynamics that are the essence of human experience before it gains definition, all that we often miss by virtue of being immersed in it. From one work to the next, he tracked the currents of exchange and tangential relationships that animate existence but are always on the margin of human awareness.

It was undoubtedly his rigorously pluralist approach that allowed him to bring these overlooked and undervalued aspects of human experience to life. He patiently analysed a series of different modes of intervention — 'projects', 'devices and desires', 'ruses', 'theories and practices', 'traversées du quotidien', 'legacies', 'uses of the archive' — and allowed his subject matter to emerge gradually from the gaps and interstices between these diverse techniques. This pluralism was his tacit but insistent *ethos*. It allowed him to approach his subject matter without diminishing its multiplicity or ambiguity; to appreciate that the vivacity of an individual life, a city street, or a historical moment was inseparable from its indeterminacy and its openness, its availability to new forms of interpretation. In *Everyday Life*, reflecting on Henri Lefebvre's writings, he observes 'critique is maieutic' 'it seeks to give birth to what is already there in embryo'. Micky was acutely aware as he wrote that he was activating something that was already given, that he was giving it a new lease of life, but that its vitality could only be respected if his interventions remained one of many possible 'births'. In this way, he managed to revitalize age-old *topoi* — the self, memory, everyday life — and he did so precisely because he allowed them to remain what they are or what they should be: a common good, accessible to all, inviting new modes of participation.

That is the Micky Sheringham of the page. Micky Sheringham in person was continuous with that: his contribution to what one might describe (pun intended) as the everyday life of his department, his college, and more expansively his discipline, was a reflection of the appetite for thinking things through and linking them up that we see in his books and articles. This book reflects this too, in the way it gathers together people from the worlds of poetry and criticism, both inside and outside the 'academy', who worked with Micky over the years. The book contains poems, prose pieces, essays, memoirs and items that have no special genre, but whose reasons for being as they are Micky would have understood implicitly and explained to the rest of us with his customary geniality.

We chose the title 'The Made and the Found' as a starting point that might catch something of these concerns: where does finding end and making begin? Are the two really so different after all? And aren't good writing and good teaching, like anything else that is enriching, about the moment that two merge and can no longer be told apart? About the moment in which critique reveals itself to be a creative or 'maieutic' process?

What we have tried to produce here, first in honour and now in memory of Micky Sheringham, is a reflection of him and his work, of his interests, his enthusiasms and his affections.

P.M., E.M.L., Oxford, March 2017

— 1 —

São Domingos, après l'incendie

Yves Bonnefoy

Est-ce encore une église? Ces colonnes
Ont vacillé dans l'étreinte du feu.
Rien que plâtre noirci ce que fut leur faîte.
Anges et fruits y ont fermé les yeux.
Et déserte est la nef. Une statue,
De sainte, à demi-nue, y veille seule.
Le feu sur elle aussi a fait son œuvre.
Dehors, pourtant, la ville, tout son bruit.
Qui désespère, qu'il entre ici, c'est plus qu'un dieu
Cet absolu qui erra dans la flamme.
Ce fut presque de l'être, ce vent qui prit
Dans la calcination d'une lumière.
Aimez ce sanctuaire, mes amis,
Quand se dénouent les signes, c'est presque l'aube.

São Domingos, After the Fire

Is it still a church? These columns
Have wavered in the fire's embrace.
Their summits are but blackened plaster now,
Where angels and fruits have closed their eyes.
And the nave is deserted. Half-nude, the statue
Of a saint keeps her vigil here alone.
On her, the fire has also done its work.
Outside, even so, the city with all its noise.
Whoever despairs should enter here: this absolute
That wandered in the flame was more than a god.
This wind was almost being, as it burned
In the calcination of a light.
Love this sanctuary, my friends:
When signs unravel, it's almost dawn.

— *translated by Hoyt Rogers*

— 2 —

Cairo Creole

Marina Warner

In twentieth-century Egypt, when Michael Sheringham's mother Yvette was growing up in Cairo, the Coptic community to which she belonged and the circles in which she moved spoke French among themselves. Many other languages — Turkish, Farsi, Italian, Greek, Ladino — were also part of the lingua franca of the several different communities living together there at the time. But complex snobberies twisted attitudes to Arabic itself, a dismal state of affairs which has, needless to say, inflicted deep scars. Edward Saïd remembers meeting a tennis coach in the United States, who was of Arab descent, had lived in Cairo, and spoke Arabic; Said tried to engage him in their shared mother tongue, only to be hushed: 'No brother, no Arabic here. I left all that behind when I came to America.'[1]

The discomfort of the immigrant speaking the mother tongue is one thing; at home it is a more humiliating prejudice, inculcated by the 'masters', absorbed in turn by the 'subalterns' (Caliban says, 'You taught me language and my profit on't | Is I know how to curse'). In Egypt, the issue became much sharper as the old powers lost their grip and Arabophone nationalists grew in strength. When the new young king Farouk succeeded his father in 1936, he was welcomed with immense hope and joy because he was the first ruler of Egypt who spoke Arabic as his mother tongue, and the dismal disillusionment of his reign was exacerbated when he failed to live up to this patriotic promise. As an early sign of the changing times, after the coup of the Free Officers under the leadership of Gamel Abdel Nasser in 1952, French was banned for official business of any kind and Arabic established in its place.

My parents left Cairo that year, after my father's bookshop was burned down in the uprising. They also spoke French when they went about in society, while I, left at home in the block of flats where we lived, picked up Arabic (of a kind, a childish kind) in the playground, and spoke it with my nanny, who came from Upper Egypt, and from the suffragi, the butler figure; later, after we left Egypt, everyone agreed it was important to keep up my French (stays with French families, the *Cours des étrangers* at the Sorbonne) but nobody gave a thought to my Arabic. So I forgot it — though the sound of it still gives me odd waves of happiness, as if I were back in the souk with the almond and honey sweets my nanny would give me. At home, my parents spoke to each other in English — and sometimes in Italian (my mother's mother tongue). Their English, however, was liberally sprinkled with Gallicisms: this use of French terms was intended to add class; it included words for social structures and types (*bourgeois*, *le gratin*, *le beau monde*), for nuances of character and occupation (*voyou, soubrette, aventurier, demi-mondaine, grande horizontale*); it made snobbishness sound sophisticated, and naturalized it by setting its dictates in the language of urban, enlightenment culture, gilded by association with Paris, the metropole of taste and *savoir faire*. In this dandyish macaronic which my parents adopted — until my mother's death eight years ago, she would still say, disapprovingly, 'Oh, she suffers from such *nostalgie de la boue*', or, more enviously, 'She's a *jolie-laide* but still, she has a *je ne sais quoi...*') — I can now read, as if in a faded and stained etiquette manual (*etiquette* itself being one of these French terms) a whole world of relations and values (*comme il faut, noblesse oblige, de rigueur, convenances, gout* — and *nuances* themselves).[2] *Placement*, a word which still survives for seating guests around a dinner table, carries the traces of the social sensitivities of this lexicon. So does *gaffe*. Certain characters who possessed *allure* also attracted French expressions: *à la mode, chic, soignée, distingué/e, raffiné/e, correcte, bien dans sa peau, en beauté, haut ton, bon ton, mignon/ne, gamin/e*; this conferred on them covetable privileges which gave them permission to behave in certain ways, ways that were fervently envied, while others were to be mocked at best, shunned at worst (*arriviste, parvenu, louche, outré, richissime, nouveau riche, declassé* or simply, with a look down the nose, *nouveau*). My father loved Proust, but chiefly as a guide to social niceties and the rich comic contretemps they brought about — in the book and in the world.

Trop prononcé was a favourite phrase — especially for women with opinions. The language of love also adopted certain proverbial turns of phrase, of course (*cherchez la femme*), but this was not dominant in the exchanges that have stayed with me from Cairo and its creole. Yet, at the same time, the structure built by the vocabulary was subject to a subtle distancing, as if the pageant were always a little absurd, the foreign lingo serving to italicize the concepts, to deliver them with an ironic shrug, with a little *moue*, in a spirit of *insouciance* mixed with *hauteur*, and a *bef! paf! enfin, bref, ouf!* She's a little *plantureuse*. He's rather *rastaquouère*. French was a *façon de parler*.

Any such glossary of class freighting, however, should begin with that adage, *noblesse oblige*, as it provided the fundamental ethical principle of my upbringing, invoked by both my father and my mother whenever they weren't themselves keen on doing something. Although I wouldn't have expressed or grasped it as such when I was young, the repetition of the phrase raised my rebellious hackles, provoked my teenage sulks, and made me quarrel with my father again and again.

Until just the other day, when I began thinking about what it meant, and realized that I had misunderstood it all along, and that the meaning is even more complacent. I'd heard *oblige* as transitive — that is, 'nobility is obliging' — and I resisted indignantly the condescension in this. But *noblesse oblige* doesn't mean that; it doesn't evoke an action towards another, but applies only to the subject: nobility requires something of the person who is 'noble'; nobility entails responsibilities; the speaker is presuming nobility on his/her own behalf and is regretting, vaingloriously, that this involves responsibilities.

This phrase made a claim based on class affiliations which I wanted to delete from my own family's sense of itself. But the motto also embarrassed me because

I wasn't at all convinced that my family could make such a claim (in this sense the snobbery of it all was coiling me into its premises). This parlance that my southern Italian mother adopted turned her into an impersonator, a foreigner posing as an insider. Yet women enjoyed more licence to practise this form of social ventriloquy than men: a wife could pass, as it were, when a man might be viewed askance as an impostor. A class infiltrator. Not rich and successful enough, perhaps, to be labelled *parvenu* or *nouveau*, but still not entitled. The French phrase, adopted as different from native parlance, was part of a role, a kind of fancy dress.

'*Rastaquouère*' was one of my father and mother's favourites, as I mentioned, used on and off to brand an acquaintance or a friend, uttered with relish at the scandalous nature of the individual in question. It didn't sound quite like other French words, but it belonged on the same spectrum of meaning as other derogatory but somehow seductive terms — with *poète maudit*, *raté*, *négligé*, *enfant terrible*, *monstre sacré*. It evoked piratical, scapegrace, much-travelled men, steeped in self-delusion, living on the edge of respectability, often only just this side of the law, unpredictable, morally dangerous, and with an unreliable relationship to credit. Scoundrels. Women couldn't be *rastaquouères*.[3] Such men were always handsome, with a tendency towards sexual unscrupulousness.

Current French–English dictionaries, I see now, give 'flashy foreigner' as the definition.[4] *Le Petit Larousse* offers 'a stranger living in grand style whose means of existence are not known'. Francis Picabia, who in 1920 published an exuberantly outrageous Dada rant called *Jésus-Christ Rastaquouère*, thought God qualified.[5] Today Wikipédia glosses '*rastaquouère*' as 'un personnage exotique étalant un luxe suspect et de mauvais gout,' and goes on to state that in the 1880s it was used to stigmatize a parvenu, and has come to be synonymous with a gigolo. The word is derived, it is thought, from Spanish/Portuguese for *rastrar* (scrape) and *cueros* (hides), and was contemptuously used of Argentinians and Brazilians who had prospered in the skin trade, arrived in Paris for the Exposition Universelle of 1889 and, spending freely, arrayed in splendiferous jewels and clothes, made a splash (in Portuguese *rastacüeros* are closer to poor 'good-for-nothings').[6] But the *rastaquouères* whom my father knew — and who always provoked him to chuckle richly with delight at their delinquencies — were English-born; unlike himself, however, they were glamorous, often subtly 'Oriental'. One such was an old school friend, always called 'the Burglar' behind his back because, a penniless descendant of fallen gentry, he had sailed for America to make his fortune, and on board the ocean liner met an heiress and was mysteriously able to present her with a magnificent engagement ring. His exploits provided my father and his friends with endless entertainment — they speculated that since Ian Fleming, another school chum, remained a close friend of the Burglar's, his hero James Bond had assumed some of his charms — and his methods.

II

The word itself when spoken in English resonates with a sound cluster from the basic stem *ra-*, which also gives *rascal* and *rapscallion*, *rackety* and *raffish*, rabid and rank (strong-smelling), *rattle* and *roar*; *hurrah* and *ra-ra* reverberate on the outer rings of these chords. In French today, it's also usually shortened to *rasta*, as Picabia had done when he coined *rastadada* in the titles of paintings he made in 1920.[7] But as *rasta* it overlaps with — on no etymological basis whatsoever — a wholly distinct cultural milieu, the Rastafarians and, by happy acoustic conjunction, it now radiates Bob Marley's sacred aura.

Stéphane Mallarmé was another poet who was also fascinated by possible connections between words' sounds and with their meanings, working sometimes through simple onomatopoeia but not always. In his long and very strange essay *Les Mots anglais* (1877), Mallarmé gathers together aural clusters and speculates on their semantic aptness — the slitheriness of 'snake', the dampness of 'damp'. He was especially attracted to the associations of body parts; this is another form of language logic: sn- sounds, for example, belong to the nose, and give words like 'sniff' and 'snot' and 'snore'; gr- expressions to the throat, as in 'gruff', 'groan', 'growl' and 'grumble'. On words beginning with R, he comments on the letter's closeness to L, then glosses the sound, 'finally, through onomatopoeia, a tearing (*déchirure*), and following from the importance of the letter, something radical...' He includes in his list of words 'romp, rouse, ramble, rap, rack, ratch [*sic*, for ratchet], rife, raid, rap, rock' and, in a further list 'rabble, rash, raw, rend, roar, rush, run, rustle, roll, rot and rumble.'[8]

Although Mallarmé's dense acoustic chains have little purchase on linguisticians' interests now (not that they ever had much), they make their own peculiar music, striking notes that are surprisingly well-tuned to the trailing sound associations of *rastaquouère*. I think it's possible to hear in the word itself how the rackety roaring boy meets the queer fish — in a satisfying, unconscious translingual sensory conjunction.

Picabia's use of nonsense music in his Dadaist phase and Mallarmé's earlier curiosity in sound-sense conjunctions, have a little-known and most entertaining precursor: the polyglot *belle lettriste*, long-serving translator for Christian missionaries, journalist, dragoman, philologist, publisher, lexicographer, and novelist Ahmad Faris al-Shidyak. Shidyak was born a Maronite in Syria (now Lebanon) in 1805 or 1806, and died a Muslim convert in Cairo in 1887; he spent most of his life on the move, travelling throughout the Middle East and visiting Europe, including Paris, and London, Oxford and Cambridge, where he worked on the oriental collections of manuscripts, and dangled after a university chair. He is also the author of an exuberant fiction, called *Leg over Leg*, published in Paris in 1855, written in response to 'Frankish' literature, as he called the European tradition.[9]

Leg over Leg braids together many genres: memoir, sexual confession, travel journal, diatribe, satire — as well as digressions within digressions investigating the properties and richness of Arabic. Shidyak is a lexicographical virtuoso, funny, obscene, lively, heartfelt, and he brandishes his immense vocabulary as a gonfalonier waves the huge colourful banner of the clan on which a fantastic animal is emblazoned. Anticipating Mallarmé's philological interests (the French poet was gathering the material for *Les Mots anglais* twenty years after *Leg over Leg*), Shidyak dedicates many pages of bravura wit to the unpromising topic of Arabic lexicography and grammar. In wild improvisatory passages, much of his vocabulary is so particular it can't be transposed into English even by the unsurpassable ingenuity of Shidyak's translator, Humphrey Davies. As a result certain pages of his work present a poetic, blended language, a kind of new creole in which the words' original music resonate for the reader: '...there are also different varieties of love, such as *sababah*, which is love and longing in their most delicate form; *gharam*, which is love as surrender; *huyam*, which is insanity born of passion; *jawa*, which is the love one holds inside oneself; *shawq*, which is the struggle with the self; *tawaqan*, which means the same; *wajd*, which is the affection the lover receives from the beloved person (by which I mean, again, of course, the beloved woman); *kalaf*, which is craving; *shaghaf*, which is what happens when love reaches the pericardium, which is to say the tissue that enwraps the heart or the fat that surrounds it or the kernel or core of it; *sha'af*, which is when love coats the *sha'afah* of the heart, which is the top of it, where the aorta is attached, or *sh'af*, which means the same; and *tadlih*, which is then one loses one's mind from love...' After this torrential single sentence paragraph (I have only quoted a bit of it) comes to a stop, Shidyak adds tartly, 'This contrasts with the languages of the non-Arabs, in which there is only one word meaning love, which they apply to Creator and created alike.'[10]

Shidyak's unique work bears on the question of foreign jargons or creoles in another way. It's irresistible to identify qualities in Shidyak of writers he could not have yet read, such as James Joyce, but he also invites comparison from people he could have read, and he was certainly influenced by the writers he had read, including Sterne and Flaubert. He is often Swiftian in his mordancy and hyperbole, frankness and misanthropy. He also burlesques his own preoccupations: on grammar, his great love, he riffs absurdly in this passage, where he returns to the question of sound sense, here rendered by the dauntless Davies:

> Certain scholars have said that metaphors may be divided into [and] ... sub-divided into the aeolian, the ornitho-sibilant, the feebly chirping, the tongue-smacking, the faintly tinkling, the bone-snapping, the emptily thunderous, and the phasmic, while the aeolian itself may be sub-divided into the stridulaceous, the crepitaceous, and the oropharyngeal, the crepitaceous may be sub-sub-divided into the absquiliferous, the vulgaritissimous, the exquipilifabulous, the seborrhaceous [etc. etc.] ...the anal-resonatory, the oro-phlebo-evacuative, the capro-audio-lactative...'[11]

I shan't give the notes of the translator to each one of the terms in Arabic, except his general comment that 'the nomenclature leaves the realm of reality and devolves into a series of fanciful and bizarre-sounding terms based largely on onomatopoeia... or, toward the end of the list, on hapax legomena known only from a single line of ancient verse...'[12]

This first translation into English, accompanying the first meticulous edition of the original Arabic text, will help change some of the simple ignorance that underlies the underappreciated status of Arabic and its literature today.

III

In a recent, fascinating study called *Rastaquarium: Marcel Proust et le 'modern style'*, the literary scholar of orientalism, Sophie Basch, applies *rastaquouère* characteristics to a crucial, distinctive sphere of the *fin de siècle*; her play on words takes a leap, however, and attaches the term to aesthetics, and specifically to the bizarre, aquatic obsessions of late nineteenth- and early twentieth-century decorative arts. While art nouveau effloresced with terrestrial forms, burgeoning into luscious fruit and flowers, leaves and grasses, its offshoot, *le 'modern style'* transformed interiors into mysterious sea-caves, covering wallpapers and fabrics, street furnishings and theatre sets, book bindings and fashionable apparel with marine wonders — seaweed, jellyfish, polyps and octopus, crustaceans, shells, sea anemones et al. *Rastaquouère* style, as evoked by Basch, gives this *'modern style'* a distinctive, even grotesque strangeness: it was intended to be mixed, impure, monstrous, and was received as such by admirers and detractors.

English was the idiom used in the phrase 'modern style' because Maple's was one of the innovatory suppliers, as Liberty's was of *le style Liberty*. But the use in French of the foreign expression does something more: it again helps to exoticize the idiom of the design — to estrange it. After the invention of bathyspheres and underwater photography, the world beneath the sea beckoned as a zone of supreme, undiscovered mystery — twilit, surprising, inhabited by rare, monstrous creatures, irreducibly alien and fascinating. The aquarium was a prime Surrealist realm of *le merveilleux*, explored by the film-maker Jean Painlevé, who turned underwater documentary into a new artistic genre when he recorded the doings of hermit crabs, octopus, and seahorses; his films count among the weirdest and most wonderful examples of the Surrealist quest for convulsive beauty.[13] Paul Valéry and Roger Caillois, amongst others, joined in these marine mysteries.

Basch has identified two sources for the word *rastaquarium*: Willy (Henri Gauthier-Villars) claimed to have made it up,[14] but more significantly, she traces it back to a journalist who became a Dreyfusard.[15] Her inquiry opens up a field of inquiry into Proust, taste, foreigners in general, and specifically anti-Semitism and the Dreyfus crisis. It seems to me that her view of the '*rastaquarium*' intersects uncomfortably with my parents' usage of the category *rastaquouère*, and the combination of deep prejudice and envious admiration which she diagnoses reflects their attitudes. They would absolutely recognize the elements of exoticism, luxury, aesthetics and fantasy (it's a coincidence that 'the Burglar' built a beach house in the Bahamas; it was a crescent-shaped pavilion made of coral and mother-of-pearl, and the bed was a four-poster of narwhal tusks). Just as giving up English in favour of French added tone to conversation, sparkle to wit, so *le style rastaquouère*, usually combined with a dash of performative fancy dress, offered a way of self-fashioning that singled someone out from the crowd.

Basch presses more deeply into the politics of strangeness on home ground, as it were. In Paris, as reflected in Proust's novel, upholders of tradition who loathed the new aesthetic also deplored the defence of Dreyfus: she writes, 'la condamnation du "modern style" par le duc et la duchesse de Guermantes comme par Charlus est une facette de leur antidreyfusisme.... L'Art nouveau, perturbateur des schémas nationaux, agent du socialisme, du cosmopolitisme judéo-belge et les Ballets russes qui reflètent tous les courants, trahissent la tradition comme le capitaine Dreyfus la Nation.'[16]

In the British empire, the *rastaquouère* aesthetic also sets rippling conflicting emotions; fear and curiosity — and repressed identification — grew differently from xenophobia and anti-Semitism at home.

Colonists who deliberately adopt local dress, reject the generally accepted tribal marks of identity and 'go native' have not been much explored, but the stratagem, used by many scholars and artists, has been recognized. By contrast, David Cannadine has explored the central place of mimetic fancy dress in the empire. In his witty and polemical study, *Ornamentalism*, he observes how Viceroys and High Commissioners were not to be outdone by local maharajahs or tribal chieftains in their panoply and splendour, and British court dress and military uniforms sprouted feathers and furs, and gleamed with gold and jewels, festoons and sashes and galloons.[17] And yet, even while no less a figure of grand respectability than Lord Mountbatten arrayed himself in gems and feathers, the whiff of something faintly ridiculous — and something a little *rasta* — clings about these bedizened figures of power. In 1938, in her furious essay, *Three Guineas*, Virginia Woolf denounces male peacockery as a display of unearned prerogatives and male authority, but her shafts also tilt at the indecency of such self-pleased exhibitionism. There is something absurd, yes, but also something not quite *comme il faut* about all these jewels and feathers, braid and enamel and gold. When John Singer Sargent's tremendous portrait of the colonial administrator Sir Frank Swettenham (1850–1946) inspired Rebecca West to comment that 'he looked as if he wasn't quite a gentleman', was she showing her sensitivity to the excess of his display? To the unfurling, regal brocade drapery behind him (from his collection of Malayan fabrics), the swagger of his hand on his swivelling hip, the sheen of his white uniform and the grandiose hauteur of his whole mien?[18]

IV

The most ornamental fellow of All Souls, Oxford, in the pantheon hanging on the walls of the Coffee Room, was an early servant of imperial interests abroad, an orientalist and a sophisticated traveller. Charles Augustus Murray (1806–1895), elected a Fellow of the college at the age of 21, in 1827, turns out, on inquiry, to be a specially strong candidate for a niche — a grotto? — in the rastaquarium. His long life is almost unbelievably colourful, packed with adventures out of the yarns of imperialist derring-do by Rider Haggard, G. H. Henty, and John Buchan.[19]

Murray was born a younger son in a web of powerful and rich aristocratic connections; he was a classical scholar, gifted at acquiring languages (he read

Portrait of Charles Augustus Murray by Willis Maddox, *c.*1850, by kind permission of the Warden and Fellows of All Souls College

and spoke fifteen, the DNB tells us), became a diplomat and embarked on his tumultuous life, which carried him to the United States, where he lived among Pawnee Indians, and later, to the Middle and Near East, where after some trouble over a highly placed woman, his embassy seems to have been the cause of the first Anglo-Persian war. The DNB entry mentions Murray's charms no less than twice in what is not a very long account.[20]

The portrait in All Souls (hanging first on the left on the walls of the Coffee Room), testifies to an exceptional dress sense of a rather orchidaceous kind, very much in the footsteps of his great-grandfather, William Beckford.[21] The author of *Vathek*, connoisseur bibliophile and eccentric aesthete, became known as 'the Sultan of Fonthill', and was notorious for the theatricality of his Gothic home, Fonthill Abbey, where the temple-height front doors were opened by a dwarf footman in order to accentuate the spectacle. Murray knew him well when he was a child, and Willis Maddox, the artist who painted his portrait, was a young protégé of Beckford's.[22] However, William Beckford himself, in spite of his orientalist passions, never travelled in the east. By contrast, his descendant became consul-general in Egypt from 1846–1853, where he made friends with the ruler, Mohammed Ali, and with whom he arranged the construction of the railway line linking Cairo to Alexandria. Murray's studied self-presentation, in every detail deliberately Orientalist, may well be an act of homage to his forebear's notorious theatricality.[23]

Murray is posing in an Ottoman interior, wearing a luxurious striped silk *robe de chambre*, seated on silk cushions. The tasselled cane — or is it a staff of office? — the loosely knotted cravat with a large jewel in the pin, the index finger carefully crooked in a gesture like a baroque court dancing master beginning to make a *révérence*, add to the exotic *mise en scène*.[24] It is likely the sitting took place in Egypt, and Murray may indeed have invited Maddox out to the Middle East when he was in post as consul-general; the artist was travelling in the Levant in the period and, soon after making Murray's portrait, died aged forty of a fever in Pera, Constantinople, in 1853. A Cairene location would also explain a disturbing and crucial element in Maddox's portrait, which greatly complicates the seductive *rasta* aura. I thought at first that the figure on Murray's right just behind him was a sculpture, a prize collectible of the mid-century, such as one of the busts of Moors that were carved in polychromatic marbles by Charles Cordier.[25] On a closer look, however, I realized this figure was not an effigy, but a real child posing like a slave in oriental costume. This young boy doesn't look altogether alive because he's standing very stiffly in attendance, keeping his gaze lowered, the mien of deference.

In Cordier's sculptures the North African men and women whose portraits he is preserving stand alone, often magnificent. But Murray has staged a social spectacle of hierarchy and erasure — nearly two decades after Abolition. Abroad, playing the foreigner could give access to other traditions no longer countenanced at home; affecting a foreign, *rastaquouère*, aesthetic style might issue a defiant defence of cosmopolitanism in the metropole; elsewhere, it could turn into *çi-devant* nostalgia.

V

In 1849, Murray achieved his greatest claim to fame, when he captured a baby hippo for the London Zoo. Wilfrid Blunt describes the melancholy circumstances, which interestingly echo the opening of *Babar the Elephant*, when Babar loses his mother: 'A posse of hunters set out for the White Nile. On the island of Obaysch, they came upon, and mortally wounded, a large female hippopotamus. The dying animal was observed to be struggling towards some bushes growing beside the river bank. This heroic gesture defeated its object, which was to rescue her infant; for one

Obaysch at London Zoo, photographed by
Don Juan, Comte de Montizón, in 1852

of the hunters, following her tracks, soon caused the youngster to break cover and then gaffed it with a boat-hook as it was about to enter the water.'[26] The delighted consul-general in Cairo took delivery of the 'little monster' and, the following May, arranged for the animal's passage to London, in a boat specially equipped with a pool. Two former snake-charmers were hired to attend him, alongside his keeper who had looked after him from the time of his capture.

Named 'Obaysch' after the place where he was hunted, this was the first hippo to be transported from the animals' native habitat to Europe, and his appearance caused a sensation. Visitors flocked to the London zoo to see him — numbers doubled the year he arrived. There were no less than five royal visitations. There was a brief craze for a dance, 'The Hippopotamus Polka'. As a result of his gift to the nation, the consul-general in Cairo became known as 'Hippopotamus Murray'.

After Cairo, we went to live in Brussels, and there I began reading Tintin — Hergé was a kind of national treasure in Belgium, and I can't recall if my parents ever discussed him or expressed a view on my enthusiasm for his adventures. Tintin himself, Milou his little dog, the endearingly vague professor Calculus, the explosive capitaine Haddock with his wild torrents of expletive, the Tweedledum and Tweedledee scientists Thomson and Thompson and above all the locales (Caribbean piracy, the pyramids, Aztec human sacrifice, Andean sun worship) gripped me, made me laugh and gasp and keep reading. When I've worried, as I often have in the past, that my colonial background and the adventure yarns of the empire have corrupted my mind, when I've looked at my appetite for exotic places and highly coloured language, I forgot how crucial Tintin was in this story. Tintin has an arch-enemy, whom I had completely deleted from the files of my memory. Until Sophie Basch prompted me, I had forgotten that the villain in the books is called Roberto Rastapopoulos, and that he first makes an appearance as a principal character in *Cigars of the Pharaoh* (1934)[27] and expands into full blooded villainy in another Orientalist adventure, *The Blue Lotus*. The story opens on a cruise ship called M.S. Isis which has docked in Egypt, and on board Tintin comes upon Rastapopoulos as he is physically abusing the Egyptologist, Sophocles Sarcophagus. Tintin recognizes Rastapopoulos, commenting that he is 'the millionaire film tycoon, king of Cosmos Pictures'. The tycoon's private yacht is called the Scheherazade, and a fancy dress ball is being held on it the night of one of the most dastardly crimes Tintin withstands.

Rastapopoulos's appearance accords with many cartoon images of Jews, the stuff of Nazi propaganda. Hergé protested that the character wasn't Jewish and that he himself wasn't anti-Semitic, but readers' doubts have not been laid to rest. Hergé reworked his own opinions and writings over and over, as his interpreters have carefully tracked, but 'despite these careful rejiggings, Hergé's sense of guilt keeps pulsing through'.[28] Roberto Rastapopoulos, Marquis di Gorgonzola, is strongly coloured Italian and Greek, but these — wonderfully absurdist — handles of the comic villain serve as a form of disguise, adopted by a personality capable of infinite deceptions, a figure of many wiles, *polytropos*, and many faces. In a similar fashion, the whole concept of the *rastaquouère*, of whom Hergé's enemy is a prime example, thrives on the exclusionary tactics of a social group, identifying itself against the stranger, the foreigner, the outsider while avoiding disclosing open racist or anti-Semitic feelings.

I began thinking about the word *rastaquouère* because I wondered why my mother and father loved this odd-sounding epithet, and I wanted to explore something that Michael Sheringham and I shared, an Egyptian background of a sort. I knew there was nothing particularly relevant to Micky's literary interests or indeed, his own style, but he was so interested in the byways of the everyday, in which parlance plays such a crucial part. We often spoke about Francophone writers from the Maghreb and he was marvellously generous and perceptive, as always. The word has led me in an unexpected dance very far from Micky's own fine sensibility, but I think that through the tensions between rejection and imitation, its layers catch something about times past.

A variant of this essay appeared under the title, 'Anglo-Egyptian Attitudes' in the *London Review of Books* in 2017; I am very grateful to Mary Kay Wilmers and her team for comments and for permission to reproduce it here; it will eventually become part of a work-long-in-progress, *Inventory of a Life Mislaid*, inspired by the years 1947–52 when I lived with my parents in Cairo.

Notes

1. Abdelfattah Kilito comments on this passage: 'We are in the presence of a phenomenon, which may be summarized thus: I will not speak my language. I will never speak it because I am ashamed of it. I am ashamed of Arabic and of the Arabs. Let us note here that Mr. Alexander interrupted Said, raising his right hand. He interrupted him by word and gesture, a defensive gesture, as if he was warding off an attack or uttering an oath — I swear not to speak Arabic and not let you speak it either. The expected outcome was not only did he avoid Said this time, but he would also treat him with contempt after that. Said recounts this incident in his book, *Reflections on Exile and Other Essays* (2000). It must have affected him and stayed on his mind since he recounts it as well in some detail in *Out of Place*.' See Abdelfattah Kilito, 'A Portrait of the Intellectual as Porter', trans. by Mohamed-Salah Omri, in A Journey of Ideas Across: In Dialogue with Edward Saïd, <http://journeyofideasacross.hkw.de/between-places-al-muthanna-and-undermining-dichotomies/abdelfattah-kilito.html> [accessed 1 September 2016].
2. Alison Finch, 'Aesthetic Form and Social Form in *A la Recherche du temps perdu*: Proust on Taste', paper given at the conference 'What Forms Can Do: Attending to the Real in 20th and 21st century French Literature', held in honour of Michael Sheringham at All Souls, Oxford, 11–13 January 2016, in which she reflected very richly on the multiple appearances of the word '*gout*' in the novel, and its many nuances.
3. Sophie Basch has identified two exceptions: Rachel and Sarah Bernhardt. See her *Rastaquarium: Marcel Proust et le 'modern style': arts décoratifs et politique dans 'A la recherche du temps perdu'* (Turnhout: Brepols, 2014), p. 171.
4. 'Rastaquouère', in *Oxford Dictionaries*, <http://www.oxforddictionaries.com/translate/french-english/rastaquouere> [accessed 1 September 2016].
5. Sarah Hayden, '*Jésus-Christ Rastaquouère:* Francis Picabia's Anti-Art Anti-Christ', *The Irish Journal of French Studies*, 13 (2013), 41–67; Frances Richard, 'I am a beautiful monster', <http://www.bookforum.com/inprint/014_03/878>. Picabia also made a Tableau Rastadada the same year.
6. Silviano Santiago, 'The Cosmopolitanism of the Poor', trans. by M. Edwards and Paulo Horta, in *Cosmopolitan Ideas*, forthcoming. He quotes from Gilberto Amado, *Mocidade no Rio e Primeira viagem a Europa* [Youth in Rio and First Voyage to Europe] (1956), in which the contrast lies between the outsider's lack of polish and French *gout*: 'I began, naturally, to be delighted by the masterworks of French cuisine. I raised my already reasonable aptitude for opining knowingly, and not approximately, like a *rastaqüero* or *meteco*, on these matters of sauces and condiments.'
7. See Hayden, p. 41, note 1.
8. Stéphane Mallarmé, *Les Mots anglais*, in Stéphane Mallarmé, *Œuvres complètes*, ed. by Bertrand Marchal, 2 vols (Paris: Gallimard, 2003), II, 958–59.
9. Ahmad Faris al-Shidyak, *Leg over Leg*, ed. and trans. by Humphrey Davies, 4 vols, Library of Arabic Literature (New York: New York University Press, 2015).
10. Shidyak, *Leg over Leg*, I, 156–57.
11. Shidyak, I, 166–69.
12. Shidyak, I, 337, note 194.
13. Jean Painlevé, *La Pieuvre* (1928); *Bernard-L'hermite* (1930); *L'Hippocampe* (1934).
14. Basch, p. 171. See *Les Histoires les plus spirituelles de Willy* (Paris: Nabu Press, 2011), p.60. Basch dates it, on the grounds of typography, to circa 1915.

15. Georges Maurevert, *L'Art, le boulevard et la vie* (Nice and Paris: N. Chini –H.Floury, 1911), p. 331. Maurevert had worked on Drumont's *La Libre parole* but changed his views. See Basch, p. 171.
16. Basch, p 153.
17. David Cannadine, *Ornamentalism: How the British Saw their Empire* (Oxford: Oxford University Press, 2001).
18. Painted in 1904, and in the National Portrait Gallery collection. See Alison Smith, David Brown and Carol Jacobi, *Artist and Empire: New Dynamics* (London: Tate Publishing, 2015).
19. The DNB records that, when he had been gated, Murray made a bet that he could spend a day in London and return to Oxford in time; he and a friend then 'rode to London, changed their clothes, mounted two hacks and rode in the park, dined at a club, saw the first act of a play, and were back at the gate of Oriel three minutes before midnight. They had relays of horses at Henley and Maidenhead.' Sir Herbert Maxwell, *The Honourable Sir Charles Murray, K.C.B.: A Memoir* (Edinburgh and London: William Blackwood and sons, 1898), pp. 58–60; and H. E. Maxwell and Rev. H. C. G. Matthew, 'Murray, Sir Charles Augustus (1806–1895)', *Oxford Dictionary of National Biography* <http://www.oxforddnb.com/view/article/19596> [accessed 1 July 2014].
20. At the beginning, he is described as 'a very handsome and charming young man with a strong interest in literature, and an excellent classical scholar, [who] formed many friendships with people distinguished in both fields.' And again, later, towards the end: 'His charming manner, immense and varied store of reminiscences, and strikingly handsome appearance combined to make him a very well-known figure in society' (Maxwell and Matthew, *Oxford Dictionary of National Biography*).
21. Another copy is kept in the National Portrait Gallery: *Charles Augustus Murray* by George Zobel, published by Paul and Dominic Colnaghi & Co, after Willis (Willes) Maddox, mezzotint, 1 July 1853.
22. Beckford commissioned Maddox to paint the *objets de vertu* in Beckford's last home, the Lansdown tower, Bath, which he built to be his mausoleum. When Beckford died in 1844, Maddox also painted him laid out in state on his Napoleonic bed.
23. Murray also followed in Beckford's literary footsteps: before he became a specialist in oriental affairs, he wrote a two-volume, lightly fictionalized account of his adventures among American Indians, *The Prairie-Bird* (1844) which includes the tragic story of his forbidden love for an heiress (her father disapproved — no doubt he sensed the *rastaquouère* beneath the charm of the young English aristocrat). Murray continued to write throughout his long life — though he's even more forgotten as an author than he is as a diplomat. (I seem to be the very first member of the London Library to borrow a copy of *The Prairie Bird*.) Murray also wrote *Hassan:* or, *the child of the pyramid; an Egyptian tale* (1857).
24. Murray posed again in *c.* 1851 for a Daguerreotype by Antoine Claudet. This image is less formal, but includes two attendants, both of them adults, acting as props to set the oriental scene.
25. See Laure de Margerie and Edouard Papet, *Charles Cordier: Les Nubiens 1848–1851* (Le Havre: MuMa, 2011).
26. Wilfrid Blunt, *Country Life*, 13 November 1975; Wilfrid Blunt, *The Ark in the Park* (London: Hamish Hamilton, 1976).
27. 'Les Aventures de Tintin', *Le Petit Vingtième*, 8 December 1932 to 8 February 1934.
28. Tom McCarthy, *Tintin and the Secret of Literature* (London: Granta, 2006), p. 45.

— 3 —

Sujets de modes d'être

Marielle Macé

On n'est pas seulement le sujet d'un récit, toujours particulier; on est aussi le sujet de formes de vie, plus générales, plus génériques: de modes d'être, de rythmes, de gestes, de régimes et de façons, autrement dit de styles anonymes et partageables, qui nous attachent et nous arrachent les uns aux autres bien autrement que les événements et les carrefours de nos biographies. Qui l'on est s'y décide et s'y débat à la surface même de la vie sensible, à la surface du 'comment': comment on vit, comment on fait, comment on s'y prend pour vivre...

L'ouvrage que Michael Sheringham a consacré au quotidien, *Everyday Life: Theories and Practices from Surrealism to the Present,*[1] m'a aidée à me forger ces convictions; son travail sur le quotidien, mais aussi, plus généralement, le choix de ses objets de recherche successifs, du 'soi' à 'l'archive': des objets qui font d'emblée prendre l'air à la littérature du XXe siècle, et obligent toute œuvre littéraire à changer ses voisinages immédiats: à se savoir contemporaine de telle réflexion anthropologique, de telle proposition sociologique, de telle interrogation éthique, à se mesurer à elles, et à prendre par conséquent son parti sur la vie comme sur le style.

Vaste synthèse historique, *Everyday Life* expose avant tout l'enchevêtrement théorique et artistique des évolutions d'une notion disparate, dont il situe l'origine dans le surréalisme, et la transformation en concept dans la France de l'après-guerre, mettant en lumière une véritable 'tradition du quotidien'. Mais j'ai été surtout emportée dans ce livre par la proposition que Michael Sheringham y fait en son propre nom (et qui tient sans doute à une fidélité sans faille à Perec, à Barthes, à Foucault, et à un goût médité pour les catégories de l'ancienne rhétorique): le cœur du quotidien, pose-t-il, c'est le *générique*, cet ordre de récurrences situées entre l'individuel et l'abstrait, entre le 'soi' et le commun, entre le propre et l'impropre. Habitudes, habitats, emplois du temps et régimes du vivre, formes de l'attention, gestes, conduites, projets, manières anonymes et partageables, figures de régulation souple de l'existence, états minimaux de la forme où le sujet ne définit moins comme celui qu'il est (comme une réponse à la question *qui?* — et il n'y en a alors qu'un seul) que comme celui qui 'fait ainsi' (réponse à la question *comment?* — et nous sommes en ce cas beaucoup, et un seul de nous est d'ailleurs, en ces matières — en ces matières des 'manières' — , comme le disait si bien Michaux, une véritable 'foule').

Ce 'générique', qui court à la surface de la vie sensible, est dans le livre de Michael Sheringham saisi au cœur de quelques 'figures'. La première de ces figures est la 'Journée': 'forme porteuse de sens', comme l'a dit Jean Starobinski à propos de Rousseau (mais aussi de Baudelaire, de Ronsard, et des régulations de la vie religieuse ou de succession des saisons).[2] Cadre général d'un façonnement du sujet et de trouvailles tactiques d'arts de vivre, la journée oriente l'analyse vers les 'technologies de soi' foucaldiennes (et l'on se souvient que chez Foucault, prendre soin de soi n'est pas prendre soin d'un 'moi', mais de ce qui dans le soi excède le sujet, le moralise, le politise), et vers une 'esthétique de l'existence' bien différente de 'la merveille' surréaliste; on en perçoit la composante dialectique: entre la contrainte et la liberté, le singulier et le collectif, le moment de vérité et l'ennui, la journée apparaît comme un instrument et un horizon partageable de 'stylisation' des sujets. Si la figure de la journée est pensée dans le voisinage de Foucault, la deuxième, celle des 'Noms de rue', qui fait l'objet de l'analyse suivante, l'est plutôt dans celui de Henri Lefebvre et de ses réflexions sur les façons de vivre la ville, Lefebvre à partir de qui tout un passé littéraire est reparcouru, qui va de la ville baudelairienne à 'l'intoxication' benjaminienne des noms propres (et qui se prolongerait de belle façon dans les réflexions actuelles de Jean-Christophe Bailly sur les 'phrases urbaines',[3] ces lignes dans lesquelles nous devons engager notre sens des nuances syntaxiques et des métamorphoses). Michael Sheringham y souligne à nouveau la force de dispositifs situés en deçà du récit, qui ont sa préférence. Avec la troisième figure, celle des 'Projets attentionnels', la filiation est résolument perecquienne — on songe à la *Tentative d'épuisement d'un lieu parisien* — : ce sont ces cas où des dispositifs pratiques, des performances et des situations d''expérimentation anti-sociologiques' conduisent des artistes à rouvrir le visible, tel écrivain notant tout ce qu'il perçoit depuis sa fenêtre dans un trajet de train hebdomadaire (François Bon avec *Paysage Fer*), tel autre se faisant l'ethnologue de sa ligne de métro quotidienne, tel encore partant à la recherche de ce qu'il y a 'en vrai' là où les cartes restent muettes et laissent des vides (Philippe Vasset avec *Un livre blanc*)...

La *Préparation du roman*, de Barthes, formerait peut-être le plus bel exemple de cette conscience de tout ce qu'engage une attention intensifiée au plan du 'comment'; le cours aura porté en grande partie sur une réflexion sur l'organisation qu'il faut à une vie quotidienne pour qu'advienne une œuvre. Étonnante réflexion *littéraire* (oui, encore littéraire) que celle qui ne porte pas sur le genre de l'œuvre, mais sur le genre de vie qui pourra lui faire place. Barthes appelle cela, avec Chateaubriand, la 'vie méthodique' ('Les romains sont si accoutumés à ma vie méthodique que je leur sers à compter les heures', écrivait Chateaubriand en ambassade à Rome), et avec Nietzsche la 'casuistique de l'égoïsme'. Au départ de ce cours se trouve une interrogation sur 'la vie qu'il faut mener' (interrogation qui n'a rien d'abstrait, mais qui fut dictée par le deuil, dont Barthes précise qu'il lui a justement imposé une 'rééducation' des habitudes). Et Barthes d'interroger longuement les aspects techniques de cette vie nouvelle, ouvrant une multitude de 'dossiers' (c'est lui qui les appelle, génériquement, ainsi) sur les 'styles de nourriture', la '*gestalt* des menus', les vêtements, la maison, l'installation, l'horaire... Dans toutes ces analyses, Barthes revient obstinément à Nietzsche. Non pour viser une anthropologie des hauteurs et de l'éclat, mais pour tourner son attention vers les enjeux éthiques de ces régimes du vivre, car les techniques du quotidien sont autant de configurations morales:

'Pour moi, alliance de l'Esthétique (de la Technique) et de l'Éthique; son champ privilégié: l'infime quotidien, le "ménager"'.[4] Oui, le 'ménager', l'*éthos* (manière d'être et séjour), c'est-à-dire l'aménagement éthique du vivre que réalise toute constellation régulière de formes.

Rythme, vitesse, récurrence, les régularités *temporelles* sont au centre de ces catégories génériques, car le quotidien est 'dans le temps' — non dans le grand temps des narrations, mais dans celui de chacune de ces pulsations pratiques, et la grande matière de l'Histoire, ou du roman, s'y transforme en une pluralité de *tempi* qui seuls nous la rendent effectivement habitable. (Ici encore, Barthes est en plein, lui qui a proposé comme premier sujet de cours au Collège de France cette interrogation générale: 'Comment vivre ensemble ?'[5] — oui, 'comment?', 'comme' quoi? — , et qui a engagé pour y répondre une réflexion morphologique et poétique sur la catégorie générale du *rythme*, c'est-à-dire sur la façon dont les sujets accordent et désaccordent leurs pratiques du temps dans une vie en commun. Savoir de littéraire, et pratique d'écrivain que cette mise en avant, dans une interrogation politique, de ce qu'il entre dans nos vies de rythmicité, de lutte rythmique, c'est-à-dire de prises de formes dans le temps.) De là sans doute les préférences affichées par Michael Sheringham pour les petites formes de la littérature contemporaine, où l'expérience est justement rendue à sa précarité et à sa fluidité rythmique: notation, répertoires, récits de méthode qui n'ordonnent pas l'expérience mais la suscitent ou la traversent, qui n'accumulent pas les actions mais forment une mémoire mobile ouverte à l'événementialité légère de l'occasion, et à une invitation à l'appropriation pratique.

L'essai plutôt que la fiction; Montaigne, Rousseau, Michaux, Barthes, Foucault; les manières, les régimes et les rythmes plutôt que le récit; le générique plutôt que le biographique (le générique qui n'est décidément pas l'abstrait, mais cette vibration de possible, de commun, qu'il y a au cœur de nos vies intimes), les formes de vie donc (que l'on documente, que l'on archive, que l'on juge — que l'on protège ou que l'on accuse), plutôt que les vies (dont, un peu différemment, on 'témoigne'): j'enracine là, moi aussi, mes préférences. Pour ma part en effet, si je travaille sur la littérature, c'est parce que de la vie (de la vie individuelle, de la vie commune, de la vie sociale) je veux comprendre justement cela: que quelque chose en elle tient à ses formes. *Littéraire*: celui qui veut voir les formes, à même la vie. La vie humaine, au plus intime comme au plus politique, est effectivement faite de régimes: régimes d'objets, régimes de conduites, régimes de relations, régimes d'attention, 'manières impropres'[6] (manières impropres pour ses singularités quelconques, comme le dit Agamben de ces régularités qui nous traversent sans nous définir), impropres et pourtant fermement qualifiantes, formes collectives qui font la vie de chacun et passent de l'un à l'autre, investissant un corps, puis un autre, cherchant des corps...

Et ces questions de formes de vie méritent d'être définitivement arrachées aux rêveries complaisantes sur l'esthétisation de soi. Car c'est à ce plan des formes du vivre que se formulent aujourd'hui la plupart de nos espérances, de nos revendications, de nos jugements. Et toi, comment fais-tu? comment vis-tu? comment t'y prends-tu? Et ailleurs comment vit-on? et pourrions-nous vivre autrement, 'comme ça', 'comme ça', et encore 'comme ça'?... Voilà les questions que nous avons à nous poser, à nous adresser les uns aux autres, et que la littérature, qui est experte en 'comment', est très bonne à affûter (c'est sa vertu, son souci). 'Vouloir défendre sa forme de vie en se contentant de la vivre malgré tout, de manière tenace et discrète, la défendre comme une vérité éthique qui s'éprouve dans le fait même qu'on la donne en partage, en faire non pas une doctrine ou une idéologie, mais une vérité sur ce qui nous lie'[7] — vouloir défendre sa forme de vie donc, mais aussi savoir en douter, et en réclamer de tout autres: l'histoire récente des terreurs survenues notamment à Paris a redonné à cela beaucoup de gravité.

On est le sujet de formes de vie donc. Penser à quelqu'un comme au sujet d'une forme de vie, se rapporter à lui de cette façon, ce n'est d'ailleurs pas tout à fait penser à lui comme au sujet d'une histoire. Se souvenir de lui comme du sujet de quelques manières de faire, de quelques gestes, de quelques habitudes, de quelques manies même, et non pas exactement comme du héros d'une histoire, ce n'est plus une affaire de mémoire, de temps qui passe et ne reviendra plus: c'est l'écoute de la 'pensée' que diffuse toute vie, qu'elle délivre à même ses formes, et c'est la promesse d'une sorte d'élongation de cette pensée, que l'on s'efforce de faire durer, de prolonger dans ses propres modes d'être, dont on honore ainsi la généralité. Un peu comme un visage reflété par la surface convexe d'un 'miroir de sorcière', qui, plutôt que de se trouvé répliqué avec exactitude, se voit placé dans une perspective aérienne, reculé, approfondi, généralisé: rapporté à tout le réseau des choses anonymes, privées et historiques, dont il participe.

— *La première fois que j'ai vu un 'miroir de sorcière', ce n'était ni à la National Gallery ni à Venise (où ils sont chez eux et deviennent des 'miroirs de banquier'), mais, comme élu pour sa légère étrangeté, dans la belle maison de Michael et Cilla Sheringham à Canterbury, cette maison à l'intérieur (au 'ménager') si nuancé, cette maison à la pensée prolongée en un étroit jardin ressemblant à une piste ouverte, une piste à suivre.*

Notes

1. Michael Sheringham, *Everyday Life: Theories and Practices from Surrealism to the Present* (Oxford: Oxford University Press, 2006).
2. Jean Starobinski, 'L'Ordre du jour', *Le Temps de la réflexion*, 4 (1983), 101–25.
3. Jean-Christophe Bailly, *La Phrase urbaine* (Paris: Le Seuil, coll. 'Fiction & Cie', 2013).
4. Roland Barthes, *La Préparation du roman I et II, Cours et séminaires au collège de France (1978–1979 et 1979–1980)* (Paris: Le Seuil, coll. 'Traces écrites', 2003), p. 51.
5. Id., *Comment vivre ensemble: simulation romanesque de quelques espaces quotidiens, Cours et séminaires au collège de France (1976–1977)* (Paris: Le Seuil, coll. 'Traces écrites', 2002).
6. Giorgio Agamben, 'Manière impropre', dans *La Fin du poème* (Paris: Circé, 2002).
7. Patrick Boucheron & Mathieu Riboulet, *Prendre dates. Paris, 6 janvier–14 janvier 2015* (Lagrasse: Verdier, 2015), p. 125.

— 4 —

Little Cuts in Time: Photography and the Everyday

Suzanne Guerlac

1. The Elusive Everyday (Receiving Attention)

For Michael Sheringham, the everyday is not simply a tradition of writings and practices that he braids together into a specific texture of modernism; it is also an ethical field, one that concerns productive reciprocities between people and their worlds. *Everyday Life: Theories and Practices from Surrealism to the Present*, we could say, is a novel in Barthes's sense: 'a discourse without arrogance' that implies love of the world.[1] Sheringham cares for the Everyday and wonders about its future. Does this tradition, tied to the cultural space of the European city, even have a future, he asks?[2] In the penultimate sentence of *Everyday Life*, he calls upon us to attend to it: 'Inherently performative,' he reminds us, 'the everyday comes into view — is appropriated (Lefebvre), invented (Certeau), acknowledged (Cavell), affirmed (Nancy) — when it receives attention'.[3]

This apparently ordinary sentence is not so simple. It cannot be a question of paying attention to something that sits before us, for the everyday 'dissolves when it is made an object of scrutiny' (E 361). Everydayness must first receive attention in order to come into view, emerging just long enough to establish a common world before disappearing again behind the things and instrumental actions that get taken up in the transactions of power and knowledge that so easily take over the cultural field. Sheringham's closing sentence, then, performs the reciprocity between subject and object, emergence and mutual constitution, that he theorizes in relation to the elusive Everyday — *être de fuite* as Proust puts it of Albertine.[4]

But what does it mean, in this context, to *receive* attention? Might it be something like what happens when a photosensitive plate receives a light impression? Might 'coming into view' be understood in terms of photographic development?

2. Receiving Shadows: All Things Equal Before the Sun

Here is Jules Janin on the newly announced discovery of the daguerreotype in 1839:

> M Daguerre [...] a composé un certain vernis noir; ce vernis s'étend sur une planche quelconque, la planche est exposé au grand jour, et aussitôt, et quelle que soit l'ombre qui se projette sur cette planche, la terre ou le ciel, ou l'eau courante, la cathédrale qui se perd dans le nuage, ou bien la pierre, le pavé, le

> grain de sable imperceptible qui flotte à la surface; toutes ces choses, grandes ou petites, qui sont égales devant le soleil, se gravent à l'instant même dans cette espèce de chambre obscure qui conservent toutes les empreintes.[5]

Before Surrealism, then, and before Baudelaire's painter of modern life, Janin speaks a language of everydayness — a language of the *quelconque*, the *quel que soit*, and of the virtual substitutability (*ou ... ou ... ou*) of elements such as running water, a stone, or an imperceptible grain of sand, all of which he gathers together as: 'toutes choses égales devant le soleil'. It is as if these things, in their utter singularity (their minute detail) receive light as a mode of attention and leave their shadows upon the prepared plate, which, when developed, brings images into view. Janin continues:

> Songez donc que c'est le soleil lui-même [...] qui produit ces travaux incroyables. Cette fois ce n'est plus le regard incertain de l'homme qui découvre au loin l'ombre ou la lumière, ce n'est plus sa main tremblante qui reproduit sur un papier mobile la scène changeante du monde, que le vide emporte.[6]

It is not a matter of the artist's hand retracing the contours of the fleeting image projected by the *camera obscura* and incorporating it into a tableau composed in the imagination. It is not even a matter of a discerning human gaze. The sun figures an impersonal mechanism of attention that the prepared plate receives automatically.

Not only does the sun replace the human hand, as André Bazin will reemphasize a century later, it miraculously produces the photographic impression all at once.[7] The daguerreotype receives impressions at one go, indiscriminately, in all their heterogeneity. The miracle (*le prodige*) of this image production is that it is 'aussi prompt que la pensée'.[8] Indeed, 'aussi rapide que le rayon de soleil qui va frapper là-bas l'aride montagne ou la fleur à peine éclose', it occurs at the speed of light.[9] It seems to run ahead of itself into the future, the future of a will-have-been-past, which is to say the future perfect of photographic time.[10] The automatic image presents more than the human eye could see, even if it paid attention: 'nul regard humain ne pourrait plonger aussi avant dans ces flots de lumière, dans ces ténèbres profondes'.[11]

In this response to the daguerreotype, Janin emphasizes various aspects of everydayness, not merely indiscriminate subject matter, or its heterogeneity, but also the nuances of atmosphere — of *no-thingness* — that float between subjects and objects. 'Pas un de ces tableaux exécutés d'après le même procédé,' he observes of daguerreotype views,

> ne ressemble au tableau précédent: l'heure du jour, la couleur du ciel, la limpidité de l'air, la douce chaleur du printemps, la rude austérité de l'hiver, les teintes chaudes de l'automne, le reflet de l'eau transparent, tous les accidents de l'atmosphère se reproduisent merveilleusement dans ces tableaux merveilleux.[12]

Two of Daguerre's earliest images present an identical urban scene — the same corner view of the Boulevard du Temple — taken at two different times of day, one in the morning [Fig. 1] and the other at noon [Fig. 2].

FIG. 4.1. Boulevard du Temple, 'huit heures du matin'

FIG. 4.2. Boulevard du Temple, 'midi'

All things may be equal before the sun, but the 'attention' of the sun, though automatic, is not constant — it is now thin, now thick, now warm, now cool, depending on the shared horizons of time of day, air quality, season and site. Early technical manuals acknowledge that there can be no fixed rules for photographic exposure or development protocols because everything depends on nuances of concrete material conditions, felt details of atmosphere — of howness and whenness, and whereness that constitute a thereness — that are contingent and variable. As Bergson argues, the time of duration — of qualitative heterogeneity — escapes measurement precisely to the extent that it is linked to attention as well as time.[13] The photograph not only lets us see these changeable nuances of everyday life that usually escape our awareness, it comes into being through them. They participate in the chemical mechanism — the very automatism — of photographic practice.

3. The Moon and the Teapot

'Ce sera le propre de la photographie que de mettre en scène à la fois le fini et l'infini, ce qui est intéressant et ce qui ne l'est pas, ce que je regarde et ce que je ne regarde pas', writes Roland Recht, speaking of the impression a daguerreotype of the moon made upon Alexander von Humboldt.[14] I submit this as a 'haiku' to the everyday. It notes that a photograph does not simply record what the photographer sees, as a drawing might, it also registers or receives what s/he does not (yet) see, or has no interest in seeing. It exceeds the subject/object relation. Fox Talbot made just this point in *The Pencil of Nature*, concerning an image of the entry gate of The Queen's College, Oxford:

> It frequently happens, moreover — and this is one of the charms of photography — that the operator himself discovers on examination, perhaps long afterwards,

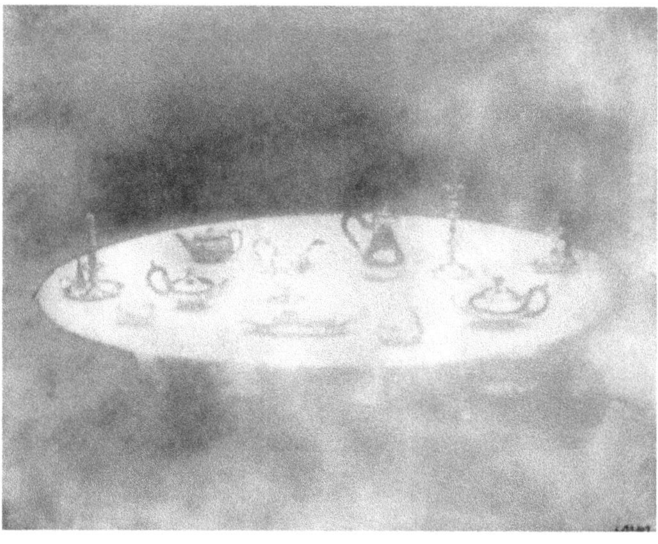

FIG. 4.3. Table du petit déjeuner, 3 octobre 1840

> that he has depicted many things he had no notion of at the time. Sometimes inscriptions and dates are found upon the buildings, or printed placards most irrelevant are discovered upon their walls: sometimes a distant dial-plate is seen, and upon it — unconsciously recorded — the hour of the day at which the view was taken.[15]

It is in this sense that the Everyday (here instantiated by the unremitting framework of clock time) emerges into visibility (in its own time) when (by chance) it receives attention. This is what photography registers. I offer a quirky image from the *Pencil of Nature* as a token of photography's contribution to the everyday — its reach from the moon to the teapot [Fig. 3].

4. The Call of the Photographic: *la touche réelle*[16]

Did the call of the photographic engage Théophile Gautier (early spokesman for what becomes known as art for art's sake) with everydayness? Gautier is captivated — even astounded — by the Bisson brothers' large-format photographs of an expedition into the Alps [Fig. 4].

Not an everyday event at the time, to be sure, but Gautier directs his attention to the ordinary elements of these photographs — 'les glaces [...] en blocs, en prismes, en polyèdres, en cristaux de toutes les formes imaginables', and the ant-sized humans that traipse through the snow.[17] 'Aucune description de poète, pas même le lyrisme de lord Byron [...] ne peut donner l'idée de ce prodigieux spectacle', he writes, speaking of the Alps, but also, implicitly of the photographs themselves, which manipulate scale in a way never before imagined.[18] Gautier will take the challenge; he will visit the mountains, following the itinerary of the expedition the Bisson brothers photographed, and write about them.[19] Gautier refers to himself as

FIG. 4.4. L. et A. Bisson,
'Savoie 35. Ascension du Mont-Blanc. Départ des grands Mulets'

a 'daguerréotype littéraire'.[20] Of the travel writing he produced on a visit to Italy he says: 'nous n'avons parlé que de ce qui est visible [...]; il a fallu nous contenter de tirer sur notre papier de simples épreuves photographiques qui n'ont d'autre mérite que leur sincérité'.[21] It is not a modest claim, given his esteem for photography:

> Le mérite de la photographie, c'est sa véracité absolue [...] Elle ne saurait mentir, non plus que l'astre son collaborateur. Elle transporte sans intermédiaire le tableau même qu'elle copie sur la plaque de son cliché. Vous avez le dessin direct, *la touche réelle* [...]. Aucune interprétation, aucune fraude agréable ou désagréable: c'est la chose même.[22]

The 'touche réelle', 'aucune interpretation', 'la chose même' — all these photographic features anticipate what Roland Barthes will say about the haiku in *L'Empire des signes*.

5. The Haiku: 'griffure de lumière'[23]

Barthes celebrates the short literary form of the haiku in photographic terms from the start. The haiku is 'un moment où le langage cesse' (ES 98); it performs a fragile apparition, a flash. Exempt from meaning, it merely designates a feature of the external world. It gives us suchness, an attestation of what is, that leaves the reader speechless. Fox Talbot spoke of the 'touch' of light on paper in the calotype.[24] Gautier spoke of the 'touche réelle' of photography. The haiku, like the photograph, touches the real. Barthes figures the photographic touch, attributed metaphorically to haiku notation, as a 'griffure de lumière' (ES 113). He speaks photographically of the haiku when he describes its content, what he calls the 'incident' (ES 109), as a little cut into time — 'sorte de balafre légère tracée dans le temps' (ES 111). In *The Preparation of the Novel*, this cut becomes a sting, the 'essential sting' that poetry produces, Barthes writes (citing Claudel), adding: 'admirable definition of the haiku'.[25] This is how we arrive at the sting — the little wound — of the photographic *punctum* Barthes will theorize in *La Chambre claire*.[26]

6. The Moment of Truth — Sliding into the Past

In *The Preparation of the Novel* (notes for a course he presented at the Collège de France between 1978 and 1980) Barthes proposes to consider literature as a practice (from the perspective of the desire to write) and to approach the 'fantasized Novel' (PN 19) from the dual optic of 'the Haiku/Proust' (PN 19). He works with the surprising proximity of these two terms, not their opposition. Unexpectedly, Proust enhances Barthes's appreciation of the literary short form. 'The haiku', Barthes writes in *The Preparation of the Novel*

> is produced by the bedazzlement of a personal, involuntary Memory (not: applied, systematic rememoration): it describes an unexpected, total, dazzling, happy recollection — and, of course, produces in the reader the very memory that produced it. (PN 39)

Barthes refers to the reader's memory experience as a *moment of truth*, an affective response he claims to have fully experienced himself only twice, once while reading Tolstoy and once while reading Proust's account of the death of the grandmother in the *Recherche*. He depicts the 'moment of truth' as

> a sudden knot in the path of reading that assumes an exceptional character: conjunction of an overwhelming emotion (to the point of tears, to the point of distress) and a self-evident truth giving rise, within us, to the certainty that what we're reading is the truth (has been the truth). (PN 104)

The affective response that occurs through the moment of truth (something that only *great* novels produce) coincides with a shutting down of meaning: the sudden '*bursting forth* of the uninterpretable, of the last degree of meaning, of the *after which there is nothing more to say*' (PN 107). Hence, Barthes writes, its 'affinity with the haiku' (PN 107), which precipitates miniature moments of truth, appropriate to its short form.

In Barthes's treatment of the haiku, the appeal to the *moment of truth* introduces a shift of perspective from the production of the text (the practice of notation he emphasized earlier) to the act of reading. The 'moment of truth' adds a strong affective charge to the encounter with exteriority — the suchness of the real — that, as we shall see, initially distinguishes the haiku for Barthes. Even more importantly, however, the appeal to memory the 'moment of truth' triggers in the reader reorients us away from the horizon of the present toward the past. We shift to the register of a '*has been* the truth' (PN 104, my emphasis) that will become crucial to Barthes's philosophical analysis of photography in *La Chambre claire*. Relayed through Proust, then, the *moment of truth* prompts a revision of the haiku event. Initially presented as an intense experience of the real, one that elicits our sense of 'tel!', or 'ça y est', it becomes attached to the truth claim of 'ça a été' (CC 120). In *La Chambre claire* reference becomes 'l'ordre fondateur de la Photographie' (CC 120) and 'la chose a été là' its norm (CC 120). In *La Chambre claire*, in other words, photography gets stuck in the past because the past adheres to it through the referent's imprint. Photography loses the everyday character which first drew Barthes to the haiku, and which Jules Janin and Fox Talbot had so appreciated in early photography. Because of Proust's imprint on Barthes — the slippage we have traced from the *moment of truth* to the punctum — photography loses the subversive agency de Certeau attributed to the everyday in his elaboration of what he called 'the right moment'.[27]

7. Barthes: *Ça a été*

Barthes writes *La Chambre claire* in between the first and second sessions of his seminar on the *Préparation du roman* at the Collège de France. The first begins on 2 December 1978. In January 1979 Barthes publishes 'Ça prend' in the *Magazine littéraire*, an essay on Proust that presents key passages from his lecture course. Session one of his seminar ends on 10 March 1979. Between 15 April and 3 June 1979 Barthes writes *La Chambre claire*, 'a book based on analyses presented in the lecture course', especially the seminar of 17 February 1979 in which Barthes noted the 'very great' (PN 73) proximity of the haiku to the photograph.[28] The course resumes with Part II of *La Préparation du roman* on 1 December 1979. The last session of the seminar takes place on 23 February 1980. Barthes dies approximately one month later. The published edition of *The Preparation of the Novel* includes notes for a new seminar Barthes intended to offer, 'Proust et la photographie', and the material of that seminar's reflection: a collection of photographs by Nadar of Proust's social world.

Although the association between the haiku and photography, implicit since *L'Empire des signes*, becomes explicit toward the end of the first session of *The Preparation of the Novel* — 'the art form that enables us to conceive of the haiku = Photography' (PN 70) — the relation between the two is far from seamless. As his orientation shifts from the happening of present time in *L'Empire des signes* to a capture of past time, which predominates in Barthes's theory of photography in *La Chambre claire*, the living vitality associated with the early writings on the haiku congeals into a horizon of death. It is as if the energy of the *Vita Nova* (associated with Barthes's engagement with literature from the perspective of its practice) had dissipated and a bout of *acedy* had set in. Acedy has been specifically triggered by Barthes's mourning for the death of his mother of course, but he associates it more broadly with a general disinvestment from life, revealing that he had pushed back against it (even after the death of his mother) specifically by investing in the project of the 'Novel Fantasy' (PN 13) — a genre he associates with emotional (and ethical) investment, that is, with love of the world.[29] When, tired of intellectual commentary, of codes, of teaching the same kinds of courses over and over again, Barthes takes up 'the moral and humble experience of Writing' (PN 21) an ethical imperative is at work. 'For me', Barthes writes, 'there's an alliance between the Aesthetic [...] and the Ethical; it's a privileged field: the minutiae of daily life' (PN 22). The Novel (the upper case 'N' endows it with magical authority) 'is fantasized as an "act of love"' (PN 14), indeed an act of 'ontological love' (PN 14). He sees it as a means of 'combating [...] hardness of heart, acedy' (PN 14) because it 'loves the world' (PN 14). It is in this sense that Barthes will conclude that literature 'is always made out of "life"' (PN 17).

When he considers his own 'aptitude for writing a Novel' (PN 15) from this perspective, however, Barthes confronts a serious problem: he has a very bad memory. How could he make literature out of life if he can't remember his life? At best he can access short 'flashes' of memory, but these are 'instantly exhausted by the short form' (PN 16). As if making the best of his situation, Barthes explains that his 'novelistic "drive"' (his love of the world) 'is not directed toward [his] past' (PN 17). 'It's not that I don't like my past', he clarifies, 'it's rather that I don't like the past [...] The affective link is with the present' (PN 17). This affective link with the present, tied to his inability to remember in any sustained way, would explain his 'desire for haiku', (PN 29). The 'enchantment of haiku' (PN 29) has to do with the fact that it 'is made directly from life' (PN 33). It offers 'an exemplary type of Notation of the Present' (PN 19), one that 'notes [...] a tiny element of "real", present, concomitant life' (PN 23). At the same time, the haiku remains 'insufficient' (PN 29): 'this is the argument of this Course, there's a call for the novel' (PN 29). Clearly the question that orients his seminar — 'how to pass from the Notation (of the Present) to the Novel' (PN 23) — is not an abstract, or theoretical, issue for Barthes. When he begins to turn from the haiku toward the past, to identify it with the 'that has been true', he begins to prepare not the Novel as love of the world but a theory of photography that, remote from the everyday, leads to melancholy — 'la mélancolie même de la Photographie' (CC 124) — to a 'forclusion du Tragique' that 'exclut [...] toute catharsis' (CC 141).

In *L'Empire des signes* Barthes considered the haiku from the perspective of its production. He spoke in terms of actions and events. It is not the reader who says 'tel!' but the haiku itself — 'Le haïku s'amincit jusqu'à la pure et seule désignation. C'est cela, c'est ainsi dit le haïku, c'est tel' (ES 113). The haiku speaks like a photograph, through its touch: 'Tel! dit-il d'une touche si instantanée et si courte (sans vibration et sans reprise) que la copule y apparaîtrait encore de trop' (ES 113). The short literary form 'reproduit le geste désignateur du petit enfant qui montre du doigt quoi que ce soit [...] en disant seulement: "ça!"' (ES 133). In its notational practice, in other words, the haiku operates like a camera as it takes a snapshot, cutting into time as it happens. In *La Chambre claire*, however, when Barthes sets out finally, to explicitly theorize photography, he declares himself unqualified to speak about taking photographs and announces he will address only the experiences of being photographed — a 'micro-expérience de la mort' (CC 30) — and of looking at photographs.[30] In both cases the photograph becomes heavy and static — the referent sticks to it and draws it toward death.

In *La Chambre claire*, the whole series of touches that we introduced through Jules Janin, Fox Talbot and Gautier, the series of scratches and cuts that we have traced in relation to the photographic depiction of the haiku, from *L' Empire des signes* to *The Preparation of the Novel*, condenses into the punctum of the photograph. But with a difference. The 'griffure de lumière' of the haiku involved a grazing contact with the outside, as did the 'balafre' of the haiku that cuts into time itself and generates 'an absolutely fresh Instant' (PN 49). But the punctum (as a development of the notion of the *moment of truth*) is a wound ('*blessure*', CC 42) that cuts inward, affecting the viewer. The punctum 'me pointe [...] me meurtrit, me poigne' (CC 49). This violence bleeds rhetorically back into the photograph itself through which 'nous voyons les morts' (CC 56).

By the end of Part I of *La Chambre claire* Barthes reaches a dead end in his philosophical quest. Even the dynamics of the punctum have not helped elucidate 'la nature (l'*eidos*) de la Photographie' (CC 95). In Part II he takes another tack. He looks at more personal images, photographs of his recently deceased, and much beloved, mother and finds one that serves as the 'médiateur d'une vérité' (CC 109). What it offers, soaked through with death, is the truth of the referent. The photograph presents the singular identity of Barthes's mother, 'qui elle était' (CC 117) in her irreplaceable being, her unique value. 'Comme le Narrateur proustien à la mort de sa grand-mère', Barthes writes, '"Je ne tenais pas seulement à souffrir, mais à respecter l'originalité de ma souffrance"' (CC 118). It is a question, he explains, speaking now of his own mother, 'de ce qu'il y avait en elle d'absolument irréductible, et par là même perdu d'un seul coup à jamais' (CC 118). With Proust as pretext, and with the survival of his mother's unique identity seemingly at stake, we arrive at the privilege of the referent when it comes to the truth of photography: 'toute photo est en quelque sorte co-naturelle à son référent' (CC 119).

Whereas the haiku 'walks — discreetly, elegantly, rapidly — along the "tightrope of Time"' (PN 55) in a field of ordinary events — in this everydayness lies its vitality and its power of enchantment — the Photograph theorized in *La Chambre claire* freezes in the grammatical mode of the substantive: the singularity of persons, places and things. It is a question, once again, of subjects and objects, of 'la chose *nécessairement* réelle qui a été placée devant l'objectif, faute de quoi il n'y aurait pas de photographie' (CC 120). If the everyday, as Michael Sheringham insists, 'dissolves when it is made an object of scrutiny' (361), then it dissolves here, with Barthes's theorization of the photographic, a far cry not only from the dynamics of the haiku but also from the charm of photography that Jules Janin and Fox Talbot conveyed. Perhaps it is the philosophical gesture — the pressure to think the *essence* of photography — that drives away the magic of the everyday, which has been flattened into banality — 'n'est-ce pas l'infirmité même de la Photographie, que cette difficulté à exister, qu'on appelle la banalité?' (CC 41).

This banality is salvaged, if at all, only through 'tout un élan d'une émotion qui n'appartenait qu'à moi' (CC 119). It is salvaged, then, only through the kind of narcissism that Barthes disparages both in *The Preparation of the Novel* and in *L'Empire des signes*, a narcissism, we could say, that the practice of the haiku, as an engagement with the everyday, was evoked to dispel.[31] From the haiku's horizon of the present we slide into the past in Barthes's theorization of photography in *La Chambre Claire*, from an investment in life, and love of the world, we sink into *Mélancolie* (CC 124); from the dynamic energies of the happening of time we pass to an immobilization of time (CC 142), from a scratch of the real we shift to an encounter with 'un réel qu'on ne peut plus toucher' (CC 136) and from the liveliness of the everyday we end up dead-ended in a 'théâtre mort de la Mort' (CC 141).

8. Photography and the Love of the World: 'Proust et la Photographie'

But *La Chambre Claire* is not Barthes's last word on photography. In his projected seminar 'Proust et la photographie' Barthes plans to return to the question of relations between literature and life — Proust's great question and the question that oriented his own discussion of the haiku in *L'Empire des signes* and *The Preparation of the Novel*. But he intends to return to it from a slightly different angle. 'The Novel loves the world', Barthes wrote in *The Preparation of the Novel*, 'because it stirs it up [*il le brasse*] and embraces it [*l'embrasse*]' (PN 14). We could say that Barthes's new question becomes: how does Proust's novel open a world by loving it, which is to say by (re) mixing it, by stirring it up? To pursue this question, Barthes turns to Nadar's photo portraits of people Proust knew and spent time with to mediate relations between the Novel and Life — and to stir them up.

By asking Nadar's photographs to play this role Barthes lifts the burden of reference that stuck to photography in *La Chambre claire*. It is no longer a question of 'la science impossible de l'être unique' (CC 110). Barthes does not turn to these photographs to get at the truth of the novel. Indeed he insists that it would be 'pointless, absurd, and almost ridiculous' to use Nadar's photographs to 'reconstitute the keys' of the novel, to 'believe in them [the photographs as keys] in a positive (and positivist) way' (PN 313). As we know from Brassaï, Proust used photographs in his writing process; as springboards for dreamlike transactions of condensation and displacement in the constitution of his characters.[32] Nadar's photo archive provides a field of conjecture concerning the various ways in which Proust might have combined elements from various individuals he knew to create his fictive characters, characters whose self-identity notoriously breaks and scatters over the course of thousands of pages in Proust's novel.

The world the novel opens, as revealed through the mediation of Nadar's photographs, renders the boundaries between literature and 'life' porous. Nadar's photographs support remixings that Proust performed in his writing. 'The Photograph', Barthes writes, '[...] will function as a confrontation between the Dream, the Imaginary of reading and Reality' (PN 314). We are dealing with at least three levels, here, the historical world, the fictive world of Proust's novel and Nadar's photographic world, all of which Barthes condenses into one aggregate he calls 'Marcel' (PN 309). The photographs enable a *va-et-vient* between fictional and historical registers grounding the essential relation of the novel to life. The authority of the referent breaks down in the transit between literary and photographic worlds. The world the Novel opens up is the world the Novel loves — the one it mixes together and stirs up. Photography, here, provides an exteriority to the world of the novel, but it is one the novel shakes up — this is how the novel loves the world and how it opens one.

'The aim of this seminar isn't intellectual', Barthes writes of 'Proust et la photographie': 'it is to intoxicate you with a world, as I'm intoxicated by these photographs and as Proust was by the originals' (PN 310). This is where we return to an aspect of haiku enchantment. Nadar's photographs fascinate us. 'To be fascinated = to have nothing left to say' (PN 31). Here the photographs perform like haiku, but only thanks to their interaction with the scattered subjects of Proust's novel. We could say that in the notes that prepare the seminar 'Proust et la photographie' Barthes performs an articulation of 'Proust/haiku' quite different from the one suggested in his seminar on *The Preparation of the Novel*. Perhaps this is where Barthes began to solve the riddle of the passage from the haiku to the novel as love of the world. Perhaps this is where he began to write his novel. Next to the photograph of Prince Boson de Sagan, for example, we read: 'frequents the foyer of the Comédie Française' (PN 364). Of Dr Samuel Pozi we read, as if a *fait divers*, 'died in 1918, murdered by a deranged patient' (PN 363). Of Lydie Aubernon de Nerville (1825–1899), whose image we see, Barthes notes '= Mme Verdurin; one of the most homogeneous and convincing keys [...] She — who'd done so much talking, invested so much in conversation — died of tongue cancer' (PN 319). We are back in the register of the Everyday, which, thanks to transactions between Proust, Nadar and Barthes is hardly banal. 'Proust and Photography', promised to be a most interesting engagement with Proust, with photography and with the question of realism, which it raises as a problem of subjects distributed between and across the novel and the world, that is as a problem of scattered subjects and moments of truth. Thanks to Proust and Nadar, Barthes has opened photography back up to the world; he has peeled off their referents, and rendered photographs mobile again as agents that activate worlds.

9. Snow and Ice, Turkeys and Peaches

The bicycle rider may be the new hero of modern life — the solitary dandy who speeds by, surprising everyone but never appearing surprised — but where is the common horizon of the everyday? Is there a future for the Everyday when electronic devices embed urban individuals in their own informational micro-worlds that traverse space and time? When he responded with fascination to photographs of the Alps was Théophile Gautier on to something? Is the everyday migrating from the city to the country — even to the wild?

Perhaps the wild is the site today of the kind of heightened attention across thresholds and frames that the city once offered Constantin Guys. Take the case of the man who raised wild turkeys from their birth, mothering them full time with undivided attention.[33] When he walks into the countryside with his brood in single file, the everyday of the wild comes into view. This is not because of the attention he gives but rather because of the attention he receives, which brings him into view differently for other creatures such that they then reveal themselves to him. His attunement to his turkey family has transformed his presence such that aspects of everyday livingness become discernible in a world shared by many species.

Or take the peach farmer making the transition to organic farming:

> Pat and I enter the field. Sounds envelop us, birds call and sing, insects buzz and flutter. Each step sounds distinct. Underfoot lies a rough collection of stalks and stems, sticks and twigs, leaves and wildflowers [...] We [...] experiment with the mechanics of walking and looking. I crouch low [...] I try listening to my footsteps and establish a deliberate, methodical cadence that forces me to go slower. It's uncomfortable [...] I hear myself breathing and discover a type of efficiency in movement. With a slow, patient stride I can check the vigor of the cover crop, the dryness of the soil, the health of the leaves. I begin to notice the slumping peach shoots where a worm has struck, the different shades of green where mites establish their home [...] I try to move even more slowly, turning my head from left to right, right to left, consciously panning the orchard.[34]

The field receives attention and the everyday comes into view — a new scene of the everyday that emerges as the peach farmer adjusts his attention to a world of livingness he no longer seeks to master.

Perhaps what is required in our Anthropocene Age is a shift in scale. Perhaps it is the biosphere that needs to receive our attention in its very finitude and complexity, enabling an everyday that comes into view through multiple rhythms of livingness, from that of the mite to those of the outermost reaches of earth's atmosphere.

Perhaps for the everyday to have a future — to come into view — it must receive attention as something other than an exclusively human precinct.

Notes

1. 'The Novel', Roland Barthes writes, 'loves the world', in *The Preparation of the Novel: Lecture Courses and Seminars at the Collège de France, 1978–1979 and 1979–1980*, ed. by Nathalie Léger, trans. by Kate Briggs (New York: Columbia University Press, 2011), pp. 15, 14. Subsequent references to this work will refer to this edition and will be given in the text, marked PN.
2. Michael Sheringham, 'City Space, Mental Space, Poetic Space: Paris in Breton, Benjamin and Réda', in *Parisian Fields*, ed. Michael Sheringham, Critical Views (London: Reaktion Books, 1996), pp. 85–115.
3. Michael Sheringham, *Everyday Life: Theories and Practices from Surrealism to the Present* (Oxford and New York: Oxford University Press, 2006), p. 398. Subsequent references to this work will refer to this edition and will be given in the text in parentheses, marked E.
4. Marcel Proust, *À la recherche du temps perdu*, ed. by Jean-Yves Tadié (Paris: Gallimard, 1999), p. 1671.
5. Jules Janin, 'Le Daguerotype', *L'Artiste*, 2 (1839), 145–48. This original version is reprinted, and cited here, in *La Photographie en France: textes & controverses, une anthologie, 1816–1871*, ed. by André Rouillé (Paris: Macula, 1989), p. 46. An English translation of 'La Daguerreotype,' trans. by Bartholomew Stritch, appeared in *Court and Lady's Magazine, Monthly Critic and Museum*, 17 (October 1839), 436–39 and is available online <http://daguerreotypearchive.org/texts/P8390002_COURT_LADYS_MAG_1839-10.pdf> thanks to the research archive of Gary W. Ewer; Ewer Archive P8390002.
6. Rouillé, p. 46.
7. André Bazin, 'The Ontology of the Photographic Image', trans. by Hugh Gray, *Film Quarterly*, 13.4 (1960), 4–9, DOI:10.2307/1210183.
8. Rouillé, p. 46.
9. Rouillé, p. 46.
10. 'Le photographe vit le présent de son experience comme le passé d'un futur. Ce n'*est* pas, ça *aura été*', Jean-François Chevrier, *Proust et la Photographie* (Paris: L'Arachnéen, 2009), p. 51.
11. Rouillé, p. 46.
12. Rouillé, p. 47.
13. Henri Bergson, 'Essai sur les données immédiates de la conscience', in *Œuvres*, ed. by André Robinet (Paris: Presses Universitaires de France, 1959), p. 39. See also Suzanne Guerlac, *Thinking in Time: An Introduction to Henri Bergson* (Ithaca, NY: Cornell University Press, 2006), pp. 54–60.
14. Roland Recht, *La Lettre de Humboldt: du jardin paysager au daguerréotype* (Paris: C. Bourgois, 1989), p. 150, cited by Pierre-Henry Frangne, 'L'Image déhiscente: Théophile Gautier et la photographie de montagne des frères Bisson', *Études photographiques*, 25 (5 May 2010), 210–42.
15. William Henry Fox Talbot, *The Pencil of Nature* (London: Longman, Brown, Green and Longmans, 1844), p. 40, <https://www.gutenberg.org/ebooks/33447>.
16. Pierre-Henry Frangne speaks of 'l'appel photographique' in 'L'Image déhiscente'. Bernd Stiegler cites Gautier concerning the 'touche réelle' of photography in 'La Surface du monde: note sur Théophile Gautier', *Romantisme*, 105 (1999), 91, DOI:10.3406/roman.1999.4352.
17. In 'L'Image déhiscente' Frangne cites Théophile Gautier, *Les Vacances du lundi: tableaux de montagnes* (Seyssel: Éditions Champ Vallon, 1994), p. 166.
18. Frangne, in 'L'Image déhiscente' cites Gautier, *Les Vacances du lundi*, p. 166.
19. 'Quand Gautier découvre dans l'atelier des frères Bisson, qu'il fréquente régulièrement, leurs clichés des Alpes, il décide aussitôt de s'y rendre [...] Son itinéraire suivra exactement les lieux photographiés', Stiegler, 'La Surface du monde', p. 94.
20. Gautier, p. 91.
21. Gautier, p. 91.

22. Gautier, p. 91.
23. Roland Barthes, *L'Empire des signes* (Geneva: A. Skira, 1970), p. 113. Subsequent references to the work will be to this edition and will be given in the text, marked ES.
24. 'The photogenic images of glass articles impress the sensitive paper with a very peculiar touch', Fox Talbot writes of Plate IV, Articles of Glass, in *The Pencil of Nature*, p. 21.
25. Barthes, *Preparation of the Novel*, pp. 75–76. Subsequent references to this work will refer to this edition and will be given in the text, marked PN.
26. Roland Barthes, *La Chambre claire: note sur la photographie* (Paris: Cahiers du cinéma, 1980), p. 73. Subsequent references to this work will refer to this edition and will be given in the text, marked CC.
27. See Sheringham, *Everyday Life*, chapter 6, for a discussion of de Certeau and the right moment. As Barthes's account of what he calls 'the moment of truth' (cited above) makes clear de Certeau is implicitly appealing to Proustian involuntary memory to energize (and render subversive) his notion of the everyday.
28. Nathalie Léger, 'Editor's Preface', in *The Preparation of the Novel: Lecture Courses and Seminars at the Collège de France, 1978–1979 and 1979–1980*, ed. by Nathalie Léger, trans. by Kate Briggs (New York: Columbia University Press, 2011), p. xix.
29. 'So, to change, to give a content to the "jolt" of the middle of life — that is, in a sense a life 'plan' (a *vita nova*) [...] there can be no other Vita Nova [...] than the discovery of a new writing practice', Barthes, *Preparation Of the Novel*, p. 5.
30. The association of being photographed and being put to death has a long history. See Champfleury's comic treatment of the theme in 'La Légende du daguerréotype' (1863).
31. Barthes distinguishes the haiku from the mirror, 'En occident [...] un objet essentiellement narcissique' (ES 106). The question of narcissism comes up in passing in Barthes, *Preparation of the Novel*, p. 23.
32. Brassaï, *Marcel Proust sous l'emprise de la photographie* (Paris: Gallimard, 1997).
33. See the video 'My Life as a Turkey' (PBS Video, 2011) <http://video.pbs.org/video/2168110328>.
34. David Mas Masumoto, *Epitaph for a Peach: Four Seasons on my Family Farm* (San Francisco: Harper, 1995), p. 58.

— 5 —

Micky's Thing

Gilles Ortlieb

pourrait bien prendre, ce dernier samedi de septembre, la forme d'une balade à mi-course d'un été indien durable et donc miraculeux, qui s'emploie à ravaler les façades et s'apprête à allumer plus tard, dans les hauteurs, balcons et baies vitrées. En dédaignant, pour point de départ, le Café du Faubourg, le bien nommé, pour le Café des Blouses blanches, à la sortie de l'hôpital Saint-Antoine et à l'enseigne soulignée par la ligne brisée d'un électrocardiogramme. Destination du jour, deux configurations extrêmes et opposées, à savoir l'avenue la plus longue de Paris — si l'on accepte qu'elle franchisse le périphérique — et, *intra muros*, sa venelle la plus courte. La première s'étire sur plus de six kilomètres, longe un zoo, traverse un bois et va mourir devant un château, l'autre se présente comme une volée de marches (treize, exactement) en accordéon entre deux rues, et sa longueur totale n'excède pas six mètres. Si le monde ne vaut que par les extrêmes et ne dure que par les moyens, comme le soutient Valéry, voici le cadre posé, à l'intérieur duquel inventorier un morceau de vie normale, à égale distance d'une quincaillerie, d'une agence bancaire, d'une pharmacie et d'un salon de coiffure pour dames. En y incluant la sévérité des églises de briques se dressant sur certaines avenues ombragées, avec une dignité de veuves faisant l'aumône à la sortie de la messe, à l'ombre d'un pilier; ou la chute d'une feuille de platane sur le trottoir, aussi sonore ou presque qu'une cagette vide tombant d'une camionnette de livraison; et les vibrations telluriques, tout juste perceptibles, d'un métro souterrain à la hauteur de la station 'Michel Bizot'; et les déjeuners entre collègues, amis ou associés, d'une bonne humeur à peine forcée, juste autant qu'il faut pour devenir communicative puis, la fillette de vin rouge aidant autant que le beau temps en terrasse, contagieuse. Au garçon en tablier, qui arbore à la ceinture un monnayeur aussi luisant qu'une cartouchière:

— Il va avec quoi, le carré de porc?
— Chou-fleur et gratin dauphinois.
— Parfait, magnifique, extraordinaire..!

J'aurai malgré tout aperçu, après avoir parcouru l'avenue Daumesnil dans son intégralité — puisque c'est d'elle qu'il s'agit — un Atlas en béton moulé soutenant le ciel à travers des feuillages, tout comme le rocher des singes émergeant au-dessus de la végétation du bois de Vincennes, frôlé au passage le quartier cossu de Saint-Mandé bordé de villas qui ne le sont pas moins, bu à une fontaine d'eau pétillante dans le jardin de Reuilly, non loin de l'ancienne gare des Chemins de fer de l'Est,

pris pour un corbeau un pigeon prenant son envol à contre-jour, et partagé pendant quelque temps l'insouciance somnolente d'une poignée de liseurs affalés sur une pelouse en pente. J'aurai aussi pensé à Sainte Rita, la patronne des causes désespérées, dont l'église qui lui est consacrée, dans un tout autre quartier de Paris, est menacée d'une destruction imminente (cause entre toutes, sans doute, parmi les plus désespérées), puis au passage Dieu et à l'impasse Satan visités dernièrement dans le XXe arrondissement, et qui certains jours devraient plutôt s'appeler l'impasse Dieu et le passage Satan. Etait-ce vraiment un hasard si l'œil bombé d'une caméra de vidéo-surveillance avait été fixée sur un mur de la première, et si le second arborait la boîte aux lettres d'une certaine Mlle Souad dont le battant précisait: 'Ô Jardin des Sens'?

La vie le fard de Dieu
La vie comme un passeport vierge
Une petite ville comme Pont-à-Mousson
Et comme tout s'est déjà dit
Plutôt la vie

Les vers sont d'André Breton, cités par Michael Sheringham dans un chapitre de *Traversées du quotidien* consacré à la notion de 'magique circonstanciel'. Et tout est dit, ou presque, d'un enchaînement mental reliant la petite ville de Pont-à-Mousson aux plaques d'égout estampillant les trottoirs d'une arche miniature griffée *PAM.*

Car si je devais additionner le nombre de plaques de fonte emmagasinées dans sa mémoire, prélevées sur je ne sais combien de trottoirs d'Europe et d'ailleurs, le poids de mon téléphone portable, qui ne doit pas atteindre celui d'une plaquette de beurre sur une balance de cuisine, se mesurerait en quintaux sur un pont-bascule pour camions. À croire que ces empreintes en relief encastrées dans le bitume ou entre des pavés agissent à la façon d'un aimant, en présence duquel le regard ne se comporte pas autrement que de la limaille de fer. Les tâches dévolues par en dessous à la plupart d'entre elles sont quelquefois explicitement indiquées ('Gaz', 'Service des eaux', 'P&T', *Water*, 'EDF' , *Kanalisasyon*, etc.), d'autres fois codées, chiffrées jusqu'à l'énigmatique: autant de portails vers des activités secrètes, invisibles. Leur compagnie est constante, pourtant, omniprésente, internationale — je l'ai dit — et rassurante souvent. Pourquoi? Pas seulement parce qu'elles disent l'homme et la ville, et les complications (en câbles, fils, conduites et canalisations) que cette association entraîne, ni parce qu'elles parviennent, en les cryptant ainsi, à dissimuler les réalités souterraines du monde à la surface duquel nous marchons. Pas seulement, non plus, par la confiance que leur solidité et leur stabilité inspirent, ni au nom, le cas échéant, de leurs qualités annexes (*Etanchéité 100%*, *Fonte ductile*, *Bouche d'incendie*, etc.), mais aussi bien par la variété de leurs formes et de leurs motifs, qui tendent parfois vers la rosace gothique, ou leur capacité à capter les incidences de la lumière, d'où que vienne celle-ci.

Quoi de moins éthéré, de plus prosaïque qu'une plaque d'égout? Et comment ne pas voir malgré tout dans cette collection, reconvertible à l'infini, de dalles, de grilles, de trappes, autant d'entrées vers les mondes souterrains qu'elles scellent par leur existence même? Je pourrais, pour lester l'argumentation, citer ici Hegel: '*Was ist bekannt ist nicht erkannt*' ('Ce qui est familier n'est pas pour autant connu'), essayer de convertir ladite plaque en métaphore, paradigme ou parabole du quotidien à inventer (à la fois trop proche et trop éloigné, chanson connue), voire de l'immanence des sens cachés, mais cela ne ferait que nimber d'une intellectualité sûrement discutable la démarche toute simple qui consiste, dans certaines circonstances, et sous réserve que le paysage mental s'y prête, à vouloir désanesthésier le banal, extraire le quotidien de sa gangue, en bref, le désincarcérer — et nous avec. Et je ne pense pas seulement ici aux dalles de fonte et à la signalétique des eaux usées, du gaz naturel ou des réseaux électriques, mais aussi bien au hasard et à la profusion des formes, motifs et inscriptions que la moindre promenade fait naître sous les pas d'un flâneur moyennement attentif.

Les plaques d'égout pourraient être ici reproduites par dizaines, pour avoir été capturées dans les lieux les plus divers, à toute heure du jour et de la nuit, sous le regard parfois décontenancé de passants de diverses nationalités. Qu'ajouteraient-elles à ce qui se présente plutôt comme une piste de réflexions possibles, aux ramifications sans nombre? Tenons-nous en, en guise d'illustrations, à l'une de celles qui ont émané de la grande matrice mussipontaine et au minuscule poinçon qui, malgré ses efforts, ne sera pas parvenu à passer tout à fait inaperçu sur un trottoir de la rue de Gesvres, devant la préfecture de police de Paris.

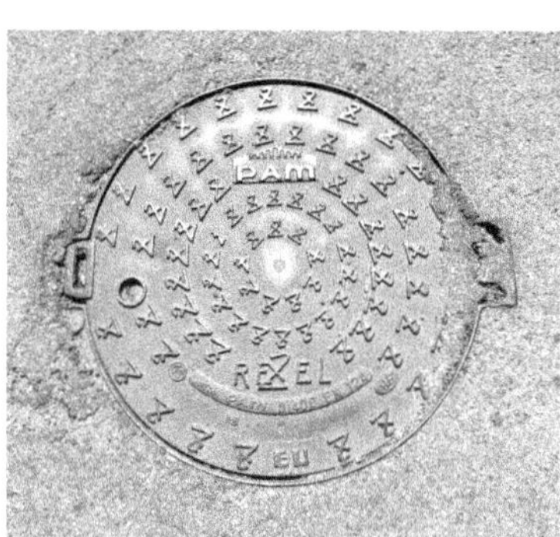

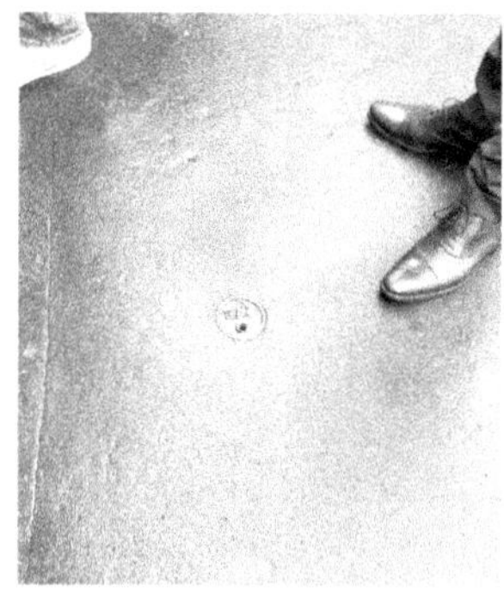

Et rendons-nous, pour finir, dans le quartier du Sentier, à quelques pas de la porte Saint-Denis (ses pigeons, ses prostituées chinoises et ses primeurs, dans la trépidante proximité des grands boulevards) et de la rue des Degrés, la plus courte, donc, de Paris. Mais, comme cela se produit souvent, c'est une chose que l'on cherche et une autre que l'on trouve. En l'occurrence, *avant que l'heure en cercle promenée / Ait posé sur l'émail brillant, / Dans les soixante pas où sa route est bornée, / Son pied sonore et vigilant,* il me fallut bien tomber en arrêt, au coin de la rue Beauregard et de la rue de Cléry, devant une maison qu'Eugène Atget avait photographiée en son temps, portant la même plaque au-dessus de l'unique fenêtre du premier étage: *'Ici habitait en 1793 le poète André Chénier'*, l'auteur des vers précités. Un point d'équilibre parfait, entre les deux célèbres postulations simultanées formulées par Baudelaire un siècle et demi plus tôt, et qui ne sont pas près de se démoder: la balade et la journée n'auraient pu mieux s'achever.

— 6 —

Diabolical Wit in Nineteenth-Century French Literature: Its History and its Successors

Alison Finch

In *Jokes and their Relation to the Unconscious* (1905), Freud hesitates about the degree of control the speaker or writer has over jokes and the comic.[1] He inclines to suggest that the joke is more accidental than the comic. It springs out, its meanings not fully available even to its mouthpiece: 'the person who makes jokes or, to put it in the only correct way, the person to whom they occur' (pp. 133–34). Or:

> What happens is not that we know a moment beforehand what joke we are going to make, and that all it then needs is to be clothed in words. We have an indefinable feeling, rather, which I can best compare with an '*absence*' [in French in Freud's text; his italics], a sudden release of intellectual tension, and then all at once the joke is there — as a rule ready-clothed in words. (p. 167)

For Freud, it is almost as if jokes are 'found' whereas the more consciously elaborated forms of humour are 'made': say, a writer's creation of an entertaining character, or the self-aware construction of a sardonic or parodic tone.

However that may be, all forms of humour play on the incongruity between what is expected or imagined (the 'made'?) and what is actually encountered (the 'found': the 'real' or the 'given'?). This incongruity shapes jokes, wit, irony, the comically exaggerated or preposterous.

In this (tentative) essay I want to look at one manifestation of French humour, 'diabolical wit' — humour created by devilish characters or devilish voices — starting with its flowering in the nineteenth century. Two scholars have made particular contributions here: Max Milner and Henri Rossi. Milner's 1100-page work of 1960 explores the figure of the devil in French literature in the late eighteenth century and the first sixty years of the nineteenth, while Rossi, some forty-five years later, examines the role of the devil in nineteenth-century vaudeville.[2]

Milner exhaustively analyses the literary appearances of the devil or devils during nine key decades. His insights are by now taken so much for granted that it is difficult to remember how pioneering his study was at the time, but to recap: Milner points out that belief in the Prince of Darkness had already, in the eighteenth century, diminished to vanishing point; even the clergy no longer promoted it. For a few in the post-Revolutionary period, like Joseph de Maistre, the devil continued to represent an abhorred atheism, indeed represented the Revolution and Terror themselves; but for most, the devil had moved into the realm of the imaginary, his persona becoming thereby increasingly malleable. The early nineteenth century might not, in fact, dislike the 'Esprit du mal': it could symbolize the liberation of the individual, and the rejection of mediocrity and of humanity's restricted condition; the devil pointed the way to intellectual adventurousness, to willpower. Milner discusses the presentation of the devil in Balzac, Nerval, Vigny, Hugo, Flaubert and many others; he describes the influence of Goethe's *Faust*, Hoffmann and the English Gothic, and the new fashion for the medieval that also contributed to the remarkably visible presence of the devil or devils at this time. En route, he departs from his purely literary brief, referring to musical works like Meyerbeer's opera *Robert le diable* (1831) as well as to 'opéras comiques' and other productions figuring the devil. Milner observes that the devil's very proliferation renders him relatively inoffensive; but he claims also that however minor some of the authors concerned, and however slight their treatment, light is briefly shed on the way 'le mal les touche, les angoisse ou les révolte' (I, 622).

Milner's culminating chapter is on Baudelaire, of whose Satan he remarks: 'sa voix ressemble parfois à s'y méprendre à celle du poète' (II, 424). Again, after Milner, it is by now a truism that in Baudelaire's writings the self is both celebrated and derided by protean narrators whose shape-shifting slides from sadism to masochism back to sadism. Protean shape-shifting is one of the traditional characteristics of Satan; additionally Baudelaire's wit is frequently imbricated with the citing of Hell, Satan and other manifestations of the infernal. Even more than *Les Fleurs du Mal*, *Le Spleen de Paris* — as has often been remarked — is permeated with a gleeful Schadenfreude towards others and the 'I', mediated by the demonic or devilish. From 'Le Mauvais Vitrier':

> J'ai été plus d'une fois victime de ces crises et de ces élans, qui nous autorisent à croire que des *Démons malicieux* se glissent en nous et nous font accomplir, à notre insu, leurs plus absurdes volontés [...] cette humeur, hystérique selon les médecins, *satanique* selon ceux qui pensent un peu mieux que les médecins [...]. (my emphases)[3]

In the prose 'L'Horloge' the narrator expresses an anxiety that 'quelque Démon du contretemps' may arrive to disturb his contemplation of the cat-like eyes of his mistress; by the end the narrator has become that demon, the last paragraph constructing its own double-edged contretemps:

> N'est-ce pas, madame, que voici un madrigal vraiment méritoire, et aussi emphatique que vous-même? En vérité, j'ai eu tant de plaisir à broder cette prétentieuse galanterie, que je ne vous demanderai rien en échange. (p. 81)

In the famous prefatory letter to Arsène Houssaye, Baudelaire describes the whole collection as a tortuous fantasy from which a vertebra or vertebrae could be unproblematically removed ('Enlevez une vertèbre, et les deux morceaux de cette tortueuse fantaisie se rejoindront sans peine', p. 6): this sinuous vertebrate is surely a snake. Is the work itself, then, *the* Serpent?

Rossi fills out a more populist picture. His appendices (pp. 284–310) show the sheer number of nineteenth-century vaudevilles, published and unpublished, as well as journals, in whose title the devil features — from *Les Pillules du diable* to the rather ingenious *Belz et Buth*. Rossi emphasizes the parodic treatment of the devil in many of these vaudevilles. They could lampoon plots imported from abroad, say the satanic pact of Faust, or home-grown figures like Robert le Diable. Rossi, through this stress on parody and in other contexts, claims a long-standing French specificity, referring for instance to a self-conscious nineteenth-century inheritance of 'l'esprit satirique français' ('écrire des vaudevilles, c'est aussi remettre au goût du jour l'esprit gaulois', pp. 11–12), and contrasting French light-heartedness of the late eighteenth century with dark English works of the same epoch: 'Cazotte et Gueulette [author of pseudo-Oriental tales] sont en effet encore bien distrayants et joyeux à côté des auteurs d'outre-Manche [...]' (p. 62). Rossi picks out various articulations of 'l'esprit français' linked with infernal characters or situations. Thus a vaudeville of 1809 stages Jocrisse, a traditional comic character who now finds himself in hell (*Jocrisse aux Enfers, ou l'Insurrection diabolique*): the benevolent demon Colifichet decides that Jocrisse, as a representative of 'l'esprit français', 'vif et léger', can be returned to Earth in order to carry on entertaining his contemporaries (pp. 231–32). (There are, indeed, quite a few benign devils or demons in nineteenth-century vaudeville.) In another vaudeville, *Le Diable boiteux à Paris* (1814), the devil of the title says how much he appreciates 'le vaudeville, enfant du plaisir et de la gaieté [...] [dans lequel] brille l'esprit français' (p. 94); and other devils present, as Rossi puts it, 'l'allégorie de l'esprit gaulois', adapting various 'personnages traditionnels de la verve française, Figaro, Molière, etc.' For — says Rossi — 'le vaudeville diabolique est bien l'héritier des fabliaux, de la farce [...], une résurgence opportune de la vieille littérature médiévale authentiquement gauloise et française' (pp. 108–09). Rossi points out, too, that vaudeville writers were thoroughly conversant both with classical French literature and with demonic literature and its themes from the medieval period on; they were knowledgeable as well as knowing. Thus there was overlap between popular and elite appeal. (Many audience members might be at an evening of vaudevilles one night and a performance of Racine the next.)

To sum up Rossi's argument: now, in the nineteenth century, the devil could be a 'good guy'; the well-worn scenarios of the pact with Satan, or the council of the devils (that is, their assembly to discuss diabolical projects), might be exploited to almost any purpose, but very often to comic ends; Satan himself could be, and was, self-parodying and witty. Rossi concludes, more frequently as his book goes on, that all this was at least in part designed to tame the image of evil, to 'reassure' the audiences flocking to the boulevard theatres.

These two landmark studies suggest, then, that nineteenth-century France saw a peak of representations of the devil, Baudelaire being the supreme artist in this respect. Yet Milner perhaps underestimates the pre-existence of paradoxical or flexible devils, and — whilst appreciating that they can be instruments of humour — he at times minimizes or ignores their comic side. We may also query Rossi's stress on the 'reassurance' needed. Nineteenth-century audiences were doubtless more robust and sophisticated than this interpretation implies; from an early stage they became accustomed to spectacles that invited the espousal of humorous devilry, and they saw that espousal as part of the very 'esprit français' that Rossi himself invokes.

But is France unique here? Devils have of course figured in other national cultures since the beginning of Christendom. Thus 'demonologies' flourished in early modern Europe.[4] These demonologies were often used to grim ends, defining for example how one might expect witches to behave — definitions that then led to arrest, torture and execution. Going beyond that, however, the intellectual historian Stuart Clark has argued that 'thinking with demons' should also be interpreted as an activity central to early modern thought, furnishing as it did some key conjectural functions: those of dual classification, contrariety and inversion in particular.[5] Through these, a broad range of disciplines was pursued — theology, science, history and politics. A properly historicized survey of 'demonology' should not, then, be limited to its most notorious practitioners; it is at times entirely dissociable from the historical witch craze, and is, rather, an important stratum of the conceptual bedrock subtending not only the witch trials but also the trans-Europe intellectual edifice of modern life.[6]

Moreover, 'sympathetic' devils occur in literatures other than French, the most renowned being Milton's Satan. Nor has France been the only home for amusing or witty ones. John Cox, in a discussion of the devil and his minions in late medieval and early modern English drama, observes that playwrights could add devils to a serious doctrinal 'main course' as a sort of 'comic dessert'.[7] And English literature provides many verbally inventive exemplars. In Shakespeare's *Othello* (1602–04), Iago, characterized as a 'devil' or 'hellish' by himself and eventually by others, refers to Othello as 'his Moorship', or tells Othello that Cassio is to 'cope your wife' — a pun, 'cope' meaning both to meet and to copulate with (Act I, sc. 1, l. 32; Act IV, sc. 1, l. 87). Jane Austen's self-centred and amoral Mary Crawford is both wily and funny (*Mansfield Park*, 1814).

In *The Devil as Muse: Blake, Byron, and the Adversary*, Fred Parker explores other representations of the devil in English literature.[8] The devil, he points out, can be seen not simply as the embodiment of evil but also as a worthy debating opponent, even approved in that role by God. The Old Testament word 'satan' means 'adversary'; such 'satans' appear in belief-systems other than the Judaeo-Christian; and, contrary to what is generally supposed, Genesis makes no direct link between the Serpent and the Devil, relating only that Eve was led to break God's command by a highly intelligent snake: in the words of that text, 'more subtle than any beast of the field, which the Lord God had made'. Nor, says Parker, is there any firm assimilation of Serpent to Devil in the New Testament; it was subsequent Christian tradition that made this identification a deeply rooted presumption. Satan is in his origins, as it were, an ambivalent figure; and Parker discusses this continuing ambivalence in Blake's narrators, who draw us into their seductive Schadenfreude, and in other witty figures like Byron's Don Juan.

Robert Louis Stevenson's *The Master of Ballantrae* (1889), too, stages a villainously jocular hero, a member of the Scottish gentry: the Master of Ballantrae himself. He deploys a grim humour: a travelling companion of whom the Master wishes to dispose finds himself sinking in a quicksand, and cries for help:

'Lend a hand,' said he, 'I am in a bad place.'
'I don't know about that,' says Ballantrae, standing still.[9]

When the main narrator tries to convey his hatred of the Master by saying that his belly moves if a certain person comes near him, the Master cries: 'Here is news indeed! I wonder — do I flatter myself? or am I the cause of these ventral perturbations?' (p. 163). Even when the Master's life is at risk, he sits 'like some easy, witty householder at home by his own fire; an answer he had for everything — as often as not, a jesting answer' (p. 197). Stevenson noted that this character was meant to be 'all I know of the Devil' (p. viii), and numerous words and phrases in the novel reflect his intention. The Master has 'a mere delight in cruelty such as cats display and theologians tell us of the devil [...] I was included in his diabolical amusement' (p. 77). The Master is rhetorically skilled: 'so devilish was his impudence, he twisted [his brother's speech] the other way' (p. 75); he has 'a devilish grace of insinuation' (p. 90). Such comparisons become ever more direct as the novel develops and as the Master becomes a rival and spell-binding narrator.

There are thus competing claims in anglophone culture. Similarly in German literature: the Mephistopheles of Goethe's *Faust* (1808) is the wittiest character in the play. Early on, he talks with impudent humour about God: 'I like to see the Governor now and then, | And take good care to keep relations civil. | It's decent in the first of gentlemen | To speak so friendly, even to the devil.'[10] Goethe's play, soon translated into French in more than one version, is one inspiration not only for the diabolical but for diabolical wit in nineteenth-century French works. Looking forward and further afield, Bulgakov's devil Professor Woland is urbane, his cat Behemoth clowns around (*The Master and Margarita*, 1928–40).

Given that the devil himself, his acolytes, and humans associated with him, have been key players in Western literature for centuries, from the mystery and other early dramas to Gothic works like Matthew Lewis's *The Monk* (1796), it is scarcely surprising that some of them include in their armoury not only persuasive guile but also wit. Nineteenth-century France does not have a monopoly on the diabolically amusing character.

And yet it may still be possible to sketch out a scenario in which the 'witty devil' has long been an unusually self-conscious, even prominent, actor in France's literature, becoming especially prevalent in the nineteenth century but ranging beyond it. Besides Baudelaire's verse and prose poetry, two masterpieces in particular stand out: Laclos's *Liaisons dangereuses* (1782) and Valéry's 'Ébauche d'un serpent' (1921) (described by the American poet and critic Yvor Winters in 1956 as the single greatest poem ever written). It is difficult to think of a renowned work in another national literature that gives an amusing voice to its villain/s as sustainedly and consistently as *Les Liaisons*. Mme de Tourvel addresses Valmont towards the end of the novel as 'Être cruel et malfaisant' (letter 161): the devil, in her eyes at least.[11] But the reader's uneasy espousal of Valmont's and Merteuil's perspective is encouraged (if not created) by their verbal dexterity, their wit. (Valmont to Merteuil: 'depuis que, nous séparant pour le bonheur du monde, nous prêchons la foi chacun de notre côté, il me semble que dans cette mission d'amour, vous avez fait plus de prosélytes que moi' (letter 4, p. 12); Merteuil to Valmont, sketching her self-formation by way of 'bons mots' that could grace any salon conversation: 'Vous jugez bien que, comme toutes les jeunes filles, je cherchais à deviner l'amour et ses plaisirs: mais n'ayant jamais été au couvent, n'ayant point de bonne amie, [...] je n'avais que des idées vagues [...]'. She consults her confessor: 'le bon Père me fit le mal si grand, que j'en conclus que le plaisir devait être extrême [...]' (letter 81, p. 176).)

Valéry's 'Ébauche d'un serpent', the longest poem of *Charmes* after 'Fragments du Narcisse', also solicits the reader's identification with this devil who 'writes' the work with his mocking account of himself and the fall of man. His bravura display of linguistic virtuosity seeks to persuade us that God is a humourless (and rather inarticulate) bungler, that humans are stupid, and that he, the Serpent, is the one to admire — certainly the one to amuse us. Phonetic buffoonery is the stuff of the poem, as for example in the lines about the theft by 'Master Serpent' of man from God: this parody of La Fontaine parades a more hyperbolic wordplay and more derisive tone than we find in La Fontaine: 'Sitôt pétris, sitôt soufflés, | Maître Serpent les a sifflés, | Les beaux enfants que Vous créâtes! | Holà! dit-il, nouveaux venus! | Vous êtes des hommes tout nus, | Ô bêtes blanches et béates!'[12]

A lineage exists between these egregious cases. Laclos was admired by Baudelaire, and the 'snake' form of *Le Spleen de Paris* may have helped suggest Valéry's serpent. But in French literature it is not only Laclos, Baudelaire and Valéry who have developed with panache the trope of the witty devil. In Diderot's *Neveu de Rameau* (about 1760) the memorably entertaining Nephew promotes a perverse ethics, and famously has the upper hand in the dialogue. In the same century Voltaire's disrespectful satire popularized Enlightenment ideas; Beaumarchais's Figaro, no longer merely the cheeky servant of yesteryear, is at moments a jesting and troublesome radical.

The devilishly enjoyable also finds favour with pre-Enlightenment French thinkers and writers. Hugh Roberts and Timothy Chesters outline the entertainment that could adhere to images of the mischievous mind and of the devil in early modern France. Roberts and Chesters explore, respectively, presentations of mental activity and of demons in the seventeenth and sixteenth centuries. I summarize their work in reverse chronological order, since Roberts looks at a more general picture, while Chesters returns us to our devils. In 'La Tête de Bruscambille et les métaphores mentales au début du XVIIe siècle', Roberts discusses the work of Bruscambille, a famous early seventeenth-century 'farceur' and prologue-maker at the Hôtel de Bourgogne (the principal seventeenth-century theatre of Paris, which entertained 'low life' as well as the elite).[13] A hundred of his prologues survive, in numerous editions that spread around the country: 'Ce succès éditorial donne une indication sur le goût de l'époque pour cette forme d'humour parmi un public assez lettré ainsi qu'au parterre' (p. 542). Roberts focuses mainly but not solely on Bruscambille's 'Prologue de la tête', describing the burlesque metaphors through which, here and elsewhere, he brought 'the head' to life, drawing in part on the sixteenth-century renewal of the science of anatomy to link mental with physical. If Bruscambille was the most celebrated comic in this genre, he was not the only one: his contemporaries also wrote amusing texts about mental activity, bringing together scientific and ribald language. 'Nous sommes loin ici,' remarks Roberts, 'de la "res cogitans" incorporelle de Descartes' (p. 544). For Bruscambille, laughter is an important strategy for providing unexpected insights into mental activity. The anatomical examination of the head, far from allowing a solid 'moi' to be constructed, waggishly suggests a hiatus between mental experience and the 'objectification' of anatomy. Furthermore, for Bruscambille and his contemporaries the head includes 'low' qualities: it is as it were an upper stomach, and may even possess a vulva and an anus. (Tabarin, another 'farceur' of the period, refers to '[le] cul de votre cerveau': p. 554.) Roberts points out that these parodic representations of the brain also appeared in Rabelais; and he concludes that such incongruous metaphors, appreciated by all strata of contemporary society, reflect tensions in the 'imaginaire collectif' (p. 555). This article, then, draws attention to an unofficial history of French rhetorical figures, savoured by both elite and populus, that represent the mind by way of the impertinent, the crude — the impish, we might say.

Plausibly, the ground was prepared not only by Rabelais but also by other sixteenth-century discussions. Chesters, for his part, argues that Robert Du Triez's *Les Ruses, finesses et impostures des espritz malins* (1563) has good claim to be the first prose demonology in the French language.[14] The work is set out as a dialogue or debate between a Protestant and a priest (and with two other interlocutors) about the status of images. Their discussion invokes Satan's power to manipulate perception and the risk of falling prey to his illusions. But Chesters stresses the importance also accorded to readerly entertainment: Du Triez describes his own work as an 'oeuvre fort utile *et delectable* pour un chascun', given 'la varieté des choses estranges contenue en icelui' (p. 402; my emphasis). It may seem perverse, says Chesters, to speak of pleasure in these texts; yet the space given over to such pleasure within demonological writing has increasingly attracted the attention of recent scholars. This writing appealed to both the moral and the aesthetic sensibility of the day: thus Du Triez not only presents the debate between Protestant and Catholic even-handedly but also has his interlocutors realize that the topic of demonic activity can be an agreeable diversion from political and religious conflict. The dialogue is full of references to the enjoyment of telling and listening to stories; digression is to be encouraged, for 'Telz joyeux discours, entremeslez de contes gracieux, et propos recreatifs, sont l'allegement des espritz troublez et fachez par soing et cure des choses graves et importantes' (p. 407). (Chesters comments on the meaningful pun or *glissement* in the use of 'esprit': the 'espritz malins' of Du Triez's title mutate here into the 'espritz troublez', the minds or spirits, of the interlocutors.) In a tale narrated by one of the respondents, the devil's presence is clear — a magician's temples sprout horns that then disappear back into his head, an event that brings 'grand plaisir et passetemps' to the aristocrat who witnesses it; thus the 'ruses', 'finesses' and 'tromperies' of demons can be a 'joyeuse invention' (p. 408). For Du Triez, thinking with demons is a way of thinking about images: their power to seduce and lead astray, yes, but also to comfort and persuade; there is an observable relation between demonology and pleasure. 'The example of *Les Ruses* suggests [...] that the "figure du lecteur en amateur curieux" [...] was present in francophone demonology from the very beginning' (p. 410).

Can we say then that there is after all something specifically francophone about the enjoyable presentation of devils — that France has deployed more wickedly amusing characters, given them more highly wrought roles, than other national literatures? Rossi clearly thinks so.[15] The tradition has continued into the twentieth and twenty-first centuries. A 'diabolical wit' shapes, for instance, the voice of Céline's narrator in *Voyage au bout de la nuit* (1932) and the darkly humorous Hell of Sartre's most dramatically successful play *Huis Clos* (1944). Other descendants are *film noir* and Michel Houellebecq (and *Charlie Hebdo*?).

We have seen counter-examples from other cultures. Yet Iago, for instance, is not consistently witty. To be sure, he is a manipulator of language, able to insinuate Desdemona's infidelity with repeated phrases like 'I think that'. But, as critics have pointed out, his rhetoric is also vulgar, with its bestial sexual imagery, and he can be deliberately platitudinous; his speeches are cunning but not generally humorous. Milton's Satan is anguished, dignified, verbally creative, but too tragic a figure to be amusing. Mary Crawford is not the main character of *Mansfield Park*, and lacks the prestige of the first-person voice given to key French devils.

No doubt we are looking at a sliding scale on which the difference between national cultures is not absolute. However, we find hints in non-French works that the funny devil is part of the image that other cultures had, and have, of France. Cox remarks that the devil as fool, rather than knave, in late medieval and early modern English drama had his ancestry in the 'soties' and 'fabliaux' of France; English courtly humanist playwrights would have been familiar with French farce and 'might well have abstracted mere mirth' from its dramatic personification of Vice or Vices (pp. 77, 79). Another contrasting circumstance to be adduced from Cox's study is that England, with the Reformation, went down a different path from France: in post-Reformation English drama, devils were often identified with the Pope or with Catholicism. Their depiction might thus take a more polemical and serious turn than in France (pp. 87, 88, 93).

Two of our later non-French writers, Goethe and Stevenson, indicate that a 'French' aura may adhere to amusing devils. Goethe's Mephistopheles would seem to have the subject of 'Frenchness' in mind. He refers to his own fashionable, cavalier-like or nobleman's dress, describing it narcissistically in its dashing detail: for eighteenth-century Germany, fashion or 'nobility' meant French-inspired. For example:

> [C]ulture which licks out at every stew
> Extends now to the Devil, too:
> Gone is the Nordic phantom that former ages saw;
> You see no horns, no tail or claw.
> And as regards the foot with which I can't dispense,
> That does not look the least bit suave;
> Like other young men nowadays, I hence
> Prefer to pad my calves. [...]
> I am a cavalier with cavalierly charms [...]
> [Ich bin ein Kavalier wie andre Kavaliere.][16]

When Faust talks of seducing the 'little thing' Gretchen, Mephistopheles remarks: 'You speak just like a Frenchman' ['wie ein Franzos'] and recommends erotic literature in French as a guide to adventurous sex ['welsche Geschicht'] (pp. 258–61). Gretchen later rejects Mephistopheles's suggestion of keeping a lover, a 'gallant' ('ein Galan') as foreign, 'not the custom around here' (pp. 284–85).[17] Does Mephistopheles's 'French' air include his deployment of an impudent wit? The connection is more overt in *The Master of Ballantrae.* The Master speaks good French, accusing his brother of having '*cette lenteur d'hébété qui me fait rager*', exclaiming (again of his brother) '*Quel lourdaud!*' (p. 93), and so forth. He is said to have French manners, French learning; he lives in Paris for a time, and his clothes are 'of a French and foppish design' (p. 72). The work establishes other links between the Master and France: for instance, the Master 'had some design of a fortune in the French Indies' (p. 85).[18]

From Goethe and Stevenson to anglophone literary studies: strikingly, the American critic Wayne C. Booth picks out *Voyage au bout de la nuit* as the prime example of ethically dubious fiction in his *Rhetoric of Fiction*; if taken seriously by the reader, Céline's novel 'must corrupt him'.[19] It is as if a French work automatically sprang to mind in this context.

Let us leave devils aside for the moment and focus on 'wit' — French wit. In their book *That Sweet Enemy*, the historians Robert and Isabelle Tombs explore the contrasting images that the English and French have built up of each other.[20] They trace the use of these images in national propaganda as well as the occasional adoption by the English and French themselves of each other's stereotypes. (If in the nineteenth century the English were thought by the French to be bluff and direct, that bluffness could appear in, say, Punch cartoons by and about the English.) The images mutated according to period and political circumstance. However, despite some fluidity and interchangeability, a few stereotypes remained constant: France, in both its own eyes and those of other nations, possessed 'civilization' and 'refinement'; England possessed 'rough genius'. One such opposition was, famously, that the English were 'humorous' whereas the French were 'witty': 'l'humour anglais, l'esprit français':

> [Nineteenth-century ideas] about why Britain and France were different went back at least to the seventeenth century, and were updated by nineteenth-century theories about climate, race and history. [...] [A] basic contrast was the idea, inherited from the eighteenth century, that Britain stood for nature, and France for civilization. This continued to be applied to culture, social conventions, and even politics. [...] The British valued 'facts', the French, 'theory'; the British favoured domesticity, the French, sociability; the British had 'humour', the French, 'wit' [...] (pp. 447, 449)

These are indeed constructions. French authors are witty, but so are Jane Austen and Dickens. Conversely, running through French literature is a rumbustious physical humour, playing its part even in the Proust once supposed to be all refinement and preciosity. France has after all given English the word Rabelaisian. From the seventeenth century on, the phrase 'l'esprit gaulois' designates a rather earthy humour, a humour which has 'la franche gaieté un peu libre des "bons vieux temps"' (Robert dictionary). And the noun 'gauloiserie' dates from 1865 (Robert), meaning both licentious, light-hearted, disrespectful speech and 'caractère gaulois'.

This being said, along with 'gauloiserie' (and often merging with it) a clever wittiness is, as Robert and Isabelle Tombs suggest, an attribute of French cultural self-awareness.[21] The very word 'esprit' plays a part with its multiple meanings, as we saw in the case of du Triez: mind, wit, ghost, spirit in moral and religious senses. There is some overlap in other languages too — in English, 'wit' can mean both humour and mental alertness ('to have one's wits about one', 'half-witted'); but generally English uses separate words for mind, for wit and for spirit. A similar partial overlap occurs in German: 'Geist' means mind and spirit, and can mean humorous wit, but again the separate word 'Witz' is normally used for 'wit'. In French, on the other hand, the concentrated and mobile word 'esprit' makes the concept of 'wittiness' coterminous with the mental and the spiritual.

French writers at intervals seek to define French 'esprit' — whether by that is meant the spirit of France, French humour, or both. These attempts are to be expected in a culture that has since the medieval period been ostentatiously self-reflexive and verbally playful, and that from the sixteenth century onwards has debated what the French language is and how it reflects 'Frenchness'. Boileau tries to pin down 'l'esprit français': 'Boileau, dans son *Art poétique* [1674], n'hésite pas à classer le vaudeville au nombre des genres satiriques, voyant en lui le produit de l'esprit français, gai, fantaisiste, débridé'.[22] Such attempts are frequent in the nineteenth century too — in part, as the Tombs indicate, arising from prevailing theories of race and environment. (English has no equivalent of the mid-century coinage 'gauloiserie'.) However fleeting or off the cuff, remarks in Gautier, Mallarmé and others enlist the concept of an 'esprit français'; it also figures in Baudelaire. Early in *Le Spleen de Paris* — in the fourth poem, 'Un plaisant' — the narrator evokes the 'explosion' of the New Year, with its chaotic street scenes: 'délire *officiel* d'une grande ville' (my emphasis). A 'beau monsieur' bows ceremoniously before a passing donkey, taking his hat off wishes it a happy new year, then turns back to his companions 'avec un air de fatuité, comme pour les prier d'ajouter leur approbation à son contentement'. The donkey trots on oblivious, but the narrator closes with this last paragraph: 'Pour moi, je fus pris subitement d'une incommensurable rage contre ce magnifique imbécile, qui me parut concentrer en lui tout l'esprit de la France' (pp. 20–21). The uncomplimentary finale leaves us uncertain whether we are witnessing the frivolous and un-funny *wit* of France, or the *spirit*, the mentality, of France, embodied here in a silly and self-important bonhomie. But what is important is the ambition to illustrate and display this 'esprit': there is such a thing as 'the wit of France', fusing with 'the intellect, the mind, of France', and, as we have seen, it often takes a far subtler form than in Baudelaire's joker.

Diabolical wit — sometimes verging on the boisterous, often sly, always entertaining — arguably does have a special place in French literature. Obvious in the nineteenth century, it may at that time particularly mesh with or allegorize the frustrations of the would-be revolutionary (Satan as sophisticated rebel). More generally, over the centuries it indicates a wide-ranging imaginative engagement with scepticism or atheism — a challenge to God, a discordantly comic view of his creation. Fiendish humour, humour 'from below', can also symbolize the incursion of lower ranks into the established order, or the break-through into consciousness of the Freudian id. Whenever it occurs, the jabbing of our devils' pitchforks mischievously creates the incongruities mentioned at the start of this essay. But somehow the jabbing merges them too: it feels both artificial and 'real', both 'made' and 'found'.

Notes

1. Sigmund Freud, *Jokes and their Relation to the Unconscious*, Standard Edition, vol. VIII (London: Hogarth Press, 1960).
2. Max Milner, *Le Diable dans la littérature française de Cazotte à Baudelaire, 1772–1861*, 2 vols (Paris: Corti, 1960); Henri Rossi, *Le Diable dans le vaudeville au XIXe siècle* (Paris: Minard, 2003).
3. Charles Baudelaire, *Petits poèmes en prose (Le Spleen de Paris)* (Paris: Garnier, 1962), pp. 42–43.
4. That is, treatises on demons; 'demonology' is also the branch of study dealing with demons or beliefs about them.
5. Stuart Clark, *Thinking with Demons: The Idea of Witchcraft in Early Modern Europe* (Oxford: Oxford University Press, 1997).
6. See Timothy Chesters's summary of Clark in 'Demonology on the Margins: Robert Du Triez's *Les Ruses, finesses et impostures des espritz malins* (1563)', *Renaissance Studies*, 2.3 (2007), 395–410 (p. 401).
7. John Cox, *The Devil and the Sacred in English Drama, 1350–1642* (Cambridge: Cambridge University Press, 2000), pp. 5, 39.
8. Fred Parker, *The Devil as Muse: Blake, Byron, and the Adversary* (Waco, TX: Baylor University Press, 2011).
9. Robert Louis Stevenson, *The Master of Ballantrae: A Winter's Tale*, ed. by Adrian Poole (London: Penguin, 1996), p. 49.
10. Johann Goethe, *Faust: Part One*, trans. by Philip Wayne (Harmondsworth: Penguin, 1960), p. 42. (Here Wayne's translation is superior to Walter Kaufman's, which I use later.)
11. Choderlos de Laclos, *Les Liaisons dangereuses* (Paris: Garnier, 1961), p. 368.
12. Paul Valéry, 'Ébauche d'un serpent', *Charmes*, *Œuvres*, 2 vols (Paris: Gallimard, 1957–60), I, 138-46.
13. Hugh Roberts, 'La Tête de Bruscambille et les métaphores mentales au début du XVIIe siècle', *Revue d'histoire littéraire de la France*, 107.3 (2007), 541–57.
14. Art. cit., p. 395.
15. See the summary of Rossi's arguments above.
16. *Goethe's FAUST*, translated and with an introduction by Walter Kaufman (New York: Anchor, 1963), pp. 246–49.
17. See also the scene in which Mephistopheles is as happy to bore into a cask of French wine as a local one (p. 227).
18. Stevenson's unfinished *Weir of Hermiston* (published 1896) extensively evokes the gleeful malice of the hanging judge Adam Weir, at loggerheads with his more humane son, and in a chapter headed 'Enter Mephistopheles' presents a dashing, amusing, fluent young man who looks set to be the final undoing of the judge's son; his name is Frank, among whose overtones is 'French'. Other evidence suggesting that 'Frenchness' somehow attached to foreigners' images of the devil from the eighteenth century on, at least, is the curious fact that in the 1780s the wealthy and well-travelled Englishman William Beckford wrote the satanic tale *Vathek* in French — perfect French; nothing else in his output was in French. Milner remarks: 'le choix de la mode d'expression ne saurait etre fortuit' (I, 131).
19. Wayne C. Booth, *The Rhetoric of Fiction* (Chicago, IL: University of Chicago Press, 1961), p. 383.
20. Robert and Isabelle Tombs, *That Sweet Enemy: The French and the British from the Sun King to the Present* (London: Heinemann, 2006).
21. Christopher Prendergast has recently drawn attention to this in his *Mirages and Mad Beliefs: Proust the Sceptic* (Princeton, NJ: Princeton University Press, 2013), pp. 29–31. (Inter alia, he distinguishes between 'esprit' and 'blague', p. 30.)
22. Rossi, p. 18.

— 7 —

L'Urbaniste

Jacques Réda

Pour Michael Sheringham

J'ai construit sans doute des centaines peut-être des milliers de villes.
Toutes se sont effondrées tantôt sous les cendres d'un volcan
tantôt dans les sables du désert ou sous un raz de marée.
Il n'en reste plus qu'une qui flotte dans le brouillard du souvenir
avec l'insistance du désir qu'elle a de trouver sa forme
définitive et hors du temps qui de nouveau la ruinerait.
On pourrait l'appeler Bin Sehir Tausendburg ou Milleville
car elle a quelque chose d'Istanbul de Berlin de Paris
et de beaucoup d'autres où j'ai rôdé tout au long de mes années
Athènes Dublin Stockholm Londres Madrid Rome Bruxelles
Vienne Munich Prague Lisbonne Alep Lausanne San Francisco
mais aussi Nancy Lyon Strasbourg Toulouse les deux plus belles
qui m'ont accueilli comme un roi passant incognito.
Ce que j'y cherchais pourtant j'en ai rarement été plus proche
que dans des patelins de troisième ordre comme celui où je suis né
et quand je bâtissais en pensée ou en rêve la ville des villes
c'était son plan qui s'imposait comme le nombre d'or.
Elle fut le modèle fondamental de tout mon urbanisme
dont je vais exposer rapidement les modes d'application.

Il faut qu'une ville soit à la fois d'une dimension réduite
et qu'on y éprouve à chaque endroit un goût d'immensité.
J'aime les villes qu'on voit surgir dans l'or des miniatures
comme des hauts bouquets de lys pointus entre tours et murailles
et celles qui n'en finissent pas de se perdre dans leurs faubourgs.
Mais la ville idéale contient l'infini dans son centre
auquel on n'accède jamais que par illumination.
Il suffit toutefois qu'elles le rendent sensible en permanence
ou vous en présentent çà et là le reflet dans un miroir.
D'un point modérément élevé on verra des collines
couvertes de bois et de prairies que l'on croirait pouvoir
atteindre en dix minutes par un itinéraire facile
qui pourtant vous ramène toujours à votre point de départ.
Ailleurs vous entrerez de plain pied avec l'orée d'une plaine

que rien ne semble empêcher de courir au-delà de Boukhara
mais c'est le faux infini-poussière et le vent se fuit lui-même
ou tente quelquefois de s'établir dans l'ennui des faubourgs.
On préfèrerait les supprimer mais ils sont nécessaires
à une bonne compréhension du sens de l'infini.
C'est là seulement que de loin en loin entre des maisons basses
qui tournent le dos mais pour brouter l'herbe fade des jardins
se dresse un immeuble étroit et sombre de cinq ou six étages,
alors que pas un seul dans la ville n'en doit dépasser trois.
Tout en haut le faux infini se tient à la fenêtre
et se regarde partir sans espoir d'arriver à son but.

Laissons-le se pendre et revenons donc au beau milieu : partout
on le devine qui s'approche et du même mouvement se dérobe,
si bien que l'on a sans arrêt l'envie de circuler
comme si l'on s'entretenait avec un compagnon de promenade
qui d'un moment à l'autre va vous révéler un secret
dont dépend non seulement tout l'avenir de votre existence
mais encore son passé comme si jamais toute la clarté
n'avait été faite sur vos sentiments, sur vos actes.
Et vous comprendrez peu à peu que votre vie aussi est une ville
avec ses rues, ses places, ses avenues et ses monuments,
y compris la gare où certains trains s'arrêtent, et d'autres passent
fracassants et à toute vitesse car vous n'êtes rien pour eux
ni la gare de cette ville que vous pensiez avoir créée
toute neuve et qui vous laisse une vague impression de déjà vu.
Vous ne saurez bientôt plus si c'est elle qui vous invente
ou si vous l'avez dessinée selon un plan préconçu
et qui tenait compte de tous vos pas à travers son espace.
Un conseil : attention aux fantômes : votre ville
est peuplée de milliers de visages inconnus indifférents
à votre présence et méfiez-vous de ceux qui vous sourient
n'attendez pas qu'ils vous adressent un signe plus familier :
C'est peut-être lui, peut-être elle
Pauvre cœur battant d'hirondelle
Dans l'air où vont les disparus
Qui n'attendent rien mais vous tendent
Une main qu'il ne faut pas perdre
Au grand danger d'être perdu.
Ce sont les doigts glacés d'une âme
qui cherche un refuge et réclame
Avec insistance son dû
Et ce fumeur qui vous arrête
Pour allumer sa cigarette
Chuchote 'm'as tu reconnu ?'

Or vous, n'est-ce pas, vous n'avez pas édifié toute une ville
pour que vos souvenirs y rappliquent touchés par la rumeur
et vous y guettent et vous y collent à tous les coins de rue.

Considérez que votre plan n'était pas aussi bon que vous le pensiez :
vous vous êtes trop laissé porter par de vieilles habitudes
et vous voilà pris au piège que votre mémoire a ourdi.

Donc rasez tout et recommencez sur des bases objectives
c'est-à-dire dépendant seulement de la règle et du compas.
Il se peut que cette méthode convienne à votre caractère
et vous donne en définitive une pleine satisfaction.
Je l'ai moi-même plus d'une fois et avec rigueur employée
et j'en étais assez content mais dès que le petit drapeau
flottait au faîte du bâtiment prévu pour la mairie
je ne songeais plus qu'à m'en aller aussi loin que possible
de cette ville désormais sans surprise et sans passé.
On n'aura pas tort de me juger changeant contradictoire
mais j'ai découvert à la longue la meilleure solution.
J'ai complètement renoncé à construire des villes et même
à vouloir parcourir toutes celles qu'on a bâties sans moi.
Ce sont elles à présent qui m'habitent et circulent comme une foule
de clochers minarets tours bulbes dômes chapiteaux
fleuves canaux ponts parcs mails ronds-points boulevards esplanades
palais temples musées théâtres supermarchés bistros.
J'en contiens chaque pavé j'en sens frissonner chaque brin d'herbe
dans des jardins secrets au fond des impasses où les yeux
des chats clignotent la nuit comme les feux le long des rues désertes
et j'entends tous les pas des gens qui vont de tous les côtés
et font un seul bruissement de pages dans une bibliothèque
où le temps insomnieux vient se relire quand la ville entière dort.
Je sais ce qu'il cherche : comment poursuivre, et ma propre attitude
n'a que l'apparence du détachement ou de la passivité.

J'écoute.
La vague bruissante et lisse et ses milliards de molécules
qui s'agitent dans le plus grand désordre obéissent pourtant
au rythme élémentaire dont je perçois le tic-tac sur l'asphalte
comme celui de deux talons aiguille qui se rapprochent à travers
la confusion les convulsions de toutes les villes du monde.
Antérieur au temps qui l'imite il a franchi d'un saut
le caniveau où se mélangeaient les ténèbres la lumière.
Et au centre infini de la ville sous l'arc de son sourire
il bat dans le maintenant-toujours d'un commencement pur.

— 8 —

Poorly Defined Goals

Ann Smock

Mrs A is the last Friend of the Library left in the circulation room at the end of a bleak March Sunday spent unpacking books and sorting them into piles. The books were brought in and donated to the annual Library Sale. A weary Mrs A gazes around her now with some satisfaction at the piles. There are six for fiction plus three extras for mysteries; three each for biography and science; a dozen or so for textbooks, reference books, how-to books and the like (*This Fabulous Century*, in 8 volumes, *Our Fifty States*, *Make Your Own Living Trust*). Several volumes lie on the table designated Miscellaneous; they are strays, from broken sets, or they are works of an unknown. Then there are a few in foreign languages. They lean against a chair in the hall, where, seated comfortably on the floor, Mrs A's eight-year-old is counting the small pieces of broken sidewalk slate she picked up earlier in the day. They will be good for marking, and will augment her collection. She appropriates a discarded styrofoam cup for use as an additional drawer in the mini-chiffarobe she has been constructing in her room to hold the slate shards and other stones, plus two crow's feathers, half an ad for fine porcelain, some pipe cleaners, a tiny eraser in the shape of a pig and some nice pencil shavings. Her eye strays to the illegible books propped nearby. She hesitates, then decides to take a dark green one home. The faded gold letters on its spine appeal to her: CONTES CHOISIS.

Mrs A turns the lights out and stands at the open door in the gathering darkness. 'Time to go, Violet.'

They leave. A dim glow from the street lamps on State Street enters the circulation room through the high windows; the piles stand in it, numb. Some stare at each other, some at nothing. Among the assembled volumes are many that once were gifts — tokens of misunderstandings — or books by relatives, unread. As night advances, the inertia to which all books are prone settles over these, and withdrawing into the pallor of the light, they let their autism show. *Sister Carrie. California State Parks.* A half-hearted gloss still adheres to a few in the Culture pile: *Gardens of Kyoto, Treasures of the Uffizi, Soups of France.*

Upon arriving home, Violet finds a letter waiting for her from her correspondent Walter B. He is her uncle.

> *Dear Colleague,*
>
> *I write regarding your several urgent queries as to your teaching schedule for the spring term at Comstock University. Your course on Birdsong will meet on Sundays from 5 to 8 A.M. in the main lecture hall located on the ground floor of Azure Hall. Unfortunately*

> *your seminar on Graphology has been canceled for lack of enrollment. However, we will continue to recommend your courses to all students. An office on the fourth floor of Azure — number 4210 — has been reserved for you. Please be so kind as to send by return mail your faculty club membership fee of four buttons, your subscription to the Comstock Poetry Review (two more buttons) and a sentence in which each of these words appears: egg, cloud, pause, shoelace, capsize.*
>
> *Salve!*
> *Uncle Walter*
> *Provost*

Violet and Walter share a collecting impulse. He is forever accumulating books, for example, and owns way too many. He has a good eye for nondescript ones. To be frank, he is drawn to useless, mismatched objects of all kinds. Anything that has got lost from some living whole and turned into an amputee is apt to appeal to him. He likes uninteresting places, too — dusty stairwells, bus stations late at night, vacant apartments. He doesn't really consider such places sad. Rather, untinged by any mood. He is fond of the idle pauses between acts, for example restaurants after the diners have gone but before the dirty dishes and wadded-up napkins are cleared away, or a concert hall when the instruments are still in their cases and the first violinist is chatting with the lighting technician or sharing a sandwich. He seems to set quite a store by boredom. Perhaps his sullen nephew, Violet's older brother Henry, from whom no one has heard lately, shares this with him — a lethargic disposition. Perhaps. It is hard to tell with Henry.

At any rate, books Walter B buys compulsively, at auctions and out of catalogues, especially when he has no money but not necessarily because he expects to read them. He just likes to collect them. It's not that he never opens one — he reads quite a lot, actually. It could just be that he isn't interested in getting anything out of them. Indeed he is dubious in general about outcomes, profits, progress and the like. He hates the idea that everything in life must lead to a result. He far prefers fruitlessness. At least, that would be one way of putting it. He says you can count on bad actions to bear fruit. That is their chief characteristic.

He is not really against fruitfulness but to his way of thinking it should stay inside whatever it is you do in life. If you want to understand a book it is best to make a hut somewhere within it and live there. You would also do well to copy the book, he advises.

In fact his nephew Henry is at this moment inching back over a long flat stretch around the middle of the fifth chapter of the book he has been living in lately — if you can call shuffling slowly back and forth across its silent terrain living. He sniffs at a slightly moist area he hadn't noticed before, lays his cheek down next to it and waits, but loose twigs scattered here and there poke his neck. So he pushes on, sighing, past the patch of star thistle, past the round hole, something's den. He touches the rim tentatively, waits, then on. At the little heap of stones he stops as usual and makes a slow circle around it, staring; then continues as far as the shed, just to scratch at the door once more before giving up. His nose is running a little, his tears fall on the dirt.

One might hope that Walter B would sympathize with the single-mindedness of this melancholic teen who devotes himself without hope to one book at a time (alone he stumbles around in it, in it alone). For whatever it is that attracts Walter to a book, it doesn't seem to be a feature that would help him map it onto a broader cultural context or complicate the history of anything.

Henry is aware that some people believe books are sanctuaries. He is too embarrassed to mention how often he finds vacant lots in them, and labyrinthine parking garages. It is unlikely that his uncle thinks books are sanctuaries. Rather, he seems drawn to particular ones as to an emergency. Notwithstanding his remark about camping inside one, it often seems to be something extraneous that draws him to a book — something like a loose page, or an unfortunate stain that makes the volume itself look as if it might like to be torn out from wherever it's been shelved or catalogued or understood — ripped out or maybe rudely summoned, to show up elsewhere, immediately.

When he thinks back on the great cities he has known, it is not so often great monuments that come to his mind, but rather blind alleys, dusty gates. They give him the impression of a kind of pause where the usual course of things appears less inevitable. He has felt — at the tumble-down entrance to a forgotten garden in Berlin's West End, say — a calm spot between things that usually jangle, like mystery and platitude, or great emotion and inertia. Instead of squaring off, in these quiet waystations opposites merge.

Not that he isn't quite attached all the same to a few illustrious works of art, for example the Isenheim Altarpiece, which he visited in Colmar as a youth. He posted a reproduction of it forever after, wherever he lived. It gives him the remote stare that things can give sometimes when you get too close — the distant look that says, "Nothing here for you."

His personal library is a mess. Partly because he has had to move around so much. On the floor stacks of books grow taller. Others never leave the crates he eagerly wrenches open. There is a lot of dust and torn paper. He doesn't mind: his books are spared the mild boredom of order. And subordination. The mild boredom of work, order, and subordination. Perhaps his library's disorder frees the books for a different kind of boredom, not so mild, maybe, and presaged by their occasional rude indifference.

Violet, for her part, is quite busy. First, she has had to catch up on her correspondence.

> *Dear Provost,*
>
> *Thank you for your lovely letter. Enclosed please find my faculty club membership fee, but not my magazine subscription, as I would prefer not to subscribe at present. Nonetheless, I dream with joy of joining you soon at Comstock, where I will bring the song of the thrush, the call of the tit and the pigeon's patois.*
>
> *Kindest regards,*
> *Violet A.*
> *Lecturer*
>
> *P.S. Regarding the puzzle you sent, here is the sentence: Time drags along the floor like a shoelace, which gives pause to a cloud blowing forward: into the delay capsizes the egg.*

Now, here is another sentence, in return. An old dog, to test a young duck's manners, gave her a runcible spoon, but whether she passed, nobody knows.

Perhaps this was written just to house a few special words. Four, to be exact. Which?
V.A.

In addition she has her seminar to plan. She has gathered some materials for it: a stapler and a tuning fork, a pocket appointment book from 1999 which someone at her house had put out for recycling, some ancient torn teacher handouts with a few smudged phrases still legible ("touches on birdsong", "Visions") that had been wedged at the back of a drawer — and heads for her office in Azure Hall. Her way leads down a narrow street in the illustrated Aesop's Fables she got for her birthday, sharp right at the tall black bear addressing a magpie on the outer wall of a hardware store, then twists and turns to an empty park with desiccated flower beds. This is the home of Comstock U. Violet passes under the stone arch, crosses the dusty courtyard where she notices some hubbub around the student theater, and climbs toward the fourth floor of Azure Hall, crossing paths with a colleague on the landing between the second and third. They introduce themselves. He is staggering under a long strip of canvas he says is to hang over the entrance arch for the start of the semester, and he spreads it out to show Violet:

LE ARNGMANGE MNT SYST M

Violet rummages in her satchel and finds a little garland of letters to add an extra touch:

S T A Y T U N E D F O R T H A T !

then resumes her march up the stairs to the fourth floor and her office, where she dumps from her satchel, along with the stapler, the torn handouts and so on, a couple of volumes which she intends to contribute to the reference room of the University Library; most of the stamp album she inherited from her mother's friend's son who died, which will make a nice atlas; a guide to Tompkins and Cortland Counties labeled "Visual Encyclopedia" and for a dictionary, a small pamphlet containing the words, in different languages, of some songs she likes, e.g. Die Nachtigallen schlagen | Hier in der Einsamkeit... Then at the bottom of her satchel she finds the box with her complete set for learning Basque: up to four can play, or one can play alone. This she sets aside for the Language Lab.

The main auditorium of Comstock University is located on the ground floor of Azure Hall. Large lecture courses are held here, as well as popular assemblies. Hanging lanterns illuminate the billboard-sized images on the walls depicting the Milky Way, the port of Algiers, the interior of a combustion engine. Outsized graphs and technical diagrams, discarded architectural drawings and engineering blueprints unfurl overhead, for picture-writing has been chosen by the poetry nuts in Letters and Sciences for the ceiling decor. Violet's class will meet here early on Sunday mornings. She is on her way home now, toward the end of the day, having attended a meeting of the Committee on Courses and got a reasonable start on her own syllabus, which lies on the desk in 4210. Weeks 1 and 2: Bird music. Recommended project: make a whistle or find one; practice your call. Weeks 2 through 4: Bird language. Research assignments: 1) interview a baby; 2) who is Bernardin de Ventadour? Weeks 5 and 6: Messenger birds. Problem: what messages are suitable? Required of all students: bring materials for a bird mask.

In the reference room of the Library, a ten-year-old consults the atlas Violet contributed, which is going absolutely nowhere on the Information Highway. He turns a page and gazes toward Libya, ochre behind its strip of sea and its palms, then contemplates the triangular Cape of Good Hope. He imagines the circulation of letters around the globe, the paths of planets in the sky. For some reason the memory of a recent eye exam comes to his mind. **Typing Manual,** the faded cover of an adjacent volume says. Inside, *A lizard enjoys vanilla ice cream. A peahen is white.* Briefly he considers the spines of a few other research tools — PMLA Index 1980–82; a guide to the Center for the Arts in Morgantown, W.Va., the handbook of a 1947 loan exhibition of French tapestries. Comstock kind of reminds me of my old truck collection, he says softly to himself. I guess I'll enroll.

He is already old enough to have figured out that people who drive trucks have to drive them, to earn money. It is not, it turns out, that truck driving is something well worth doing on its own. Toy trucks, though, and playroom cooking equipment partake of a world replete with challenging jobs and intriguing tools; rolling pins made out of mailing tubes, since they serve no purpose, preserve in the grownup world at least a hint of a world where work and its instruments, things and their use cohere. For the things are playthings and not factors in a big, colorless production process where adult-sized pastry blenders, fully functioning trucks, real trailers and aircraft carriers fade out into abstract phases of an all-encompassing value-producing apparatus, and it's never just to dig that anybody digs, never just to drive, or read. You might think that Comstock is a toy university — an Institute for Advanced Study designed for dolls. Be that as it may, few among the child students there, or the child faculty miss preschool or the pleasures of the nursery. Most are future-oriented! Their game, if you will, or their fantasy, with its bibliographies made out of ancient instruction manuals and its course catalogue glued together from a dilapidated guide to desert wildflowers, shows by the contrast it presents beside the real university's beige learning management system how unreal the real world really is at present, and in this way emits a vivid sign of a life to come.

Granted, Comstock students don't dream big. If they stick around here too long, they are unlikely to realize their full potential. Some of what they can be, probably they won't. Likewise faculty members at Comstock don't assess their options, project their goals. They are not especially creative.

Rarely are they "excited" — to participate in this, or launch that — and never do they begin a sentence "What *fascinates* me here is the way in which...." Many never seem to get anywhere at all with their research. Violet's colleague Stanley is an example: she likes to accompany him on trips to the University Library. They both have books to return every so often, and Stanley has recordings and scores to take back. He generally goes on to check New Acquisitions, with Violet at his side, and browse in Periodicals, sometimes posing a friendly question to Jane, the reference librarian. Yet what Violet especially likes is something tentative in his gait as he goes upstairs to Interlibrary Loan. He gives the agreeable impression that he is just taking practice steps, while looking for the spot where he might really begin his library work. He is more experienced than Violet, and, as someone else at some other school might put it, he is good at what he does — but he never gets past the starting point. Nobody considers this much of a problem at Comstock U., where most results, instead of accumulating, building up into something, appear to dissolve in thin air and experience, instead of making faculty members more mature, makes them even younger. When things go well for them, they have to chalk it up to beginners' luck. Indeed, at their very best they grade a paper or chair a meeting as if it were their first time ever doing it. Granted, this hardly ever happens without a lot of practice, but the way practice helps is not by making the professors more proficient. They are proficient enough already for all practical purposes. It is rather by discouraging their tendency to bust a gut, which their parents and other coaches at home are busy instilling in them — it's by sanding down their will, so that something else (their hands, for example) can take care of things for them.

Obviously Comstock faculty members, growing younger with practice, don't rediscover — revising their footnotes, going over their lectures — some enchanting, or frightful beginning, some irretrievable, one and only, long ago first time ever reading *The Yellow Dwarf* that no other time can ever quite be like. After all, they have a penchant for worn out, discarded stuff. More likely their papers and memos, their books and their flash drives slowly come to turn to them the strange face things have when habit's rhythms have ironed all the strangeness out of them. When long practice, like scales everyday, or conjugations, or like darning, or peeling and chopping has finally ceased to be preparation, because there's no time for a sequel. Then grading and meetings, chalk and i-pads and British Romanticism are released into another time: so novel! so *ordinaire.*

Nothing is likely to be at all different from the usual, when this release occurs, if it does, so it cannot be anything to aim for. On the other hand, nothing will be remotely the same, either, so you might imagine that eventually Comstock's graders and chairpersons will come to aim, yes, but at nothing, like some loony medieval lover of a lady he'll never meet — or they will start striving for something that cannot be striven for, something that no one can achieve on purpose. Once Comstock gets up to speed, there may be a lot of people young enough to be no one. Anyway, the new dispensation, should it come, will at least escape the mild boredom of order wherein work is subordinated to outcome.

Walter B jots down an idea or two suggested by Violet's shoelace and egg sentence ("Time drags along the floor like a shoelace," etc.) and puts it in a drawer. Time, he has written, with no more purpose than an untied lace, drags, forming a little eddy in the propulsive flow of things, and there the egg — material of genesis — dives.

Trailing and untidy, lagging time is the still-to-come time overcoming the purposeful and punctual, confusing their programs, watering down their dynamism. They lose their watches, neglect to process, forget to drive humanity forward. A lapse in the general course of implementations forms a whirlpool whose rhythmic pulse pulls them home.

"Couldn't you tell me what the quiz will be like tomorrow? Are you going to grade on a curve"? An anxious student visits Violet in her office hour, close to tears. "I can't remember all the birds you've mentioned. I've spent so much time memorizing but I'm afraid I'm going to flunk". Violet gives the student her copy of *Watchable Birds of California* by Mary Taylor Gray and suggests he sleep with it under his pillow.

"What's with the Sunday lectures"? another student inquires. "Sundays are supposed to be days off".

Violet answers, "We could switch to Wednesday. Wednesday was supposed to be the day for Birdsong 204 anyway, I think, but then on the University Calendar some days off changed places with days on, and Wednesday landed in Sunday's spot. So we might just as well land our Sunday on Wednesday's. If the whole class agrees.

"Will it still be a holiday? Or not?" the student wonders. Violet answers, "Yes".

A twelve-year-old called Bruno is taking a course on translation at Comstock University. His mother made him enroll in Mandarin from first grade on, and he already knows Spanish from home, so he thought Translation: Practice and Theory, offered in the Human Ecology Department, might be for him. "It's an advantage to know more than one language," his mother has often told him. His teacher brings him proverbs, songs, recipes to translate from English into Spanish into Mandarin. One of his Spanish-speaking classmates is studying Wolof, and translates Bruno's recipes translated from English into Spanish from Spanish into Wolof. And so on. Students who know only one language translate from it into it — proverbs into doctors' prescriptions or grocery lists into chronicles into poems. Bruno's mother believes that knowing multiple languages is enriching not to mention empowering because with more languages you can say more, and mean more (things you can't express in one you can in another; all the kinds of snow, for example). "I think it might be the opposite," he confides to her on a visit home, half-way into the semester.

In fact he is starting to suspect that what with all the different languages getting translated into each other or into themselves in Translation: Practice and Theory, the signifying gear in all of them could be getting worn out. In class, he has noticed, they have all been finding less and less reason to say anything whatsoever. "What about robust intellectual exchange?" Bruno's mother asks. "I don't know," he answers uncertainly.

It is peaceful in Translation: Practice and Theory. Nevertheless Bruno is preoccupied. The cause is probably a serious boy among his classmates with a devastating smile. They haven't spoken, Bruno doesn't know his name, but hopes the note which turned up on his desk recently is from him. The envelope had "To B" on it, and the note itself, written in cursive in the middle of a pale-green 3x5 card reads: *A peahen is white.*

The directions, in the book Henry is living in again, to his rendez-vous seem to indicate that it lies toward the end of the tenth chapter. But you have to take a subway to get there and transfer twice. It is late, the underground corridors between lines are almost deserted. Their white tile walls, harshly lit, regard him with mild scorn.

All at once four big heads without bodies but with huge, protruding tongues leap out to interrogate him, in unison. "*Parlez-vous* Business English?" He is proceeding in the wrong direction, having missed a turnoff. The smells of tar and urine mix in his soul and his hair is getting matted. He arrives on the wrong platform. There, vending machines stand at uneven intervals and propose unfamiliar refreshments. He hesitates, then turns back to try a different passageway. He can hear a train coming and makes up his mind hopelessly to take it. He does, lets several stops go by and then comes Belleville. Lovely City, he thinks, stumbles out and starts to climb the rue de Belleville. It is quite a long haul but unexpectedly he arrives at a vineyard with a fence around it, looking out over a metropolis from the side of the hill. Could this be the garden where she's supposed to be? Or the orchard? Could that be her standing among the short, pruned-back vine stocks, wearing jeans and a green windbreaker? Henry approaches the little gate. *C'est payant, monsieur*! snarls a guard, materializing suddenly. Henry is panting a little when he produces a large bill, the only one he can find at the bottom of his knapsack. The guard gives him a look of contempt, pockets the money, opens the gate.

"You're late," the girl in the jeans says. She is a knockout, but her face is stern. "Your poor, plodding devotion is getting you nowhere with me — which doesn't mean there's any other way. Not for you, in any case. Now get lost".

This is easy for Henry — he is lost practically all the time anyway. His nose is damp and cold, though, and his heart so heavy that Walter B senses it far away in some other book and writes to Violet.

> *Dear Colleague,*
>
> *I enclose with this letter some words which I would like very much for your brother Henry to receive as soon as is convenient. Would you be so kind as to see to this? To be perfectly clear, it is not to Henry that I wish to send these words so much as to his feet, to the oxfords Mrs. A always makes him wear on them — to his elbows, his shoulder blades — for I am confident that, receiving this missive, they will retain it for him, behind his back where he won't try to understand it, and proceed to change things for him after their own fashion.*
>
> *I am pleased to add that I hear only splendid reports of your teaching at our University, and I remain, as ever, your*
>
> *Uncle Walter*
> *Provost*
>
> *Don't lose heart,* the enclosed message goes. *There are only too many competent, purposeful people alive today. Why add to their numbers? Especially since love — which has no end — is staking all upon incompetence like yours.*
>
> *Responsible adults want to make everything in life prove itself. That is why they make you take so many tests. But don't worry. Love's unqualified faithful don't know what they are doing, or who they are, and their hapless unworthiness alone is worthy.*
>
> *Motivated people with credibility to burn, whose actions are as sure to be justified as to produce results, often say with satisfaction that they are driven, and really just about anything will serve them for fuel. They will eat anything. Don't let them get you down. Love lives without dining.*

Today Comstock's theater majors are painting a backdrop. How did they come by the midnight blue house-paint they are laying on so thick, slathering the mysterious faraway onto the nailed up, sanded boards? Scraping their hands, smearing their cheeks. A Political Scientist from a top Research Institute in California stumbles by. He is distracted, not quite himself. He'd waked up feeling under-incentivized and hadn't been able to charge his phone. Hence the blur spreading over his schedule for the day. He'd thought he would make a little headway on a grant proposal but his desk has lately taken on an odd appearance. Perhaps it is because he has neglected to clear away the agendas and minutes of past meetings. His competitors' CVs. Or to do anything at all about the promising projects whose vision statements are starting to form piles around him suggesting the uneven foundations of ruined buildings. Plus there are the stray objects which have been showing up lately among his files — the earmuffs he'd given up for lost, the teapot he once had the faint thought of offering to his administrative assistant. He sets out to find an espresso, and loses his way and ends up in a slight daze at a stagecraft class. The look of the backdrop freshly painted in thick midnight blue brings him up short. It seems a foreign landscape, stretching on way out of sight, all quiet and unmoving. Its distant stillness seems to fix him with a kind of glare and keeps on doing this even when he walks right up and gets nose-to-nose with the plain boards streaked with thick paint from Truitt's Paint and Wallpaper. He ought to get on with his day but he can't because his whole world has just got packed tight into the space of the little stage set with its frame clearly defining it. The charged atmosphere suggests he is about to receive an ultimatum, or some news, or get his first and last chance at something. The scenes that Comstock's young actors block, the figures they form entering and exiting, grouping and splitting, the fights and the chases they improvise scare him — the lightning movements, nervous Ratmansky gestures, each, he suspects, a fleeting flashing sign from some other world they're in contact with, whence they send out signals by fits and starts. They dream small as we know, not big — really they're tearing the future's jerky signs and signals *right out* of the magical realm of dreams and applying them to materials: to scene design and lighting, to pulleys and props, cardboard and paint; to scraps from their story books, to dialogues, trumpets and drums, to rounds.

Dreamers love a still, heavenly blue fading out of sight. They don't like seeing things up close because from up close nothing is still, there is movement everywhere, incessantly. Whatever they see up close disappoints them. Their delight is to command nature herself to stand still and yield to pastel images. Opposed to this dreamy pleasure, think not right off of the can-do man's satisfactions. He's rolled up his sleeves and mastered nature. Great. But think instead of the Poli-Sci professor whose whole world, as though summoned by some sudden gesture, has hurtled over the threshold between close and distant, turbulence and immobility. Its agitation and its stillness collide and stand clasped, each by the other. He is unmoved by this, and transported.

Bruno has heard from Violet's students in Birdsong 204 that Wednesday is Sunday at Comstock, and he wonders if Thursday, the day of his translation class, might not also be Sunday, or at least Saturday, or possibly Labor Day. It's not that they are idle in the class, they work a lot but all the while it feels as if they are on spring break. Bruno would not say that translation is so fascinating it's actually fun. No, certainly not. How to explain, then, his feeling when he works in Translation: Practice and Theory that the whole class has knocked off early?

The other question he has for Violet in her office hour bears on passenger pigeons. Violet thinks it would be worth asking if the starling who has been auditing her course might undertake the errand Bruno has in mind. She will look into this.

At the moment, however, Bruno, unfortunately, is sleeping through his music class. In his dream, he is in his Translation classroom where all the objects seem to be peeling: the blackboard, the coat rack, the bust of Marx, the rubber plant... Little heaps of dust and feathery detritus — nothing gross like old skin or fingernails; rather, thin strips of dried-out paint, chips of varnish or textured surface, with a frayed name-tag mixed in here and there gather at the feet of things, as if these were all shedding their colors, their shine, their look, their face. In the janitor's closet Bruno finds a bucket, a big can of liquid glue with a roller and rushes to re-attach the things' expressions (their smiles, their tears) — to re-apply their names and meanings, their colors and shapes but the glue turns out to be water and the roller shrinks to a useless size. He wakes up sweating just as the room in his dream starts filling with radiant forms he can't recognize as the forms of anything whatsoever and with unattributable reds and blues, the golds and greens of nothing. The song he thinks he hears swelling up turns out to be a CD the music professor has just turned on. Whew.

During Bruno's dream Henry — dismissed by the girl in the green windbreaker — has been trudging on along the vineyard's edge to the place where it joins the Parc de Belleville and there, because his head is bowed, his gaze descends from the little plaza lined with plastic bags full of garbage to the lawns and paths stretching away below. It is dusk. Absent-mindedly he perceives that the earth is turned over in the flower beds down the hill, ready for something new. He heads nowhere in particular, but in their general direction, which is to say, down. He is exhausted, and if it were only up to him he would probably fall, but his feet carry him along, and his loneliness seems to be watching out for him too. After a while the moon comes out. Its pale light sifting through tree leaves mixes with the sound of the evening breeze to form a fringe of glints and murmurs fluttering around the edges of Henry's attention. Now he bends down to adjust his sock which has formed a bunch around his heel inside his shoe and something rings out all of a sudden — a bird call maybe, someone hailing him, he couldn't say. But as he straightens up with a huge effort, the walls and hallways inside him crumble, his time falls in loose folds. He walks on further, past a park bench, a shovel leaning on a wheelbarrow, a giant sack of planting mix. The first stars appear and bear their names wordlessly to Henry, who forms them with his lips — names he wouldn't really think of attaching to the early evening gleams, or to anything, but which, without their ever being given, the stars just present, simply by coming into view, appearing and being themselves, only to fade away sooner or later and disappear, there being nothing to add (develop or expand), nothing else to mean. Henry thinks of the mountain peaks he once saw early in the morning on a camping trip breaking through mist, and the church spire looming up unexpectedly when he turned a corner long ago in a foreign town, and their names, too, swim to the surface of his mind, theirs and still others. Presently, on the blurred horizon against the darkening sky a great swath of pink: peonies unfolding their buds and blooming in profusion. Among them a young face shows. Violet! All at once Henry is with her, in the courtyard of Comstock U., where she and her students (one with a purple martin mask, another looking out through bobolink eyes) are decorating for an outdoor springtime general assembly, suspending overhead in the moonlight giant wings of owls and hawks beautifully constructed of papier-mâché and feathers. Some sort of impromptu ceremony is underway in a far corner of the courtyard where the students in Translation: Practice and Theory are gathered. Henry cannot recognize the language they are singing and laughing in. Maybe one not to use so much as to celebrate. In any case it looks as if they understand each other perfectly OK. A disoriented adult who clearly doesn't understand anything at all appears and stands shyly next to Henry, on the outskirts. Perhaps the stray Political Scientist? It is in his hand that a passing starling deposits something from his straight, tapered beak. A small, smooth leaf of paper. Also with his beak, and a glare from his little black eye the starling briefly yet emphatically indicates the boy among the revelers that the leaf is meant for, at least the grown-up thinks this might be so: maybe he is supposed to complete a delivery. But since he still just stands there, still kind of non-plussed, the starling pauses long enough to hiss helpfully into his ear, "El mensaje de amor". "La lettre est blanche," the young addressee comments upon receipt of it, looking up with joy.

****

If Comstock University had a Board of Trustees, its members would include:

> Th. Adorno, H. Arendt, W. Austin, W. Benjamin, M. Blanchot, E. Bloch, J. von Eichendorff, P. Fenves, W. Hamacher, E. Hocquard, S. Mallarmé, H. Melville, J. Roubaud, G. Scholem, W. Smock.

— 9 —

Mieux que nous

Jacques Roubaud

hommage à Michael Sheringham

Nous l'avons rencontré pour la première fois
Près de Kensington High Street Station, je crois,
Et nous avons parlé français car M....-L.....
Ne parle pas anglais. Parfaite, sa maîtrise
De la langue opposée, invisible parût
Si naturelle que sans s'étonner on sut
Qu'il connaissait aussi, nivernaise, l'ancienne
Forêt des Amognes. Pourquoi? Que se trouve sienne
Cette image n'était pas un des hasards fous
Mais prouvait qu'il savait mieux la France que nous

— 10 —

Crossing through Dakar at High Noon: Legend, Destiny and the Everyday

James S. Williams

> C'est d'ailleurs ce que j'aime en général au cinéma: une saturation de signes magnifiques qui baignent dans la lumière de leur absence d'explication. Voilà pourquoi je crois au cinéma.[1]
>
> M. de Oliveira

Picture this: a herd of zebus emerging from the distance in a dusty haze and drifting slowly across the asphalt of a multilane highway in daytime Dakar, shepherded by a tall, elderly man dressed in a star-studded denim shirt and cowboy boots wielding a stick. As the camera records this African urban cowboy scene in a series of long takes (from an initial, gentle, high-angle, panning shot in extreme long shot to medium long-shots at ground level), we hear the theme tune from Fred Zinnemann's 1952 Western *High Noon* by Tex Ritter who warbles in a moody baritone about love, duty, longing, destiny and vengeance.[2] He pleads: 'Do not forsake me, oh my darling | On this our wedding day | Do not forsake me, oh my darling | Wait, wait along | I do not know what fate awaits me | I only know I must be brave | For I must face a man who hates me | Or die a coward, a craven coward | Or die a coward in my grave'. Despite such tough and bruising language, the heavy, plaintive undertow of the ballad matches the slow, horizontal movement of cattle right to left across the screen blocking that of the cars now stalled up vertically in both directions. And like the ballad, the way the camera intersects directly with, and intrudes into, the brute, day to day reality of Dakar in real time (this is not a CGI simulation) creates a set of startling juxtapositions: between documentary-style footage of the new Afropolis of Dakar and the arcane sentiments of a classic Hollywood western; between ambient street noise and urban grit and the mute vulnerability of animals blocking the traffic; and above all between the generic everyday (the daily commute, the herding of cattle) and the special and unique (Dakar reborn in the sunlit glow as the high sierra). The sheer heft and heave of this provocative panorama of the Senegalese capital is thrown into heightened relief by the arrival on screen of the explosive, poetic French phrase 'Mille Soleils' emblazoned in thick, blue ultramarine lettering over a setting red sun, under which falls in slender lower-case the wisp of an African female name, 'Mati Diop'.[3]

Such is the extraordinary, magnetic, opening credit sequence of the forty-five

Fig. 10.1. A herd of zebus in daytime Dakar: the opening sequence from *Milles Soleils*, directed by Mati Diop, produced by Anna Sanders Films (France), 2013.

minute short, *Mille Soleils* (2013), written and directed by Mati Diop.[4] It's like a controlled rush: a highly charged, giddy, liminal moment of crossing where the screen becomes a generative site of flows and counter-flows, the cattle seemingly cast adrift yet always moving together loosely against the flow of the traffic, presumably on their way to the slaughterhouse. The camera operated by Director of Photography Hélène Louvart is harnessing, steadily and unflinchingly, the physical forces of external reality. Contingent on the shifting fabric of the Dakarian everyday, and framed literally by it, this exemplary frontier image dares us to ask how much of what we are witnessing is 'natural' (i.e. record footage of a chance encounter in Dakar where mounds of earth do indeed line the main roads) and how much is staged and composed for the camera. It also conveys an irresistible sense of promise — of opening up new elemental spaces in African cinema somewhere beyond the labile frame that verge potentially on the mythical — just as the stark, documentary-like beginning of *High Noon*, with its voiceless actors appearing to move in real time, once announced a new form of the Western (even if its tale of one individual (Gary Cooper as town marshal) forced to confront a gang of killers proved archetypal Hollywood). Before the narrative regions of *Mille Soleils* are even broached, therefore, we sense this is a work plugging directly into the imaginary of cinema. Indeed, these potent, resonant images of motion across the surface of the real appear loaded with the freight of cinematic memory, as if carrying in their wake the entire sweep of modern Senegalese cinema — a cinema founded precisely on the tensions between tradition and modernity, rural life and the industrializing city, nationalism and pan-Africanism. As a bold cinematic gesture and dazzling conceit, they recall inevitably Djibril Diop Mambéty's legendary debut feature *Touki-Bouki* [*The Journey of the Hyena*] (1973), a road movie that likewise took place in contemporary Dakar and which, with its modernist blend of African street culture and Western popular culture inspired by *Easy Rider* (1969), *Bonnie and Clyde* (1967),

Fig. 10.2. Magaye Niang awash in the blue light of the projector screen in *Milles Soleils*, directed by Mati Diop, produced by Anna Sanders Films (France), 2013.

American blaxploitation films and the French New Wave, offered a vivid snapshot of West Africa in the immediate aftermath of decolonization and independence.[5] The sight of a solitary, ageing, urban cowherd lost in the Dakar traffic evokes the young, rebellious male protagonist of *Touki-Bouki*, Mory, combing the streets of Dakar alone after deciding at the last minute not to embark on the boat bound for France with his girlfriend Anta. Moreover, *Touki-Bouki* concluded with the same *cinéma-vérité*-style images with which it began: a boy herder (possibly Mory in his youth) leading his cattle from the sahel to the abattoir. And wait a second: look again at the opening shots of crossing in *Mille Soleils* — it's the same man! Or at least the same actor, Magaye Niang, now forty years on, as if, like the character he played in *Touki-Bouki*, he had never left Dakar.

And it's a fact — he didn't. Like his character Mory, Niang remained in Dakar, a semi-professional actor as well as musician, photographer, even sound engineer (he describes himself in one interview as a jack-of-all-trades).[6] The twists of fate don't stop there, however, for, as we quickly learn, Magaye's co-star in *Touki-Bouki*, Marème Niang (unrelated — Niang is a common last name in Senegal), did like her character and left Dakar, though not before starring as the progressive feminist student and defiant daughter Rama in Ousmane Sembène's *Xala* (1974) — a film that also features Magaye in a bit role as a pickpocket who charms his way into the new, corrupt, political elite. This fabulous coincidence of destinies would surely have to be made up, yet truth in the cinema is always stranger than fiction. In an escalating vertigo of floating identities, Magaye and Marème in *Mille Soleils* are both actors playing themselves and the reincarnation of their fictional characters Mory and Anta, although in the case of Marème we will never actually encounter her as she is now. Magaye may or may not currently own a farm, but he is certainly not a professional herder as *Mille Soleils* would like us to believe. Hence, the two striking portrayals here of Magaye as Dakar cowboy and Marème as security guard on an oil rig in Alaska — all the more seductive for being so oddly contrasting and extravagant — are pure narrative constructions.

It's on this tightly compressed note of reversible movements and intersecting destinies — and crucially the fantasy that Mory then and Magaye now are one and the same — that *Mille Soleils* manifests itself into being. This is a film that will consciously work the borderlands between truth and fiction, the real and the constructed, by expanding the formal and thematic implications of the opening images of crossing and by staging a series of stunning reversals. And it does so precisely because it taps simultaneously into the lure of both the everyday and cinema, that is, our temptation to believe that what we see and hear unfolding in front of us is *real*. At the film's core is the extended scene of a night-time, open-air screening of *Touki-Bouki* in a square in downtown Dakar, an invited affair to celebrate the film's fortieth anniversary but with the general public also looking on. Magaye arrives late and inebriated after drinking in a nearby bar, as if reluctant to attend his second appointment with cinematic destiny after the strange, nebulous semi-fame of *Touki-Bouki*. Pictured in close-up sporting the same shirt and boots, grey-haired and rail-thin but still ruggedly handsome, he retains the outlaw cool and hip of *Touki-Bouki*. We watch from behind the audience as sequences from the latter stages of Mambéty's film are projected on a large screen amidst the everyday bustle of Dakar. Following the screening Magaye is asked how his life has changed since making it. Awash in the translucent blue glow of the projector and standing in front of a magnified image of his younger self — the moment Mory heads out of the port in his millionaire suit deflated and confused — he remains silent and sullen, his lanky frame casting a narrow black shadow on the screen. In apparent denial and delusion about his current unrecognized status, he tries in Wolof to convince a group of young boys that he's the same man they behold in the film, yet they protest: 'You're in a dream, that's not you!'. Later, his old friends, including Joe Wakam (Issa Samb), Ben Diogaye Bèye, and the celebrated jazz musician Wasis Diop (Diop's own father and younger brother of Mambéty), chastise him by pointing out that '*touki*' means to travel, yet he's stuck. Hence, Mory/Magaye has once again flunked his moment of destiny and the chance to be famous second time round. Scrounging for money and insisting grumpily 'Là où je vais, je suis une star!' while his female partner or assistant berates him, just as Mory's onscreen mother did forty years before, there seems little to separate the nervously shifting and rather louche older man from the young hustler he once played. Hence, if the beginning of *Mille Soleils* reimagines Magaye as a Western hero on the urban prairie, he is no Will Kane who in *High Noon*, after a grand and bloody shoot-out with his rival, triumphantly left town. Instead, a pale, spectral avatar of his fictional character, he seems visibly haunted by the consequences of never having left Dakar. Exiled in his legendary screen role, he appears doomed to keep paying the price for once being Mory.

The Lost and the Found

What exactly is Diop doing with the incorporated sequences from *Touki-Bouki* which feed so directly into the structuring fiction of *Mille Soleils*? For they appear to function as so many found objects, as in the film genre known as 'found' or archive footage, a standard marker of authenticity in documentary cinema. *Touki-Bouki* is, in fact, a film that was literally lost by powerful institutional forces in African cinema due to Mambéty's perceived dissidence. His utterly original and idiosyncratic style clashed with the kind of social realist cinema and overtly political, allegorical narratives produced by Sembène and others and promoted during the first decades after Senegal's independence by the African Federation of Filmmakers (FEPACI) (*Touki-Bouki* was all but ignored in Senegal on its release and not distributed in France for another ten years). Like Mory arriving at the port in *Touki-Bouki* with his dreams of future wealth and fame in Paris (ironically romanticized by the repeated refrain from Josephine Baker's jaunty *Paris, Paris, Paris* heralding paradise on earth), Mambéty had been set to embark on a glorious and unstoppable Senegalese New Wave. Yet ideologically out of favour he could not secure major funding and tragically made only one more feature film many years later, *Hyènes* [Hyenas] (1992), a damning indictment of neoliberalism and consumerism, as well as a small handful of brilliant shorts.[7] *Touki-Bouki* thus represents the stupendous promise of something that never quite materialized. The question, what if Mory had taken the ferry with Anta — and with it, what if Magaye had followed the example of his co-actor and left Dakar — also comes down to what if Mambéty, hailed locally as a 'trader of dreams', had been able to pursue his natural destiny as an exceptional, trailblazing artist. Mambéty later often talked of his sense of loneliness and exile after eventually leaving Senegal to seek success and solace in Europe, only to find that as his dream quickly disintegrated he would never be able to return home (he died in 1998 aged 53 in Paris while undergoing treatment for lung cancer). *Touki-Bouki* may be read therefore as a film already signalling proleptically the impending fate of its director.

The restrained melancholy of the opening image of urban drift in *Mille Soleils*, its existential ache and pull, conveys this shared story of abortive destinies — the regret of dreams deferred and potential unfulfilled — as well as, more generally, the forlorn history of Senegalese cinema, now in steady decline since the golden age of innovation and experimentation in the 1960s and 1970s due to the almost total withdrawal of State support — much like the capital Dakar itself, now struggling with an exploding population, increasing poverty, and the flight of young migrants to Europe (the subject of Diop's searing 2009 short, *Atlantiques*). Only a few feature films are made each year, and Dakar has effectively fallen dark with the closure or demolition of virtually all its great cinemas. Yet if *Mille Soleils* is a brooding work etched in the agonies of a nation and its cinema, part of its dynamic force derives precisely from reprojecting into the light Mambéty's forgotten masterpiece, suddenly visible again on the very streets which engendered it. For the glimpsed sequences of this legendary film have the electroshock force of early primitive cinema — a sudden bolt of energy and sensation released from the vaults as if for the first time to recharge Senegalese cinema and society. Indeed, *Mille Soleils* throbs and vibrates with the surge of affect of inherited images — rough-hewn, visceral, ravishing — in experimental compositions and vistas combining 35 mm and video.

But what sort of film really is *Mille Soleils*, with its cascading collage of images and sounds directly embedded in the heat of the everyday? Its official status is a documentary, and its hypnotic power created by the use of found footage, hand-held camera effects, and long takes in real time — given images that would seem to speak for themselves — seduces us into believing this. Yet *Mille Soleils* certainly does not perform like a conventional documentary, proceeding instead as if instinctively in a trance by means of impressionist touches, suggestions and evocations. There is no formal introduction, no commanding authorial voice-over, and no explicit articulation of an overarching critical discourse. Indeed, the stories, acts and gestures presented as factual start very soon to appear more like legendary fables or parables whose significance will only become clear as our understanding of the film's personal, cultural and historical contexts deepens. Already in the continuous long takes of the opening urban frieze — a threshold image in the process of being constructed in the live present where what seems momentous and unique is framed by everyday ritual — Diop appears to be exploring the very conditions and limits of fabulation. We quickly suspect, in fact, that the entire film may be an elaborate fiction, not just the later, more obviously staged scenes of Alaska when, as Magaye speaks in a public phone-shop to a female voice on the end of the line identified as Marème, vowing he will never let her depart again, he is abruptly transported into a frozen landscape across which he strides in hot pursuit, still clad in his denim shirt but now with bare feet which leave footprints in the snow. From out of the mist of a waterfall a naked female figure momentarily appears and walks past him. The status of this apparition and comic missed encounter is left deliberately opaque: did Magaye, attracted like all Diop's protagonists by the vague promise of an *ailleurs*,[8] indeed travel to Alaska to find Marème, or, as seems more likely, is this a wholly subjective vision by Magaye of his failure to do so (in a film where paradoxically subjective POV shots are rigorously denied)? In fact, *Mille Soleils* luxuriates in the factitious and continually invites us to speculate on its uncertain status: is it a follow-up to *Touki-Bouki* with its characters now older and wiser, or a remake that replays certain documentary-like scenes but with telling points of difference? Diop, for example, also enters the local abattoir but withholds the gruesome moment captured by Mambéty of the animals' sudden shock at their fate, preferring instead to focus on the diurnal routine of slaughter.

Mille Soleils is thus a film that refuses easy categorization, reinventing documentary reality as a polyphonic clamour of cinematic and musical subjectivities. It is essentially a fabrication that invokes reality in order to underscore and embellish its own facticity, revelling in the workaday real to guard even more jealously and assiduously its own secrets and mysteries. Here is Diop's strong authorial warning about the episode of the phone call: 'It bears reminding that *Mille Soleils* is a fiction. The sole element of reality that I kept in my film is that Magaye Niang stayed in

Dakar and Marème Niang left for Alaska. From there I took fictional liberties, but the phone conversation that is heard in the film remains *quite faithful* to the real conversation that I recorded between the two actors. Nothing is true and nothing is false in my film. The *friction and two-way shuttling* between reality and myth is the main subject of my film' (my emphasis).[9] The ambivalent nature of the reconstructed phone call is further amplified in another interview where Diop freely admits she recorded the original conversation in 2008 by stealth, for which Marème later reproached her (it would take another five years for Diop to regain her trust).[10] Folding reality and fantasy into and over each other, Diop keeps us always in a state of creative and interpretative suspense. The film's shimmering surfaces, phantasmatic textures and spectral repetitions of familiar images would appear inexhaustible.

It is precisely the poetic way *Mille Soleils* shuttles between — and potentially synthesizes — moments of raw and found footage, constructed and possibly reconstructed images, memory and fantasy, that interests me most here for what is says of the relation in cinema between the cinematic real and unreal conceived in terms of the found and the made. What makes this metapoetic process even more complex and fascinating is the biographical fact of Diop's own relationship to her uncle Mambéty — this is personal history interacting directly with the grand History of cinema. *Mille Soleils* is in large part the story of her return to Africa in search of the truth of *Touki-Bouki*. Growing up as a *métisse* in Paris with her white mother, Diop claims in one interview that she never knew her uncle and that it was only through her later discovery of his films, and subsequent dialogue with her father about them, that she made links with her own Senegalese origins (see Picard 2013). Dedicated to Mambéty, and clearly intended as a personal tribute, *Mille Soleils* unfolds implicitly as a series of reflections on the cinematic legacy of *Touki-Bouki* viewed against the backdrop of one Senegalese family across the generations and of a country's troubled past. In what appears a case study of film genealogy and cinematic succession, Diop reengages with her family history by negotiating the miraculous event and enigma of *Touki-Bouki*. The freeze-frame that ends *Touki-Bouki*, whereby the young cowherd is suddenly suspended as he moves out of frame, is effectively reanimated by Diop who releases Mory/Magaye back into the spectacle of real time in *Mille Soleils* with his herd of zebus entering the visual field (we note, too, that 'The Ballad of High Noon' which bookends *Mille Soleils* was one of Mambéty's favourites).[11] Indeed, Magaye is arguably already a stand-in for her solitary and mysterious uncle, the notorious 'poet-dandy' and vagabond of Dakar, as in the hand-held camera sequences (many filmed by Diop herself) when we follow him drunk in the streets and forever roaming. Diop's primary challenge of ensuring the transmission of a shared cultural legacy while also moving decisively out of Mambéty's all-encompassing creative shadow and influence is all the more daunting for the fact that he was a unique visionary filmmaker who regarded himself as both a *griot* for his times and creator of the future.

Yet what does it mean exactly for Diop to reclaim and redeem Mambéty's seminal work in the form of found footage, not merely as a lost and found item of family luggage but also as a jewel of modern African cinema? Put a little differently: what are the terms and conditions attached to presenting inherited images of narrative fiction as the found and real? Is it the case that in order to inscribe herself aesthetically within her family lineage and pay off with interest the artistic debt she owes Mambéty (and in the process establish herself as an individual African female *auteur* in her own right), Diop must trope directly on her uncle's work by transfiguring the real embodied by the found images of *Touki-Bouki*? And, if so, what does this reveal of Diop's general approach to the physical world which is intimately linked here with the everyday? I want to consider these questions in the express light of Mambéty's method and style in *Touki-Bouki*, for this will serve to highlight Diop's poetic strategy of reframing and reconfiguring reality and fiction as the found and made, and extending further that relation in terms of the unique event and the everyday. *Mille Soleils*, I shall argue, pre-empts and disqualifies the notion of the Big Event and single epic encounter with Destiny of the kind championed in *High Noon* by letting it stray and shatter in the creative, intoxicating borderlands of the everyday.

The Found and the Made: Live Archives, New Projections

In *Touki-Bouki* Mambéty had captured the unique rhythms of Dakar in formally intrepid and uncompromising ways, eschewing clear meaning, either overt or allegorical, in favour of an associative, poetic logic. With its recurring symbolic images of animals being slaughtered to evoke and intensify the fate of humans isolated from freedom, the film pitted the blood-red energy of urban experience against repeated shots of the ocean which become progressively more abstract, at times even occupying the whole frame. Mambéty's dialectical collage of new, cut-up, cross-fertilizing rhythms matching those inherent in the Wolof language itself was sustained by breathless ellipses, unaccounted flash-forwards, abrupt, often absurd collisions and acerbic juxtapositions, including flagrant contrasts between poverty and wealth, rural existence and the metropolis, the baroque architecture of Le Plateau and the sprawling shanty towns (Mambéty's first film was a short entitled appropriately *Contras'city* (1968)). Formal experimentation afforded Mambéty a means of not being tied down to the enormity of the present which raw documentary-style footage ran the risk of merely reproducing. Yet in challenging the fixed dictates of social realism and naturalism in order to reinvent the present, Mambéty sought always to interweave compelling fictions with punctual, audiovisual bulletins of his native city now being subsumed into dehumanizing and alienating narratives of industrial progress. He celebrated the small daily acts of survival, encounter and community, in particular of the socially excluded eking out a fragile existence on the margins. Indeed, his engagement with the real urban space of Dakar and its individual and communal activities and rituals (drawing water from the local well, public wrestling matches, the daily workings of the port), bespeak a commitment to capturing what Michael Sheringham, theorizing the quotidian and *quotidienneté* as a set of practices and relations and rhythms, has called 'a commonality of experience

FIG. 10.3. Magaye Niang and Marème Niang as Mory and Anta in *Touki-Bouki (The Journey of the Hyena)*, directed by Djibril Diop Mambéty, produced by Cinegrit and Studio Kankourama, 1973.

that is endlessly forming and reforming human activities and encounters — if only we deigned to notice it'.[12] Mambéty ensures we do precisely this, for his scorching sounds and images may be read directly as what Sheringham elegantly calls 'figures of the everyday, pathways into the apprehension of everydayness' (Sheringham, p. 363), where the communal, dissident mass of quotidian existence is revealed as a form of resistance to the control and codification of the prevailing system. Key to Mambéty's strategy was his subversive *détournement* of *cinéma-vérité* images. At one point in *Touki-Bouki* he intercuts historical footage of a presidential procession (a banner is glimpsed with the names of Senghor and, just visible, Albert-Bernard Bongo (later Omar Bongo, President of Gabon)) with a tracking shot of Mory and Anta in their newly stolen gear waving to the crowd from a Citroën decked in the stars and stripes of the American flag. Elsewhere, an outside wrestling match sequence incorporates recorded documentary images of the elders of the Lebu tribe in attendance to help fund a memorial statue to Charles de Gaulle. These incursions into objective reality privileged the long take and the slow pace of individual shots through lingering, probing pans, so allowing the viewer to become immersed, if only intermittently, in the duration of everyday reality. The force of this raw reality is further underlined in *Touki-Bouki* by being ritualistically repeated through montage, notably in the film's climactic sequence where repeated shots of animal slaughter are juxtaposed with Mory running away from the port area. The end-result of Mambéty's stylistic research was a new and radical reshuffling of documentary and narrative, experience and spectacle.

Propelled by the same fierce, experimental drive as *Touki-Bouki*, *Mille Soleils* is at once similar to, and fundamentally different from, Mambéty's practice of both honouring and (re)making found reality. For whilst Diop trades equally in symbolic images and is a naturally self-reflexive storyteller, she responds more freely to the reverberations of the real. In clear emulation of Mambéty's sensory use of sound and colour, *Mille Soleils* has the technicolour feel of a kaleidoscope — a distilled, poetic caress of reds and blues as well as combinations of green, pink and white, flashes of purple and magenta lights in the discotheque scenes, and the continual flooding of the image with a single, saturated digital colour to isolate characters from their settings. Plunging us into fully synchronous real time and tracing voluptuously 'the unfolding rhythms of the day' (to use Sheringham's phrase),[13] Diop also stays true to Mambéty's luminous vision of the everyday of Dakar as a site of glaring and surreal juxtapositions — a restless, sometimes volatile, zone of savage beauty and human hyenas. However, whilst Mambéty ensured that his viewer always understood more or less the limits and parameters of his formal and thematic method of contrast and incongruity (namely 'real' diegesis (found documentary or archive footage) versus fantasy (dream sequence, poetic motif)), Diop appears to blur and confound all such binaries. Indeed, if Mambéty always foregrounded oppositions and polarities, Diop works in reverse towards equivalence: everyday images are treated in the same manner as both found or constructed images. Indeed, *Mille Soleils* may initially coax us into thinking we know the difference between what is reconstructed reality and what is recorded directly from the convulsions of daily life due to the eminently sequential order of episodes (Magaye preparing for the event, his taxi ride through Dakar to attend, the screening followed by Q & A). We soon intuit, however, that the fictional and documentary are uncertain poles and highly elastic concepts, and that *Mille Soleils* resides ambiguously somewhere between the two. For what might seem authentic, reportage-style footage could either be a remake of previous footage (the abattoir sequence), or the incorporation of classic narrative cinema as found footage (the celluloid 'reel time' of *Touki-Bouki*), or else staged and entirely fabricated episodes, as in the Alaskan scene and the extended taxi sequence where Magaye encounters in the driver the voice of a new generation of political protest in Senegal, the real Djily Baghdad, chief rapper of the group '5kiem Underground' and a politically committed activist (he was a key figure in the 'Y'en a marre' ['We're fed up'] movement of artists, journalists and students during the country's 2012 presidential elections).

At every level, therefore, *Mille Soleils* may be regarded as an African trickster tale. Enmeshing different kinds of real (documentary, biographical, (film) historical and familial), casually distorting the lines and boundaries of genre, forgoing the formal comforts of obsessive repetition, the film impels us ultimately to disregard the particular status and source of the diegetic sounds and images at stake. We come to realize more profoundly how the real in cinema is always in the act of being found, and that the found is never just found but always already refound, remade and reimagined. It's not just that the found real, variously defined, serves as an automatic vehicle for new cinematographic forms — the very distinction between the found (the real) and the made (the artwork) evaporates in Diop's hands. Each image in her cinema, however 'natural', is always in the act of being found and disclosing itself in the present as made and constructed. As in the film's inaugural crossing where Dakar slowly comes forth in real time, the everyday has time here to unfold out of itself poetically. The act of cinematic poiesis reveals, in fact, that these two instances, the made and the found, are always already intertwined and part of a moving continuum.

What this means is that the everyday real is not some pristine, immaculate experience that can be seized upon intact by the camera but always multiply generated and composed, and always something else, even imaginary, by the time we get to see and hear it — whether a replication or reconstruction or reimagining of something anterior, source unknown. The found narrative images of *Touki-Bouki* are reactivated by Diop as a formal springboard from which to spin off into the loose, fluid, free-floating regions of fable with romantic fantasies of reunion (the driving fantasy of seeing Mory/Magaye and Anta/Marème finally together). Indeed, the simultaneous impulse towards fiction and the everyday appears unstoppable in *Mille Soleils*: the image of the everyday real is already personal or metaphorical or mythical or iconic or legendary, or flush with all things at once, and it contains within itself both the pre-movements of memory and the premonitions of desire. As Diop remarks of her crafted hybrid of cultures, traditions and styles that skirt the borders of the real and fiction, reality and dreams, reality and myth, 'nothing is true and nothing is false' (Picard 2013). More specifically, the everyday as a set of recognizable rituals and habits provides *Mille Soleils* with a clear framework for a cinematic method where reality and fantasy overlap with each other mutually and excessively in a passion play of multivalent realities. By working the rich seams of the everyday and its live archives — its intersubjective ebbs and flows, its peak times and troughs — *Mille Soleils* is able to foster and sustain the compulsive fictions and fantasies it sets in motion. One is reminded here of the late Chantal Akerman who, by means of the long take, duration and extreme slowness, radically employed time passing on-screen as a way to transform everyday experience while always remaining loyal to it. In both cases, the concrete possibilities of collapsing the real and the staged or constructed into single open-frame images create a wholly original and expressive cinematic space, and with it a new form of passionately detached engagement.

Blistering, lyrical, phosphorescent and eruptive in its hallucinatory drive, Diop's warm and vertiginous, fluid mix of sounds and images proclaims cinematic freedom and a genuinely organic way of accessing and projecting the truth of the real (familial, historical, cinematic, biographical — always constructed) which she deforms and reforms at will. Impossible to demarcate and fix as separate instances, increasingly porous, the made and the found intersect, collide, and occasionally combust in *Mille Soleils* in an alchemical process of poetic fission and fizzle, to the point that what seems different and opposed might actually constitute the same. For if all is made, all therefore is potentially true and real: the real *is* the found *is* the (re)enacted *is* the narrative *is* the poetic *is* the fantasmatic. In this live, incandescent, smouldering crucible of miscegenation and transformation, every image is loaded, literally and poetically: a compound alloy, freshly minted and equal in status (there is no hierarchy of 'real' over 'non-real'), and glowing in a continuous state of (re) apparition. Which is to say, Diop is not directly concerned with the everyday in

Fig. 10.4. A vision of Marème Niang in *Milles Soleils*, directed by Mati Diop, produced by Anna Sanders Films (France), 2013.

and of itself, but rather with opening up new aesthetic thresholds of the everyday. What matters above all are the film's numinous poetic fusions and reversals, such as the bone-dry dailiness of Dakar seguing magically into Alaskan ice floes. The more bright and white the screen appears, the more allusive and enshrouded in poetic mystery it becomes. Paradoxically, it is this absolute poetic commitment that makes Diop's naturally oneiric and rhapsodic cinema so intensively alive to embodied experience and the sensual skin of the material real, as well as to the persistence of the lived past in the immediate present. Magaye then and now is a face and figure breathing in the polluted fumes and dense particles of the heady Dakar atmosphere.

The rich deposits and concentrates of the everyday are revealed therefore by Diop as the very core of aesthetic experience and a prime site for cinematic invention, far from 'the peril, unspeakable peril, in the everyday' conjured up so apocalyptically by the American proponent of literary nonfiction, Joan Didion.[14] We are transported back inexorably to the film's opening image and its poetic collapsing of extremes in a rolling crisscrossing of reality and fiction — one that emphasizes continuity through mutability and rupture. This chiastic movement is already encapsulated in Diop's statement of her intentions for *Mille Soleils*: 'J'ai découvert l'incroyable destin des acteurs de *Touki-Bouki* qui avaient poursuivi l'exacte trajectoire de leurs personnages fictifs. C'est une *fiction qui était devenue réalité*. J'ai voulu transformer cette *réalité en fable*' (my emphasis).[15] Anchored in the real world yet always attuned to its imaginary realms, *Mille Soleils* at once indexes and transmutes recorded reality. It's only when we get to the Alaska sequence that we are allowed to draw back a little and acknowledge such fantasy as, well yes, pure fantasy, though once again Diop gives us the freedom to believe in it if we wish since no direct moral tone or judgement is adopted. *Mille Soleils* is thus a paean to cinema's capacities for projection, both real and imaginary, and Diop wants us to take seriously its fictions by projecting freely our hopes and desire for the characters onto the sounds and images. Her declared artistic project is, in fact, to restore to Africa its right to fiction and the imagination in the face of the tired, miserabilist clichés of a permanently ailing continent.

Regraft and Transfer: A Thousand Suns

Diop's fundamental trust in the aesthetic wellsprings of both the everyday and the cinematic imaginary enables her ultimately to surrender her moment of artistic destiny in *Mille Soleils* (her preordained engagement with *Touki-Bouki*) to the unstoppable figurability of cinema and so avoid a spectacular and lethal showdown of the kind glorified in *High Noon* and imaged graphically in the scenes of the slaughterhouse. Indeed, the cinematic act of reinvesting and reimagining different instances of the real — the communal everyday of Dakar, the unique event of *Touki-Bouki* — entails a transformative recalibration through reversible checks and balances and continuous fine-tuning. For rather than a definitive *crossing through and out* of aesthetic influence in a sublime, transumptive act of poetic muscle, Diop essentially extends the legacy of her benign uncle with a certain Mambétian irreverence and transgression in kind, generously replaying and regrafting *Touki-Bouki* to claim filiations of style yet also forge new lines of aesthetic dialogue in an ongoing poetic transfer of forms.[16] This affirmative double movement is made further concrete by the presence of Djily Baghdad who successfully mobilized massive street rallies to prevent Abdoulaye Wade from passing on power unconstitutionally to his son in a potential abuse of his family bloodline. Baghdad was instrumental in ensuring the relatively peaceful continuity of Senegal's precious democratic heritage — the occasion for him here to admonish Magaye and his fellow elders: 'Qu'avez-vous fait de vos luttes? Que nous avez-vous laissé en héritage?' Hence, Diop welcomes both the everyday and Mambéty into her open, inclusive frame in a spirit of celebration, at once tender, overwhelming, and profound.

If one can still talk of Diop as a 'practitioner' of the everyday in her palpitating poetry of primary colours and primal emotions and drives, it is perhaps more in the terms provided by Malcolm Bowie, invoking Freud, of an erotic force field in which the unconscious makes itself heard (cited in Sheringham's *Everyday Life* (Sheringham, p. 33)). For *Mille Soleils* takes the processes of condensation and displacement to their very limit at both a plastic and thematic level, confecting an endless play of forms, rhythms and figures in a continually mesmerizing process of binding and unbinding that offers the pleasures of perpetual reenchantment. Diop talks herself of the film's different temporalities being revealed by the very fact of combining different formats and image systems, and of herself wanting to stand at the intersection of different types of motion (Picard 2013). Moreover, while Mambéty spoke about himself in *Touki-Bouki* through the character of Mory who harks back to Will Kane, Diop aims instead for the more universal: 'Dans *Mille Soleils*, je filme *tous ces hommes à la fois* à travers Magaye. Le thème de *High Noon* représente à mes yeux leur mélodie intérieure et le fil invisible qui les réunit' (*Comme au cinéma*, para. 3 of 7) (my emphasis).[17] We have moved decisively here from the epic moment (the dream departure) and its flipside (desolation and exile) to a process of consistent dilution and defusion where any notion of a climatic personal encounter with destiny becomes an object of (inter)textual play and irony. Indeed, *Mille Soleils* offers a continual dedramatizing of the Big Event through a proliferation of micro-events — *a thousand suns* of the everyday — that radiate out centrifugally. Diop insists on such unfathomable, interlocking mysteries and fictions of the everyday, for to throw ourselves into their rich interweave is, this remarkable film suggests, perhaps the only true, lasting secret of our shared destinies and being.

For the reasons given, no single dramatic event or revelation could possibly round off *Mille Soleils*. Just as there is no final disclosure of the everyday or conclusive aesthetic reckoning, so there is no cathartic happy end or personal closure: Mory/ Magaye and Anta/Marème will never be reunited *for real*, and a graphic lifting of the regret felt by Magaye will always be denied. The closing sequence of *Mille Soleils*, where an extreme close-up of Magaye's wizened face staring blankly out into the distance is immediately followed by a reverse-field shot of zebus dribbling across the verdant landscape (a shot into which he gradually enters stage-right, viewed from behind and heading towards the horizon), is accompanied by the same Ritter ballad with which the film began, but now crucially reset to the uptempo beats and rhythms of contemporary rock — another riff on Diop's consummate play of the found as made, and once again in affectionate homage to *Touki-Bouki* which repeated its opening shot of a boy herder not with a light kora flute as before but with sheets of pounding '70s funk. In this conspicuously downbeat, indeterminate, yet quietly moving ending, Diop is taking her leave respectfully from both Mambéty and Magaye who is now returned to the sanctuary of everyday rural life. *Mille Soleils* will remain as opaque and mysterious as Magaye's inscrutable, weathered face in the unforgiving Dakar sunshine. Another way of saying that if any redemption is possible, it lies in cinematic form and intricate regrafting — at once exhilarating, rapturous, and interminable. For there is always a real to find, (re)make, and transform, and for Diop, as for Mambéty, the only free space that truly exists is in the world of cinema, even if only as a fleeting, high-octane vision on the urban rim.

Notes

1. Manoel de Oliveira to Jean-Luc Godard in *Libération*, 4–5 September 1993 (included in *Jean-Luc Godard par Jean-Luc Godard*, tome 2, 1984–1998 (Paris: Cahiers du Cinéma, 1988), ed. by Alain Bergala, p. 270).
2. *High Noon*, dir. by Fred Zinnemann (United Artists, 1952).
3. Diop states that the title derives from a jingle used in a Dakar radio programme of the 1970s declaring 'L'Afrique, le passé, le présent, le futur ... Mille Soleils!' ('Entretien avec Mati Diop', *Comme au cinéma*, <http://www.commeaucinema.com/interviews/mille-soleils,305873-note-115565> [accessed 10 September 2015]). It carries numerous resonances in French, from the phrase 'comme mille soleils', an expression from a survivor of Hiroshima, to the Indian proverb of eternal hope: 'Il y a toujours mille soleils à l'envers des nuages'.

4. *Mille Soleils*, dir. by Mati Diop (Anna Sanders Films, 2013).
5. *Touki-Bouki* [The Journey of the Hyena], dir. by Djibril Diop Mambéty (Cinegrit, Studio Kankourama, 1973).
6. Laurent Rigoulet, '*Mille Soleils*, ou le printemps de Dakar': Interview with Mati Diop and Magaye Niang, *Télérama*, 5 April 2014 <http://www.telerama.fr/cinema/mille-soleils-ou-le-printemps-de-dakar,110694.php> [accessed 2 September 2015]. Magaye Niang also features as the possessive spurned lover Lamine Diop in Joseph Gaï Ramaka's 2001 musical reworking of the Carmen story, *Karmen Geï*, set on the former slave island of Gorée.
7. In the 1990s Mambéty began a trilogy of short films entitled 'Contes des petites gens' comprising *Le Franc* (1994), a comedy about a poor musician who wins the lottery, and *La Petite vendeuse de Soleil* (1999) about a young handicapped girl surviving the streets of Dakar by selling the city's newspaper, *Le Soleil*. He was editing the latter when he died.
8. Genevieve Yue rightly states that '[t]hese evocations of distant locations [...] suffuse the concrete worlds her characters inhabit so that her [Diop's] films often seem to be in multiple places at once' (Genevieve Yue, 'Art of the Real: The Films of Mati Diop', *Film Comment*, 18 April 2014 <http://www.filmcomment.com/blog/the-films-of-mati-diop/> [accessed 5 September 2015] (para. 1 of 9)).
9. Andrea Picard, 'In the Realm of the Senses: Mati Diop on *Milles soleils*', *cinema scope*, 57 (2013) <http://cinema-scope.com/columns/filmart-realm-senses-mati-diop-mille-soleils/> [accessed 12 September 2015] (para. 9 of 27). Subsequent references to this interview will be given in the text.
10. Jacques Mandelbaum, 'La Tendresse explosive de Mati Diop', *Le Monde*, 12 July 2013. <http://www.lemonde.fr/culture/article/2013/07/12/la-tendresse-explosive-de-mati-diop_3446680_3246.html> [accessed 10 September 2015] (para. 4 of 7).
11. Mambéty later pastiched Zinnemann's film in the build-up to the collective murder of Dramaan Drameh in *Hyènes*.
12. Michael Sheringham, *Everyday Life: Theories and Practices from Surrealism to the Present* (Oxford: Oxford University Press, 2006), p. 398.
13. Sheringham, p. 71.
14. Joan Didion, *Play It As It Lays* (New York: Farrar, Straus and Giroux, 1970), pp. 99–100.
15. 'Entretien avec Mati Diop', *Comme au cinéma* (2014) <http://www.commeaucinema.com/interviews/mille-soleils,305873-note-115565> [accessed 12 September 2015] (para. 1 of 7).
16. An obvious point of comparison here is Claire Denis's *35 Rhums* (2008), a story of personal choices and destiny where Diop herself plays the *métisse* daughter Jo(séphine) planning to leave the one-parent family nest lovingly tended by her father Lionel (Alex Descas). In one interview Diop even suggests that the film lies at the very origins of *Mille Soleils*: 'This is when I discovered the thousand stories hiding behind *Touki-Bouki* [...] After having found and affirmed my own cinematographic language, I was ready to make *Mille Soleils* and to look *Touki-Bouki* straight in the eye' (Picard 2013). *35 Rhums* was such a formative cinematic experience for Diop precisely because Jo engineers her own family solution by marrying literally the boy next door, thus ensuring close proximity with her father. By deregulating and romancing the Father at pivotal moments where the screen becomes a site of multiple, intersecting lines of intertextual passage (the film presents itself as a variation on the theme of Denis's grandfather through the legendary prism of Yasujirō Ozu's *Late Spring* (1949)), *35 Rhums* successfully renegotiates familial structures and social prohibitions. Moreover, this intimate illustration of blood ties and the necessary stages in the human cycle is also rooted in the daily rituals and networks of meaning in a particular community, emphasizing the sustained benefits of immersing oneself in the patterns of the everyday (the shared rituals of cooking rice, driving a taxi, taking the metro to campus). For a detailed study of *35 Rhums* and Denis's personal correction and *shifting* of Ozu, see James S. Williams, 'Romancing the Father in Claire Denis's *35 Shots of Rum*', *Film Quarterly*, 63.2 (2009–10), 44–50.
17. The implications of Diop's reshaping of the made and found for our understanding of the construction of masculinity in *Mille Soleils* would require lengthy discussion and need to take into account how Diop reworks the queer panache and vagabondage of *Touki-Bouki* in subtle,

even tangential, aesthetic ways. In contrast to Mambéty's freewheeling, frontal, (homo)erotic images of 'soft' masculine figures (including the rich, gay fop Charlie in the central poolside scene) and the concrete found objects and male talismans (*gris-gris*) that provide Mory with multiple identities (not only stolen clothes but also the steer's skull, long horns and Targui Cross that adorn his motorbike), Diop focuses almost exclusively on Mory's final incarnation at the port as one part of a heterosexual couple with no real indication of how he was diegetically 'made'. As we have seen, however, she invokes instead the opening sequence of *High Noon* over which the Ritter song first appears — an enthralling moment with homoerotic undertones when three outlaw cowboys meet together ritualistically one by one on the high sierra in a kind of tryst. In addition, during his phone call to Marème, Magaye makes eye-contact with a masked young man in the street on a motorbike identical to the one he rode in *Touki-Bouki*, as if he were encountering his double in a Coctelian gaze, before then reciting (anonymously) the famous words about exile from James Baldwin's 1956 landmark gay novel *Giovanni's Room*: 'You don't have a home until you leave it and then, when you have left it, you never can go back'.

— 11 —

Des livres mouillés par la mer: Pensées simples III

Gérard Macé

Je me crois impropre au discours continu, comme Montaigne.
JOUBERT

Comme d'autres philosophes, Darwin a pratiqué la promenade propice à la méditation, et je me plais à penser que son tour du monde ne fut qu'une promenade parmi d'autres, un peu plus longue et un peu plus féconde.

L'habitude était prise depuis l'enfance, puisque son père avait tracé une promenade circulaire dans la propriété familiale, un *Thinking Pass* que ses fils devaient parcourir chaque matin avant le petit déjeuner. Plus tard, dans son domaine de Down House, Darwin lui-même avait aménagé un *Sandwalk*, sentier qu'il parcourait quotidiennement: 'Il avait l'habitude de faire chaque jour un certain nombre de tours qu'il comptait au moyen d'un tas de cailloux: chaque fois qu'il passait, il envoyait rouler dans le sentier une des pierres amoncelées', écrit l'un de ses biographes.

Entre temps, comme on le sait, il avait fait le tour du monde à bord du *Beagle*, un tour unique et plein de surprises, qui dura presque cinq ans.

★ ★ ★ ★ ★

'Que mon esprit se soit développé grâce à mes recherches au cours du voyage paraît confirmé par une remarque de mon père, l'observateur le plus pénétrant que j'aie jamais vu, d'un naturel sceptique et qui était loin de croire à la phrénologie; car en me revoyant pour la première fois après le voyage, il se tourna vers mes sœurs en s'écriant: 'Tiens, la forme de sa tête a complètement changé!'.

Le père de Darwin a trouvé le mot juste, au retour de son fils après un tour du monde de près de cinq ans, à bord du *Beagle* et sur terre où les escales pouvaient durer des semaines ou des mois. La navigation ne fut donc pas son occupation principale, on s'en aperçoit en lisant le journal qu'il a scrupuleusement tenu de 1831 à 1835. Pendant que le *Beagle* est amarré, plus longtemps que prévu parce qu'on attend des vents favorables, ou parce qu'on finit de dresser les cartes du littoral, Darwin remonte des rivières, franchit des plaines, passe des jours à cheval, découvre des fossiles, tend des pièges et des filets, s'active en tous sens et fait l'inventaire de la création, mais un inventaire qui continue de vivre sous ses yeux, ce qui ne l'empêche pas d'observer les humains de façon quasi ethnographique.

De quoi changer une tête en effet, pleine de merveilles, enrichie de différences, et troublée sur la route du retour par ce qui donnera au monde la théorie de l'évolution. Au grand dam, comme on le sait, des défenseurs d'une lecture littérale de la Bible, et d'une vision fixiste de l'univers.

La tête de Darwin a changé, comme si sa pensée se voyait, comme si son crâne lui-même avait *évolué*, au lieu seulement de vieillir. C'est bien ainsi qu'il l'entend, puisqu'il éprouve le besoin de rapporter le mot de son père, dans la préface à son *Journal de voyage.*

★ ★ ★ ★ ★

On les croit éternelles, mais les questions qu'on se pose appartiennent à leur époque. On ne se demande plus si l'océan va se mettre à bouillir ou si les Indiens ont une âme. Encore moins si les cyclopes ont un pays, ou si le sphinx est un mangeur d'hommes.

Darwin se demandait encore comment reconnaître une langue, lorsqu'il entendait les habitants de la Terre de Feu. Il ne se demandait pas *quelle* langue ils parlaient, mais s'ils parlaient une langue ou s'ils émettaient des bruits qui n'avaient pas de sens. Question d'autant plus étonnante qu'à bord du *Beagle*, voyageaient trois Fuégiens qui avaient séjourné à Londres, et que le capitaine ramenait au pays. C'est ainsi que les marins trouvaient partout des interprètes, sur les côtes où ils faisaient escale.

★ ★ ★ ★ ★

Des jumeaux âgés de trois ans, un garçon et une fille, déclarent qu'ils parlent anglais. Un anglais qui n'est pas celui de Shakespeare, on s'en doute, ni celui de Lewis Carroll, d'autant qu'il s'agit d'une langue imaginaire. On sent qu'ils font des phrases, avec une virtuosité confondante, mais pour nous ces phrases sont vides de sens, même si elles sont plus proches du langage que du bruit.

Quand on cherche à les imiter on n'y parvient pas, parce qu'il nous est devenu impossible de produire des phrases insensées. Notre vocabulaire est tellement lié à la morphologie de notre langue, et aux significations qui la rattachent à la réalité, que nous ne parvenons plus à dire tout à fait n'importe quoi. Au lieu du bruit articulé qui permet aux enfants de se parler, peut-être même de se comprendre, nous retombons sans arrêt sur des mots rares ou étranges, comme bachi-bouzouk, wiedersehn, acratopège ou yamanaka. Difficile de se débarrasser du sens, qui revient par la fenêtre quand on l'a chassé par la porte, comme une seconde nature.

Ou alors il faut être comédien, comme Charlie Chaplin dans *Le Dictateur*, quand il hurle en imitant Hitler, dans une langue totalement inventée qu'on reconnaît pourtant sans peine: celle de la violence insensée, de la folie meurtrière, de l'inhumain qui trouve à s'incarner.

★ ★ ★ ★ ★

— 'Je n'aime pas vos lèvres; elles sont droites comme celles de quelqu'un qui n'a jamais menti. Je veux vous apprendre à mentir, pour que vos lèvres deviennent belles et tordues comme celles d'un masque antique.'

Cette fois c'est à Gide que s'adressent ces propos d'Oscar Wilde, et c'est Gide lui-même qui les rapporte. S'ils ne sont pas forcément à son avantage, ils n'empêchent pas une délectation pleine d'ambiguïté, ce qui complète le portrait en lui donnant une touche de vérité supplémentaire.

Quant à Oscar Wilde, il exprime ainsi un reste de pensée magique, toujours prête à resurgir, même en Occident où c'est la psychologie qui l'inspire, quand on croit que la physionomie peut traduire le caractère de façon transparente, comme autrefois on voulait croire que l'âme se lisait sur les traits du visage. En Afrique la magie s'exprime plus directement, c'est une pensée agissante qui se voit dans les masques de maladie par exemple, ou dans les interventions sur le corps, comme les déformations labiales. Mais celles-ci ont d'autres fonctions: marquer l'appartenance à un groupe, ou traduire le pouvoir de l'homme sur la femme.

⋆ ⋆ ⋆ ⋆ ⋆

> Si je devais atteindre la quarantaine, j'épouserais probablement une vieille fille aux incisives supérieures proéminentes, légèrement découvertes par les lèvres supérieures.'
>
> KAFKA, *Journal*, 9 novembre 1911.

La greffe d'une face animale sur un visage humain, ou du moins la superposition des deux images: c'est le rêve éveillé de Kafka, qui tient de la hantise et du désir. Dans le cas précis, des dents qui se chevauchent lui rappellent des jambes croisées, celles d'une Mademoiselle K. Comment ne pas remarquer l'initiale, marque et tatouage de l'être protéiforme qui porte ce nom à peine énigmatique -nom réduit à une seule lettre, qui désigne aussi bien l'auteur lui-même que son plus célèbre personnage, Joseph K?

Le même jour, Kafka entreprend de raconter un rêve assez long, du moins dans le souvenir qui lui est en resté, et le récit qu'il en a fait. Ce rêve qui lui a procuré une *énorme satisfaction onirique* le menait en compagnie de Max Brod dans une longue enfilade de chambres, des chambres à coucher où des gens dormaient encore, et qu'on pouvait voir au lit. Plus loin ces chambres devenaient des bordels, et la dernière chambre donnait sur le vide, une des filles étant même suspendue tête en bas. Le plaisir du narrateur est alors si grand qu'il ne comprend pas que ce divertissement soit gratuit, jusqu'à ce que l'inquiétude et l'angoisse reviennent: 'sans remuer ses jambes, la fille dressa son buste et me tourna le dos, tout couvert de grands cercles rouges, à mon grand effroi, d'un rouge de cire à cacheter, entouré de bordures pâlissantes, entre lesquelles de rouges éclaboussures. A présent je remarquais que son corps en était couvert, que je tenais mon pouce sur ses cuisses en plein dans ces taches, et que mes doigts mêmes étaient semés de petits éclats pareils à ceux d'un cachet brisé.'

Le lecteur de Kafka éprouve une sensation de 'déjà vu' parce qu'il reconnaît l'atmosphère de ses récits, et même les corps martyrisés de *La Colonie pénitentiaire*. Mais le lecteur de Baudelaire est pris d'un vertige encore plus grand, parce qu'il a l'impression que les rêves passent d'un auteur à l'autre, que les nuits communiquent entre elles. Et les maisons, si l'on pense à cette lettre du 13 mars 1856, dans laquelle l'auteur des *Fleurs du mal* raconte le rêve qu'il vient de faire, juste avant que Jeanne Duval ne le réveille. C'est dans ce rêve devenu fameux que Baudelaire, le pantalon déboutonné, les pieds humides à cause d'une flaque d'eau, entre dans une maison de plaisir où il découvre un monstre pourvu d'un appendice 'qui lui part de la tête, quelque chose d'élastique comme du caoutchouc, et si long, si long, que, s'il le roulait sur sa tête comme une queue de cheveux, cela serait beaucoup trop lourd et absolument impossible à porter.'

On reconnaît là, sinon les ailes géantes qui empêchent de marcher, un attribut sexuel qui procure de l'embarras, comme la p... du rêveur avait provoqué sa gêne. Envers de la castration, cet appendice enroulé sur lui-même, dont on ne sait pas quoi faire à certaines heures, est aussi indispensable et encombrant que cet ami dont Kafka ne parvient pas à se débarrasser, ce Max Brod toujours là, jusqu'à lui survivre et sauver ses manuscrits. Quant à Baudelaire, il adresse son récit à Charles Asselineau, l'ami qui deviendra le principal témoin de sa vie posthume.

Les deux amis sont des excroissances des narrateurs, leur ombre fidèle et leurs premiers interprètes: à chaque fois un autre soi-même, présent jusque dans les ébats intimes, dans le plaisir comme dans la vie littéraire. Comme si Baudelaire et Kafka ne pouvaient pas jouir sans témoin, chacun à sa façon. C'est peut-être même ce besoin d'avoir un double qui en fait des écrivains, espérant voir venir un frère en la personne de 'l'hypocrite lecteur'.

★ ★ ★ ★ ★

'Un matin, Wilde me tendit à lire un article où un critique assez épais le félicitait de 'savoir inventer de jolis contes pour mieux habiller sa pensée'.

— Ils croient, commença Wilde, que toutes les pensées naissent nues... Ils ne comprennent pas que *je ne peux pas* penser autrement qu'en contes. Le sculpteur ne cherche pas à traduire en marbre sa pensée; *il pense en marbre*, directement.'

C'est encore Gide qui parle, pour nous rappeler utilement que la pensée ne se résume pas au langage, mais qu'elle doit toujours trouver une forme. Une forme qui pousse de l'intérieur pour modeler la surface, comme le style selon Proust.

★ ★ ★ ★ ★

'Pour le poète authentique, la métaphore n'est pas une figure de rhétorique, mais au contraire un substitut en images, qui lui vient réellement à l'esprit à la place d'un concept' (Nietzsche, *La Naissance de la tragédie*, traduction de Patrick Wotling)

★ ★ ★ ★ ★

Il y avait un jour un homme que dans son village on aimait parce qu'il racontait des histoires. Tous les matins il sortait du village, et quand le soir il y rentrait, tous les travailleurs, après avoir peiné tout le jour, s'assemblaient tout autour de lui et disaient: Allons! raconte: Qu'est-ce que tu as vu aujourd'hui?: Il racontait: J'ai vu dans la forêt un faune qui jouait de la flûte, et qui faisait danser une ronde petits sylvains. — Raconte encore: qu'as-tu vu? disaient les hommes. — Quand je suis arrivé au bord de la mer, j'ai vu trois sirènes, au bord des vagues, et qui peignaient avec un peigne d'or leurs cheveux verts. — Et les hommes l'aimaient parce qu'il leur racontait des histoires.

Un matin il quitta, comme tous les matins, son village — mais quand il arriva sur le bord de la mer, voici qu'il aperçut trois sirènes au bord des vagues, et qui peignaient avec un peigne d'or leurs cheveux verts. Et comme il continuait sa promenade, il vit, arrivant près du bois, un faune qui jouait de la flûte à une ronde de sylvains... Ce soir-là, quand il rentra dans son village et qu'on lui demanda comme les autres soirs: Allons! raconte: Qu'as-tu vu? Il répondit: -Je n'ai rien vu.

Cette histoire qui n'a pas d'auteur (ou qui en a plusieurs) ressemble à celles qu'on prête aux maîtres zen et se passe de conclusion, ce qui est sans doute la marque distinctive de la pensée poétique. Pensée qui procède par cercles concentriques, ou par ondes successives qui viennent se briser sur les bords du réel, pendant que l'auditeur (ou le lecteur) est saisi par l'étonnement qui donne à penser.

S'il fallait malgré tout une morale à cette fable, ce serait à peu près celle-ci: on n'aurait jamais tant parlé des licornes, si on avait pu les rencontrer. Et personne ne se serait vanté d'avoir rencontré le diable, si on avait pu le voir.

★ ★ ★ ★ ★

Rien ne sert de parler des sirènes et des licornes si personne ne vous croit, rien ne sert ne raconter une histoire vraie si elle parait invraisemblable. C'est aussi ce que veut dire Karen Blixen dans *Une histoire immortelle*, son récit adapté au cinéma par Orson Welles.

Dans la ville de Macao un vieux milliardaire se fait lire tous les soirs ses livres de comptes, comme s'il s'agissait de ses mémoires, et parce que seules les histoires vraies l'intéressent. Il n'a que faire des prophètes, et quand on lui parle d'une histoire qu'on raconte sur tous les bateaux, celle d'un marin qu'un vieil homme a choisi, puis payé pour qu'il couche avec une jeune fille et l'engrosse, il veut aussitôt que cette histoire s'incarne, qu'un marin puisse la raconter comme vraie.

Quand la volonté du vieil homme est faite il meurt, croyant son désir exaucé. Mais quand le comptable dit au marin qu'il pourra désormais raconter l'histoire en affirmant qu'elle est vraie, puisqu'elle lui est arrivée, la réponse fuse: 'Qui me croira?'

Dans ce conte admirable, Karen Blixen a condensé les rapports du réel et de l'imaginaire, ainsi que le pacte avec le lecteur, qui fonde les pouvoirs de la fiction. En moins de pages que Cervantès (mine de rien elle traite le même sujet, et le comptable est une sorte de Sancho Pança) elle a inventé au passage l'un des plus beaux récits du XXe siècle.

★ ★ ★ ★ ★

Le plaisir de l'analyse, l'esprit critique toujours en éveil, l'intelligence trop bien exercée empêchent l'aveuglement provisoire qui donnent au poète son élan, au romancier l'illusion qu'il recrée la vie. Proust en avait fait l'expérience, et en avait tiré les leçons pour écrire la *Recherche*; Lévi-Strauss et Starobinski, chacun à sa façon, l'ont refaite au point de se détourner de la création littéraire.

Tenté par le roman, Starobinski ne s'estime 'pas assez doué pour s'abandonner au rêve', et dans *La parole est moytié à celui qui parle*, il en vient d'ailleurs à parler sereinement de son échec: 'L'histoire de Phénix, dans Homère, m'avait paru un superbe canevas. Sa mère le supplie de séduire la maîtresse de son père. Il accepte, mais son père l'aveugle... L'idée valait ce qu'elle valait mais le vent ne soufflait pas dans mes voiles. Et pas davantage dans les petits récits à mi-chemin de l'allégorie que j'ai tentés, avec un regard sur Melville ou Kafka: un couple d'amants fonde une cité aux confins du désert, mais le désert se referme, insidieusement, sur cette ville. Pour étoffer cette parabole, il fallait trop de persévérance dans un unique système d'images'. Et trop porté à l'autocritique, Starobinski se retire sur la pointe des pieds, sans amertume ni jalousie.

Il en va tout autrement avec Lévi-Strauss, qui a sérieusement rêvé de gloire littéraire, et n'a au fond jamais renoncé. Adolescent il écrivait des comédies dans le genre de Labiche, un peu plus tard il admirait des romanciers conventionnels, pour ne pas dire académiques, et rêvait de couchers de soleil à la Chateaubriand. *Tristes tropiques* reprend d'ailleurs un titre de roman abandonné, mais pas totalement renié, puisqu'il en cite des pages entières dans le livre qui l'a rendu célèbre, comme si rien ne devait se perdre. Des pages qui décrivent justement des couchers de soleil, sortes de cartes postales littéraires. Lévi-Strauss a persisté en même temps qu'il signait son œuvre d'anthropologue, puisqu'il a raconté à plusieurs reprises que les jurés du Goncourt ont regretté de ne pas pouvoir couronner *Tristes tropiques.*

Des philosophes ont brûlé leurs tragédies, des penseurs se sont cru romanciers, comme si la littérature était une origine en partie inavouable, d'une liberté supérieure mais d'une autorité douteuse. Montaigne, Rousseau, Leiris ont pourtant réussi le croisement des deux traditions, l'une se nourrissant de l'autre. Mais Leiris brille par son absence, dans les entretiens de Lévi-Strauss avec Didier Eribon.

★ ★ ★ ★ ★

Quand Anna Akhmatova était jeune, elle était aussi souple qu'une acrobate (elle joignait la nuque et les talons), et sa mémoire avait la même agilité.

Nadejda Mandelstam est d'autant plus frappée par sa démarche lente, et la lourdeur de son corps, quand elle la retrouve des années plus tard à Tachkent. Mais Nadejda remarque une aggravation plus sensible, parce qu'elle est un inconvénient majeur pour un poète, qui pourrait vite devenir un obstacle insurmontable: 'Sa mémoire aussi avait commencé à décliner, et elle n'arrivait plus à composer de tête'.

Composer de tête: c'est ainsi en effet que naît le poème, qu'il continue de vivre en soi et qu'on le retient sans l'avoir appris, grâce à son rythme qui s'accorde à la pensée, et qui l'épouse au point de faire corps avec elle. C'est d'ailleurs grâce à cette mémoire en partie spontanée, en partie travaillée, qu'on peut reconstituer des poèmes perdus. Akhmatova en a fait l'expérience, quand elle a voulu reconstituer ses œuvres, aidée par ses proches après leur destruction par la police; Nadejda plus encore, qui avait vu travailler Ossip Mandelstam, et qui fut la gardienne de ses textes, de son vivant d'abord, puis après son arrestation et sa mort sur le chemin de la Kolyma: '...je me remémorais sur commande tout ce dont il avait besoin. Sa mémoire, qui était phénoménale, était d'un autre type que la mienne: il mémorisait instantanément d'énormes passages à l'oreille, mais les oubliait très vite...'

Ce rôle de Mnémosyne, qui accompagne le poète comme son ombre, et partage son inspiration au point de savoir intimement comment il travaille, lui a permis de sauver l'œuvre de Mandelstam, mais dans ses souvenirs sur Akhmatova elle fait une autre remarque, moins attendue et tout aussi importante. C'est également pour soi qu'on apprend des poèmes par cœur en cette sinistre période: 'Le plus important, c'était de tout garder en mémoire — si jamais on m'envoyait dans un camp, que me resterait-il là-bas, si j'oubliais les poèmes?'.

* * * * *

Ce que Nadejda Mandelstam garde en mémoire, lorsqu'elle apprend par cœur un poème, c'est 'le domptage artistique de l'effroyable'. La formule est de Nietzsche, et c'est ainsi qu'il définit le sublime, dans *La Naissance de la tragédie.*

* * * * *

Cernovik. C'est par ce mot que Chalamov désignait le brouillon invisible de ses écrits, rumination intérieure qui n'était pas un premier jet, mais la version quasi définitive, inscrite en creux, des *Récits de la Kolyma* . 'Le cerveau laisse remonter à la surface, ne peut laisser remonter que des phrases préparées par une expérience personnelle à un moment antérieur. Il ne s'agit plus ni de polir, ni de corriger, ni de parfaire: tout s'écrit au propre immédiatement'.

* * * * *

Les poètes ont très peu écrit dans une autre langue que la leur. Leur langue maternelle, qu'on devrait plutôt appeler leur langue natale. Sans doute parce que cette langue ne demande aucun effort, qu'elle vient de l'intérieur alors qu'une langue apprise reste toujours extérieure à soi-même. La langue poétique est comme la langue de tous les jours: son rythme est aussi nécessaire, aussi involontaire et régulier que la respiration, ses sonorités sont aussi familières que les bruits quotidiens qu'on n'entend pas plus que le battement du sang, elle est le liquide amniotique où baigne le poème. Ce n'est pas seulement la langue de l'enfance, c'est une langue prénatale, avec une forme en plus (il faut bien que l'eau soit contenue par une amphore ou un vase), et un surcroît de sens.

Un des dangers pour la poésie est la régression jusqu'au babil, jusqu'à une suite de sons où se perd le sens.

* * * * *

Composer de tête, c'est assister à l'épanouissement d'une forme en même temps qu'à l'éclosion du sens. Et le plaisir est tel qu'*écrire*, si l'on ne voulait s'adresser à des lecteurs inconnus, deviendrait alors parfaitement inutile, c'est pourquoi la poésie fut si longtemps orale, c'est aussi pourquoi certaines civilisations ont pu se passer de l'écriture. Mais le goût du secret, le pouvoir accordé à la magie ont aussi joué leur rôle.

* * * * *

L'interdit étant inséparable du sacré, l'écriture fut taboue dans plusieurs traditions, en dehors même de l'Afrique. Dans *Le Prisme des langues*, un linguiste polyglotte, Nicolas Tournadre, rappelle utilement que le sanscrit s'est transmis oralement pendant plus d'un millénaire, de même que les commentaires de la Torah dans la tradition juive. Pour préserver le pouvoir des prêtres, ou par crainte des déformations, l'écriture parfaitement connue peut être frappée d'interdit. Ailleurs elle peut être réservée à une caste, ou donner naissance à des formes cryptées, pour des raisons religieuses aussi bien que politiques.

Autant de pratiques éclairant l'absence de l'écriture au sud du Sahara, si l'on veut bien admettre que cette absence, sans être toujours un choix au sens plein du terme, peut être une stratégie, et plutôt qu'un manque une autre relation au monde.

* * * * *

En Europe même on s'est méfié de l'écriture, au point de vouloir s'en passer dans la tradition occultiste, et d'arriver à cette invention paradoxale du 'Livre muet'.

* * * * *

L'Afrique n'est pas la seule à entretenir un rapport magique avec l'écriture. Il est même émouvant de relever que des sociétés sans écriture et des sociétés où elle est inséparable depuis longtemps du sacré comme du savoir, connaissent des pratiques semblables. Ainsi la tradition juive a connu la magie, et dans les pays séfarades en particulier on a fabriqué des amulettes, on a disposé des textes en triangle ou selon le carré magique, on a usé de formules pour chasser les rats, les serpents et les scorpions. On a chassé les démons et l'on a apaisé les esprits des ancêtres, on continue aujourd'hui même d'enfermer des manuscrits dans des étuis, pour se protéger ou protéger les maisons.

* * * * *

'Les mystères, comme Dieu, ne peuvent être confiés qu'à la parole, et non à l'écriture'.

C'est Pierre Hadot qui rappelle cette phrase de Clément d'Alexandrie, dans une 'Introduction à l'enseignement oral de Platon'. Platon qui lui fait dire ailleurs: 'On connaît la célèbre fin du *Phèdre*, dans laquelle Platon laisse entendre que seul le dialogue vivant est durable et immortel parce qu'il s'écrit dans les âmes vivantes et non dans des pages mortes'.

Pierre Hadot est encore plus proche de certaines pratiques africaines lorsqu'il évoque les mystères d'Eleusis, cherchant à les comprendre non plus en termes de savoir, mais en termes d'expérience. Tout ce que nous pouvons reconstituer des rites est en effet banal (cris rituels, exhibitions d'épis, effets de lumière), mais l'essentiel est cette parenthèse sacrée vécue par les initiés, qui leur fait vivre un autre temps, une autre dimension de l'existence.

L'énigme des initiations africaines n'en est plus tout à fait une, si l'on admet qu'un secret n'a pas toujours de contenu, ou si peu. Et qu'une expérience se transmet difficilement par les mots, quand elle se résume au moment crucial qu'elle fait vivre.

Si nous avons tant de mal à entrer dans cette logique, ou dans ce climat mental, n'est-ce pas parce que la philosophie en Occident se ramène à des textes et des concepts, au lieu d'être une leçon vivante? Pierre Hadot cite à ce propos Sénèque s'adressant à Lucilius, comme quoi le problème n'est pas nouveau: 'Je pense qu'il n'y a personne qui ait rendu plus mauvais service au genre humain que ceux qui ont appris la philosophie comme un métier mercenaire, gens dont la vie est sans rapport avec les règles de vie qu'ils prescrivent.'

⋆ ⋆ ⋆ ⋆ ⋆

L'écriture n'est pas fiable, parce qu'elle est fragile. C'est ce qu'on a pensé en Afrique, ainsi qu'en témoigne William Snelgrave, un négrier anglais dont on a traduit le *Journal* en 1735. Alors qu'il vient d'acheter des esclaves dans le golfe du Bénin, les marchands noirs ont du mal à se satisfaire d'une reconnaissance de dette écrite: un papier peut se perdre, et l'écriture peut s'effacer.

A la même époque en Europe, on croit que les écrits restent et que les paroles s'envolent. Ce sont donc deux logiques qui s'affrontent, difficilement conciliables. Mais pour comprendre la défiance des Africains, il suffit de se souvenir de l'apparition du papier monnaie, ou des assignats.

⋆ ⋆ ⋆ ⋆ ⋆

Le même Snelgrave raconte qu'au Dahomey, vers 1730, il a rencontré des Malais, 'dont la nation habite fort avant dans le pays, et sur la frontière de celui des Maures; *et que ce peuple égalait les Blancs en une chose, savoir l'art d'écrire.*'

Preuve supplémentaire, s'il en fallait, que l'on connaît depuis longtemps l'écriture en Afrique de l'ouest, en dehors même de l'influence arabe. Preuve supplémentaire que si l'on n'adopte pas l'écriture, ce peut être par choix et non par défaut, au moins en certaines circonstances.

La présence de ces Malais nous rappelle aussi que par l'Océan indien, l'Afrique a eu depuis toujours des visiteurs venus d'Asie. Ce sont eux qui ont apporté le bananier, le cocotier, la pirogue à balancier, et même le soufflet de forge. Sans parler des cauris, ces coquillages qui ont servi de monnaie pendant des siècles: venus d'ailleurs ils avaient le prestige de la rareté, produits par la nature ils avaient l'avantage de ne pouvoir être imités.

⋆ ⋆ ⋆ ⋆ ⋆

Les sociétés sans écriture ont été considérées longtemps comme des sociétés 'non civilisées', même aux Hautes Etudes où l'intitulé d'un séminaire inauguré en 1888 n'a été modifié qu'en 1951, sous l'impulsion de Claude Lévi-Strauss. Mais ce changement qui faisait entrer les sociétés sans écriture dans la civilisation, n'a pas empêché qu'on les considère comme des sociétés sans histoire.

* * * * *

J'ai déjà raconté l'histoire du sultan Njoya, qui inventa une écriture autour de 1900, dans son royaume de Foumban, à l'ouest du Cameroun. Après diverses tentatives, et des tâtonnements qui le mènent progressivement à la mise au point d'un syllabaire, il fait un rêve, au cours duquel un homme lui demande de dessiner une main humaine sur un tableau noir, puis d'effacer cette main avec de l'eau, de boire enfin cette eau qui conservait le souvenir de l' écriture.

Or, je viens de retrouver la même expérience sous la plume de Mungo Park, dans son *Voyage dans l'intérieur de l'Afrique*, publié à la fin du XVIIIe siècle (l'an VIII pour la traduction française). En 1796, dans la région du Sahel, Mungo Park est hébergé une nuit par un Bambara qui fut autrefois l'esclave d'un Maure, et qui a obtenu sa liberté après la mort de son maître. Converti à l'islam, ce qui ne l'empêche pas d'avoir conservé les croyances de sa jeunesse, cet ancien esclave apprenant que Mungo Park est chrétien, lui demande d'écrire quelque chose sur sa tablette, afin d'en faire un objet doué de pouvoirs.

'Je remplis donc d'écriture toute la tablette, se souvient Mungo Park, du haut en bas et des deux côtés. Mon hôte, pour être sûr d'avoir à son usage toute la force du charme, lava l'écriture de dessus la tablette, avec un peu d'eau qu'il recueillit dans une calebasse; ayant dit dessus quelques prières, il avala ce merveilleux breuvage: après quoi, de peur qu'il lui en échappât un seul mot, il lécha la tablette jusqu'à ce qu'elle fût absolument sèche.'

Ces deux scènes semblables à un siècle de distance, et dans des régions passablement éloignées, laissent penser que la pratique n'était pas rare. Elles permettent surtout de comprendre un usage de l'écriture différent du nôtre, puisqu'elle est transformée en philtre ou en élixir; une pensée qui nous est devenue étrangère, malgré quelques formules cabalistiques et quelques symboles encore actifs. Avec le goût du secret, elles permettent aussi de comprendre l'usage restreint de l'écriture, et sa diffusion si limitée dans l'Afrique noire. On voit mal en effet comment la magie pourrait inspirer un usage parfaitement banal, une pratique à la portée du premier venu.

Si cette conception superstitieuse de l'écriture étonne aujourd'hui, qu'on se rappelle les interprétations délirantes auxquelles ont donné lieu les hiéroglyphes ('caractères sacrés' en grec), jusqu'à ce que Champollion, et quelques linguistes après lui, démontrent que l'écriture des Egyptiens était une écriture comme les autres.

* * * * *

Gaspard Mollien, rescapé de *La Méduse* parce qu'il n'était pas monté sur le radeau, profita de sa mésaventure pour explorer la Gambie et le Sénégal, un peu avant 1820. Dans plusieurs épisodes d'un récit passionnant, par un homme jeune mais curieux de tout, et quasiment sans préjugé, l'écriture est mise en scène, toujours en rapport avec la magie.

Ayant besoin d'un guide, Mollien recrute un certain Diai Boukari, qui fera en sa compagnie l'essentiel du voyage. 'Avant de s'embarquer, raconte l'auteur, mon marabout traça sur le sable plusieurs caractères arabes, pour savoir s'il reverrait un jour sa femme et sa mère; la réponse du destin étant favorable, il ramassa et mit dans un petit sac une poignée de sable, persuadé qu'à la conservation de ce précieux sachet était attachée celle de sa vie'.

Cette scène est loin d'être isolée. Beaucoup plus loin, l'auteur rencontre un homme affligé d'éléphantiasis, puis un homme presque aveugle, qui lui demandent la fabrication d'un gris-gris, d'un charme pour guérir, tant ils sont convaincus des pouvoirs magiques de l'écriture.

Plus loin encore, près des sources du Sénégal, Mollien veut remercier un chef pour son hospitalité, en lui proposant les présents habituels. 'Mon hôte de Courbari ne voulut recevoir aucun des présents que je lui offris; il me supplia, pour prix des services qu'il m'avait rendus, de lui composer un gris-gris en bonne forme, qui lui donnât le moyen d'acquérir de grandes richesses sans travailler. Je traçai sur un morceau de papier des cercles, des croix et des triangles, qui lui parurent doués d'une telle efficacité qu'il me fit présent de deux mesures de riz.'

Une conclusion trop facile, et surtout erronée, consisterait à croire que les Noirs rencontrés par Mollien sont totalement soumis au pouvoir des Blancs, parce que leur admiration serait aussi complète que naïve. 'Cependant, ajoute-t-il dans un récit qui respire l'honnêteté intellectuelle, malgré le respect que mes talents à composer des talismans inspiraient à tous les habitants, ils disaient hautement: 'Le Blanc sait lire, il sait écrire, mais il ne sait pas prier.'

Comme quoi chez l'autre, on voit toujours ce qui lui manque.

★ ★ ★ ★ ★

A la fin du récit, Mollien raconte une scène que nous avons déjà rencontrée sous la plume de Mungo Park, et plus près de nous chez le sultan Njoya.

Le guide de Mollien tombe malade, et gravement. Boukari souffrant de coliques fait des signes sur une calebasse remplie d'eau froide, qu'il avale avec autant de confiance que de résignation. A Mollien qui souffre à la fois de dysenterie, de maux de dents, de fièvre et de plaies diverses occasionnées par des piqûres de chiques, on apporte un gris-gris sur une planchette. On l'invite alors à laver l'écriture, et à boire l'eau qui contient les caractères effacés.

★ ★ ★ ★ ★

Dans l'Ancien Testament, une main tend un rouleau à Ezechiel, et une voix lui ordonne de le manger, afin qu'il puisse parler au peuple d'Israël avec les mots d'Adonaï lui-même. 'Je le mangeai donc et il fut dans ma bouche aussi doux que du miel'.

L'image s'est conservée jusqu'à nos jours, et je me souviens d'une affiche pour promouvoir la lecture, dans les années cinquante, qui montrait Gérard Philippe dévorant un livre à belles dents.

★ ★ ★ ★ ★

L'art de la divination est à l'origine de l'écriture chinoise, sur des os ou des écailles de tortue.

★ ★ ★ ★ ★

Chez le peuple lega, dans les collines à l'est du Congo, on racle certaines statuettes douées de pouvoir, et l'on met dans l'eau cette poussière afin d'obtenir une décoction que l'on avale, afin d'ingurgiter la 'charge' et sa magie. Faire la même chose avec l'écriture n'a donc rien d'étonnant: on change d'objet, mais on reste dans la même logique.

★ ★ ★ ★ ★

'J'avais mis dans une bouteille d'eau les dernières paroles de ma femme. Les lettres noires se diluèrent bientôt, et l'eau devint couleur de vase. Quelques années plus tard, la retrouvant dans un placard, l'eau s'était évaporée, et dans le fond de la bouteille les lettres avaient repris leur forme.'

Cette confidence n'est pas d'un magicien ni d'un sorcier, c'est une invention de Pierre Bettencourt dans l'une de ses fables. Il n'empêche que cet imaginaire partagé permet d'approcher l'Afrique, et même de la comprendre, autant que les voyages.

— 12 —

'Frieze' and 'The Changes'

Chris Andrews

Frieze

for Michael Sheringham

Longish lull. If there was a hold-up
at what was once the service station
run by John Howard's father, the scene
on the footage would open with Vish
(as it's simpler to be known) who turns
from MISSING GIRL FOUND HER MIND A BLANK
to the feats of a hero before
blunderless Deep Fritz wore them all down:
Zenón Franco's *Anand: Move by Move.*

But it happens after closing time:
numbers from the price sign, bags of ice
from the freezer if it's left unlocked.
They probably put air in their tyres
before wobbling away with the loot.
And then the hours of oily cement
and mute spelling GOT GAS? TUNE & LUBE
until the first simple three-note cry
of the bird that must never be seen.

For now, there's action at the station
of the State Emergency Service:
orange trousers scissor through the dusk,
a pair of ponytails bobs along.
And there they are: the empty belfries
of the Greek church: elevated frames
for gliding puzzles of three-tone sky:
cream sunlit cloud grey cloud in shadow
continually deepening blue.

The Changes

The destination of the sweetness
that hung dispersed in a cloud of drupes
against the cooling sky is a jar.
They who were drifting are now driven.
The timber that was a doorjamb is
a crocodile of ticking embers,
a self-effacing wraith and a wheeze.
Of the hands that rang the changes, two
wring a rag and hang it in the breeze.

Whatever we packed in the capsule
on New Year's Eve 1999
(we came to that river: it is swum)
lies buried under a lemon tree.
The skylit workshop with its jigsaws
and clamps, locked up for years preserving
a gentle reign of dust, is a loft.
The hanged man in the tarot pack hung
by one foot wears a serious smile.

Papers and leaves that were scraping by
singly are a drift. The sun that sank
like a lozenge in the river's throat
inspected depths of rust on a craft
slated for scuppering, still afloat.
Of the hands that rang the changes, one
that wore out a ring is waving, bare.
A draught is blowing through a keyhole.
A door that was jammed shut is ajar.

— 13 —

mon selfie avec Michael S

et la coïncidence du visage souriant dans le registre du roman
ce que la division la rue   l'établissement modèle
dans sa composition   à la recherche l'extérieur
le travail   dans les blés le plein
avec les affections   que l'on porte dans le monde physique
accorde   à retourner le dispositif
que le jardin se fasse résidence   c'est princier
ainsi des lieux réorganisés   d'une grande douceur
la relève de la de la rime   s'élargissant à tous
à savoir s'il faut dénicher   la still life vibration
des arguments des preuves   de complicité et de chaîne
il vous sera fait selon   l'exemple de la dépose
un trait dessus qui laisserait   comme en attente
d'échapper   complaisamment au flash de face du jour rentrons

Anne Portugal

— 14 —

Scots, Translation and Biolinguistic Diversity

Clive Scott

'C'est en feuilletant, pour la vingtième fois au moins, [...] C'est surtout de la fréquentation des villes énormes, c'est du croisement de leurs innombrables rapports que naît cet idéal obsédant'.[1] Browsing through a short selection of Baudelaire's *Petits poèmes en prose* just translated into Scots;[2] thinking through the title — *Traversées du quotidien* — of the French translation[3] of Micky Sheringham's indispensable *Everyday Life*, a translation first encountered in a bookshop in Madrid (2013); musing on languages threatened with extinction;[4] trying to give shape to a reading of Robert Macfarlane's *Landmarks* (2015):[5] these activities were always looking to converge in an argument about translation as a peculiarly 'urban' art, as a manifestation of the everyday, as a minoritarian art, as an instrument for the preservation of languages through permeation, as an instrument of perceptual animation.

I looked at two versions, in Scots, of Baudelaire's 'Enivrez-vous':

> Et si quelquefois, sur les marches d'un palais, sur l'herbe verte d'un fossé, dans la solitude morne de votre chambre, vous vous réveillez, [...][6]

> An if frae time tae time, on the steps o a palace, in the green sedge o a sheuch, in the dreich lanesomeness o yer chaumer, yo come tae yersel, [...] ('Get Yersel Fou', Walter Perrie, born Quarter, South Lanarkshire)

> An if, sometime, apö da steps o some palace, apö da green girse o a ditch, aa dysel in dy room I da moarneen, sood du wakken, [...] ('Be du fu', Christie Williamson, born Yell, Shetland) [7]

I realized at once that I would need to revise some assumptions. We assume that languages can be circumscribed, if not systematized, that they are accessible to acquisition, that they are constituted by describable linguistic features. In saying these things we have already made three mistakes, and particularly so in relation to Scots. True, Scots is haunted by the temptation of circumscription, of self-consolidation ('standard' Scots, 'ideal' Scots),[8] but it is a wandering, exploratory language, with an equally multifarious past still to be drawn upon, and a future ever in the process of being made; indeed, it is probably true to say that the development of modern Scots, and particularly of varieties of urban Scots, has not been — cannot be? — kept track of.[9] About the Scots poems in *Underwoods* (1878), Robert Louis Stevenson confesses: '[...] I simply wrote my Scots as well as I was able, not caring if it hailed from Lauderdale or Angus, from the Mearns or Galloway; if I had ever heard a good word, I used it without shame';[10] Liz Lochhead, introducing her 1985 translation of Molière's *Tartuffe* (1664), is not embarrassed to admit: 'Actually, it's a totally invented and, I hope, theatrical Scots, full of anachronisms, demotic speech from various eras and areas; it's proverbial, slangy, couthy, clichéd, catch-phrasey and vulgar; it's based on Byron, Burns, Stanley Holloway, Ogden Nash and George Formby, as well as on the sharp tongue of my granny';[11] we are told that Scots is best 'conceived of as a language continuum that ranges from "Broad" Scots to "Scottish Standard English"'.[12]

This already begins to suggest ideas about Scots as a translational language, indeed as a *model* of a translational language, among which we might mention the second mistake: Scots cannot be acquired, and this should be our view of all languages in their translational forms. There is the danger that translation, of all linguistic mechanisms, will draw on the known, the route to consensus, domestication, rational decisions and choices, judgement and approval; but translation is, by virtue of its intercourse with other languages, a coming to knowledge, with language in variational flight, ever to be modulated and pursued. Scots is a language designed for 'traversées', an instrument not only of pathfinding across languages, but also of finding one's way through language, as a total medium. Scots has nothing to do with a translation that is the best available option, that involves the progressive exclusion of less felicitous alternatives; it is rather a psycho-topographic journey across linguistic landscapes, more akin to Situationist *dérive*, or drifting, than to grail-questing, and like *dérive*, it is 'une technique du passage hâtif à travers des ambiances variées', with less emphasis on the 'hâtif', so as to fully savour *dérive*'s 'comportement ludico-constructif'.[13] It is a translation, too, practised in *détournement*, an appropriation or re-routing of language that redistributes cultural values, that acts outside language-systems, in unmonitored spaces of free intersection, inventive promiscuities, associative hallucination; translation is the frequenting of great cosmopolitan cities, is the weaving together of their innumerable connections. Translation thus refuses to be complicit in the standardization of language, that is, in a process in which: a freely expressive language becomes a codified one; criteria of expressivity give way to criteria of correctness; orthography, grammar, lexicon become subject to the authority of grammar books and dictionaries; the language becomes an essentially written form that loses its connection with the spoken and all the volatilities and paralanguage of the spoken; consistency of register and style become an aesthetic *sine qua non*. If standardized language makes us think of Certeau's city-planning driven by panoptic power, if *détournement* makes us think of Certeau's notion of 'tactics', then our translational model is also reminiscent of Certeau's account of the affinities between enunciation and urban walking, particularly as expressed in 'La marche affirme, suspecte, hasarde, transgresse, respecte, etc., les trajectoires qu'elle "parle". Toutes les modalités y jouent, changeantes de pas en pas, et réparties dans des proportions, en des successions et avec des intensités qui varient selon les moments, les parcours, les marcheurs. Indéfinie diversité de ces opérations énonciatrices. On ne saurait donc les réduire à leur trace graphique'.[14] If we 'walk'

Baudelaire, then we may begin in Lanarkshire and go to Shetland, still not knowing what our destination is, knowing only that each part of the itinerary, the graphic trace, cannot contain the linguistic places that the text lets loose; the city's grid cannot contain the walker, either in predicting a linguistic behaviour or in mapping out all the possible routes and spaces. It is in these senses that translation shares qualities with what Deleuze and Guattari call the 'minor' or 'minoritarian', in that, as an art of the dynamic and the refractive, it resists 'official' ('major') aesthetic criteria, pursuing the variable and variational as against the constant, testing limits, favouring the experimental, 'deterritorializing' and disequilibriating codes and conventions, a stuttering language-in-formation.

Part of the reason for Scots being a wandering language is the fact that it is pragmatics-generated rather than linguistics-generated, that is to say that it is a language of *situations of use* rather than simply a language *to use*; it is a language of shape-shifting, not merely in terms of code- and register-switches, but in terms of lexical and morphological and behavioural need. What do we mean by behaviour here? This question opens on to the third mistake, the mistake which inheres in 'describable linguistic features'. When we read Scots, we are reading not so much a written language as the transcript of a spoken one (with, of course, hugely varying degrees of transcriptive correspondence), that is to say a language which will tend to cultivate orthographic inconsistency in order to animate, dramatize, its connections with a paralanguage, with features of voice (pausing, accentuation, tone, pitch, tempo, amplitude) which written versions will want to ignore or do scant justice to; and one should quickly add that styles of pronunciation and accent in Scots are far from uniform. One might argue that, in written Scots, for example, the apostrophe has a peculiarly challenging ambivalence because it both expresses the tensions between the written and the spoken, the written's urge to become spoken, to achieve a pressing proximity, and, at the same time, looks like a deference to English inasmuch as it indicates the loss or absence of sounds where they occur in English — one indeed feels the presence or absence of apostrophe as a crux of linguistic sensitivity in these accounts of Baudelaire's prose poems. It is this commitment to orality that gives Scots its peculiar access to the everyday, by which I mean, its refusal to let sense and effect be deferred, its commitment to enunciation as an ongoing eventfulness, the solicitation of interlocution, a direct engagement of the speaker's psycho-physiological presence, proffered in an urgent here and now, a field of eco-action.

For 'foreign' readers of Scots, this oral-cultural underpinning makes the language difficult to penetrate, to reach through to. And it endows spoken accent with a non-negotiable, even exclusionary, indispensability, an indispensability that in other little used languages, or indeed in other languages *tout court*, it does not enjoy — why else, for example, change the orthography of 'house' or 'down' to 'hoose' or 'doun', if not to *demand* accent. But these observations in turn require a paradoxical correction: whatever we might say or feel about the oral sources of Scots, it is as a literary language that it has, perhaps, been most able to publicize its survival, a literary language which owes substantial debts to dialect glossaries, dictionaries, archaism and neologism, themselves seemingly bound to drive a wedge between the literary and spoken vernaculars. But if I say 'seemingly' it is to guard against hasty conclusions: Hugh MacDiarmid may have drawn on reference books and brought John Jamieson's *An Etymological Dictionary of the Scottish Language* (first publication 1808) into the linguistic purview of poets of the Scottish Renaissance, into the creation of Lallans, but his verse attests to a profound absorption of these sources into his own inimitable vocal expressionism.[15] Whenever we address the undoubted divergence of the written and the spoken in Scots, or indeed in any language, we should bear four things in mind: (i) literature clearly has obligations to the development of its own linguistic adventures in perceptual and conceptual possibility, exacerbated with the advent of Modernism: as McClure points out, Hopkins's verse has as little direct relation to spoken English vernaculars as the work of the poets of the Scottish Renaissance has to Scots vernaculars;[16] (ii) we should add that such poetry, for all its distance from the spoken language, in no sense forgoes its orality: Hopkins, too, insists that his verse is for vocal performance; (iii) the adaptability of Scots orthography allows it, when need be, to redefine its relationship with vocal realization: Albert Mackie's objections to MacDiarmid's practices are couched in these terms: 'I write on the basis of a living dialect, even indicating this in my spelling, whereas he sets his face against all dialect and writes mainly on a basis of aggregate vocabulary and idiom';[17] (iv) what is ultimately at stake is not a divergence between the spoken and the written, inevitable, nay desirable, as it is, but the persuasiveness of the assimilation of items of lexical beach-combing; as William Soutar puts it: 'Have we gathered all these words into a mortuary, or is it a literary orphanage waiting for the authors, who are foster-fathers?'[18] Moreover, as a further paradox, this liberation of Scots from the anchorage of determining origin and 'style' creates those conditions of explicit, not to say brazen, linguistic experimentation so fundamental to a progressive view of translation; one might go so far as to say that Scots is, simply, an experimental language, a translational language. There is one further qualification to add: we tend to think that one cannot be largely ignorant of a language and at the same time claim to have a meaningful relationship with it. But I precisely want to argue that such a thing is possible, and not only possible but an essential part of the thinking about the productivity of translation. My ignorance of Scots puts me in a position where my loosened linguistic grasp allows me to *imagine* Scots better, to feel for its imaginary, to make any knowledge that I get of it *emergent from it*.

If we view translation as an exercise in the relating of languages one to the other — where the notion of relating has less to do with transfer and much to do with the non-coincident reciprocation of linguistic posture and insight — then we might have no difficulty in believing that every translational act involves us in thinking, tacitly perhaps, not just the two languages of the immediate transaction, but all languages. It is not difficult to all but agree with Édouard Glissant's observation that: 'La poétique de la Relation requiert toutes les langues du monde. Non pas les connaître ni les méditer, mais savoir (éprouver) qu'elles existent avec nécessité. Que cette existence décide des accents de toute écriture'.[19] Elsewhere, Glissant speaks of this global linguistic awareness as a grasp of the imaginary of languages, rather than as a knowledge of languages: 'Ce n'est pas une question de science, de connaissance des langues, c'est une question d'imaginaire des langues. Ce n'est pas une question de juxtaposition des langues, mais de leur mise en réseau'.[20] The *applied* knowledge of languages, or polyglottism, Glissant suggests, is not necessarily a desirable form of multilingualism,[21] inasmuch as it may lead to a cognitive/conceptual separation of languages ('juxtaposition'), rather than to a sense of their interrelated poetics, which itself derives from a desire for knowledge of them, a desire for their knowledge, their mode of relating to the world. But we might prefer the notion of meshwork ('tissage') to Glissant's network ('réseau'), that is, a tissue or tangle of interwoven trails, emerging from environmental inhabitation, rather than a map, a bird's eye view, of interconnected points, points, that is, conceptually connected by straight lines.[22] While 'network' indicates languages' positions relative to each other, measures their proximities and distances, their affinities and disjunctions, while 'network' is to do with the evaluative and quantifiable, 'meshwork' encourages various kinds of promiscuity, lines bending or deviating to take account of associative mechanisms, variations and continuities, morphings from one language to another, fluid interactions, in short all the idiosyncratic paths of the individual wanderer.

To say of McClure's 'Awa ayont the swaws of the ruifs' ('Par-delà des vagues de toits') in his version of Baudelaire's 'Les Fenêtres' ['Winnocks'] that 'swaws' means 'waves' is to privilege exchange-value over use-value, and metadiscourse over discourse. So he might just as well have said 'waves'? Translation is not an answer to the question 'What does that mean?' but is a process of mutual linguistic interpenetration as a key to perceptual/conceptual education, letting the findings of one language infiltrate the findings of another in a cumulative metamorphosis: vagues/waves/Wellen/swaws/houle/swall. If there was only one way of saying 'water', Glissant observes,[23] what a terrible limitation of the human imagination it would be. On the other hand, if all the different ways of saying 'water' were deemed to mean the same thing, it would be just as bad. We do not, as Glissant reminds us, use language to codify the world, but to enter into a relationship with it;[24] and we translate in order to nuance, extend, complicate that relationship. Translation is fundamentally an ecological undertaking. If the French 'vagues' perhaps carries 'algues' in it, and is enriched by the complex interferences of its etymologies (< Old Scand. vâgr (cf. Ger. Woge); < Latin vacuus: 'terrain vague'; < Latin vagus [errant, vagabond]), McClure's 'swaws' has a palindromic 'balancement' [rocking motion], is at its heart a mirror image of 'awa', and calls to mind his use of it to render 'houle' in 'Le "Confiteor" de l'artiste': 'the chyngeless sang o the swaws' ('mélodie monotone de la houle'), making Baudelaire's monotony more eventful, more epidermic, more acoustically complex, noisier. 'Swaw' is also a verb, of Scandinavian origin (cf. Norwegian dialect *svaga*, from Old Norse), to sway or swing, cognate with 'swag', to sway from side to side, to move in a zig-zag; English 'sway' comes by another route: Low German *swâjen*, Dutch *swaaien*. 'Swall', used by Christie Williamson to translate 'vague' in 'Enivrez-vous', relates directly to English 'swell' ('houle'). In this kind of translational world, 'errors' themselves are perceptual deviations rather than inaccuracies: in his version of 'Chacun sa chimère' ('Ilkane his ain Chimaera'), Robert Calder reinvents Baudelaire's 'se dérobe' as 'taks aff her veils' — rather than, say, 'eludes/escapes from' — for obvious reasons, and (wilfully?) misreads the expletive 'ne' in the final sentence, perhaps in order more thoroughly to inhabit the poem's labyrinth of shifting negativity, and humanity's self-delusional translations of the negative into the positive.

Glissant's argument that we must work with a multilingualism, built on the imaginary of languages rather than on polyglottism, makes translation, and a particular kind of 'non-technical' translation, all the more indispensable. What we need is 'une sorte de variance infinie des sensibilités linguistiques', or, as he also puts it, a consciousness of the 'variance infinie de nuances des poétiques possibles des langues', rather than 'une connaissance des langues', with the result that: 'De plus en plus les traductions deviendront un art essentiel. Jusqu'ici on a trop laissé les traductions aux seuls traducteurs. Les traductions deviendront une part importante des poétiques, ce qui n'est pas le cas jusq'ici'[25] What I would want to insist is that translation not only activates our sense of the imaginary of languages, it is expressly designed to push languages *into* the imaginary, which for me means two things. First, it means a rejection of a present form of evaluative translational criticism which is based largely on bilingual considerations, on the assessment of decisions and choices, and on the known linguistic patrimony, a delimitative criticism, without any sense of what translation might be, other than doing a text over into another language, to extend its range of consumption. Translation has the distinctive capacity to activate linguo-perceptual comparisons, to intensify our sense of differing styles of linguistic embodiment, to make dramatically visible the continuities and swervings between languages. Second, it compels us to re-imagine languages in relation to their sources of expression, so that, under the impetus of expressive needs identified by other languages, or of needs generated by linguistic cohabitation, we might re-invent those resources. What makes one alphabet more appropriate than another? Do we need to develop new alphabets? How many graphemes/phonemes does any particular alphabet need?[26] How is punctuation to be removed from its role as clarifier of syntax and servant of discursive logic, and restored to expressive trace of voice and body in writing? What does language allow us to hear and prevent us from hearing? What would, in any particular instance, an appropriate orthography be?

The death of Scots has long been predicted, by Boswell in 1764, Pinkerton in 1786, Stevenson in 1887, and no doubt by many since.[27] It is no surprise that Glissant constantly warns against the loss of languages: he speaks of 'cette conscience ou cette prescience que nous avons besoin de toutes les langues et que chaque fois qu'une langue disparaît, meme si nous ne la parlons pas, nous sommes appauvris par cette disparition.'[28] This general case is given eloquent elaboration in the work of anthropological linguists such as Nettle and Romaine, and Harrison. Where the argument leaves me wondering is in the assumptions (a) that 'languages perform a fundamental act of identity for their speakers',[29] and (b) that 'the world's major languages are becoming more like one another through the process of intertranslation and culture contact'.[30] Identity is a static and unhelpful concept; better to be in a position of multiplicity and becoming, of transformative chemistry both with local eco-possibility and the non-local context. Even though Nettle and Romaine come back with some insistence to the idea that language is the indispensable bearer of identity, they do seem to acknowledge the dangers of 'language-related national identity politics'[31] and go so far as to say that 'We all have overlapping and intersecting identities',[32] which is to say perhaps that we should cultivate and extend those overlaps and intersections in a way that is mutually empowering. And it is translation which, far from acting as the instrument of diversity-reduction and homogenization, might, if properly conceived, have entirely the opposite effect.

There are other elements in the arguments of Nettle and Romaine which also seem to me to flirt with self-contradiction. The strength of their overall case depends on the lockstep interdependence of biodiversity/sustainable ecosystem, on the one hand, and the preservation of the linguistically indigenous on the other, an interdependence they call 'biolinguistic diversity'.[33] But their vision of increasingly bilingual and multilingual cohabitations, in the development of mutually enriching local/global relationships, seems to me to entail a dynamic of the sustainable within the changing, and the adoption of an evolutionary principle, whereby it is profitable to envisage intergenerational transmission as a productively non-coincident or self-differentiating process (previously interpreted as culture-loss), and also whereby language and eco-system enjoy sufficient separation constantly to be able to re-define each other, to generate a progressive dialectic.

Eco-niche languages have certain inherent proclivities: they are retentional, cumulative, multifunctional and integrational. Attached to oral cultures, they cannot 'outsource' information to the written word, although they may outsource certain processes to objects (e.g. counting/numbering in stones or sticks). The burden of information, as indeed the imperious needs of survival, may thus become constraining, may indeed dictate perceptual fields as much as refine them: Harrison observes: 'Certain languages, due to a process of language adaptation to a landscape, will force their speakers to notice and specify certain properties such as a direction of river flow'.[34] One might say that it is not making a written record of these disappearing oral cultures that condemns them to petrification, nor their being elbowed aside by so-called hegemonic languages, but rather that they are self-petrifying, that relative isolation and insulation, and their resistance to using their own languages to communicate with 'outsiders',[35] is the root of their inbuilt obsolescence. What such languages need is not survival, or revival at the point of extinction, but a multiplication of contacts when they are living, translation, that is, of a particularly involving and reciprocated kind, so that they have access to alternative linguistic proclivities: not retention but creation, not accumulation/aggregation but diversification/variation, not multifunctionality but functional dispersal, not integration but centrifugality. It is translation which can, as it were, enlarge the group and act as the importer of other linguistic populations. Translation can engender *langages* within the *langue*, or can find a superordinate roof for a threatened *langue* in *langage* in its other sense, the world-wide linguistic medium as a whole. In short, we perhaps need to concentrate more not on preserving the diversity *of* languages, but on encouraging diversity *within* languages.

Those who make the case for disappearing languages do not perhaps sufficiently acknowledge that their discourse (a) is too exclusively concerned with lexis and word-formation; (b) tacitly believes that what is named in a single word is not only more efficient than what is described in seven, but also more precise and more in touch with the world; (c) believes, in consequence, that these terms may be explainable, but that they are not translatable; (d) promotes too exclusively the behavioural 'ethics' of hunter-gatherers and pastoralists, rather than agriculturalists, the language of subsistence/survival rather than of surplus and re-distribution; (e) elides the implication that to maintain the full efficacy of vanishing languages we would need to maintain the ways of life they serve (this would be to make them the equivalent of adventure-vacation languages); (f) implies that the West's apprehension of time, space, number is impoverished, or too abstract, or too scientific, compared with that of vanishing languages, even though each of our arts — sculpture, painting, cinema, photography, etc. — explores a different relationship with time, while Cubism, Surrealism, Land Art have taken us on different adventures in the perception of space.

Anthropological arguments about vanishing languages overlap in many respects with the lost languages of our own country lore and the deleterious ecological and conservational consequences of that loss. In *Landmarks* (2015), Robert Macfarlane argues that within those specialized vocabularies developed by speech-communities/dialects to deal with the landscapes and life-patterns in which they are locally embedded, we find a lexicon sharply sensitive to, and empathetic with, the distinctive characteristics of objects, through their 'accessory' or complicating features, thus: *bungel* (Shetland) 'clod of turf used as a missile'; *haggering* (North Sea coast) 'distortion of objects by atmospheric refraction'; *sussing* (Suffolk) 'noise made by pigs when feeding'. Words like these, the argument runs, bear testimony to a quality of attention, a 'vibrancy of perception',[36] a lyricism of relationship, an ecological intimacy, which are progressively going missing. Where, then, are the risks run by this particular argument? First, it once again approaches language too lexicographically (word-list, glossary, lexicon, phrase-book, thesaurus); it implies that individual words, in themselves, carry knowledge, not that they help to provide the contexts for knowledge, nor that those contexts include not only other vocabulary but kinds of speech act, kinds of dialogic interconnection, kinds of characteristic collocation, kinds of discourse. Second, it once again implies that because the words are single (rather than phrases, like their explanations) they are more exact, more responsive to the phenomena they capture. Besides 'exact', Macfarlane describes these words as 'scalpel-sharp', 'super-specific', 'precise', 'untranslatable'. It is as if the singleness of the word were proof of a process of distillation rather than of economy, of an unerring and revelatory compression of perception rather than of linguistically determined selector mechanisms. Besides, does *smeuse* (Sussex) really make me more knowingly or knowledgeably aware of gaps in the hedge than the phrase 'the gap in the base of a hedge made by the regular passage of a small animal', which is presented to me as the meaning of *smeuse* — that is, as clumsy metadiscourse — rather than as a phrase in its own right. In fact, considered in its own right, as itself a literary construct, one can see how expressive this phrase is of a certain dragging, rustling, squeezing, squirming awkwardness of thoroughfare: /(g)æp/ acoustically reverses in /pæ(sɪdʒ)/; the hard, voiced, velar stop /g/ twice (gap, regular) softens to voiced alveo-palatal affricate /dʒ/ (hedge, passage); voiceless /s/ (base, passage, small) tries to slip by unobserved, or quietly squeaks; the /ɔ:l/ of 'small' undergoes a further dramatic compression — /m(ə)l/ — in 'animal'; none of these vicissitudes of progress, one might argue, is captured by *smeuse*. Third, Macfarlane does not address the question of the transferability of these terms. Can we just adopt them haphazardly, as if they belonged indelibly to the phenomenon, as if no other word were possible, even though we know from the word-lists supplied that different regions each develop their own terms, even for shared natural features. If we were to use the word with any real sense of inhabiting it, would we not have also to digest the whole corpus of a particular area's cultural *Weltanschauung*? Fourth, while distinctions in the matter of word-derivations are made in passing, the consequences of those distinctions are not addressed. *Sussing* (above) is clearly onomatopoeic; but any user of English has the licence to create nonce onomatopoeias or adapt those already in existence (see comic books and graphic novels), whereas words with traceable etymologies and histories of usage acquire a certain semantic transparency and linguistic status and transferability. It is words whose origins and derivations cannot be recovered that take on the mystique of the 'revealed' that Macfarlane would wish for them. And let us be clear: onomatopoeic words do not have meanings; they are imitative of sounds; if they do have a meaning it is because they are inadequate as imitations. Fifth, by dint of what do we distinguish the virtue of words in these glossaries from that of (a) any foreign word that makes us newly mindful of phenomena by the oddness of its meaning or the intricacy of its relationship with its meaning (French: *cippe* 'a foreshortened funeral column'; *méduse* 'jellyfish', *riquiqui* 'tiny, stingy') or of (b) any highly specialized terminology, e.g. the language of bicycle frames, or of screws, or of vacuum cleaner attachments, or of verse-metrics?[37] Sixth, it is assumed that the experience provided by *natural* phenomena is deeper than that provided by others: 'a leather-covered steering wheel bearing the marks of hand-sweat'(?); 'trousers creased at the sides rather than at front and back' (?). Seventh, we must ask where the items in these glossaries stand in relation to Saussure's case for the arbitrariness of the sign. Can a word be 'scalpel-sharp' if the relationship between signifier and signified is not a necessary one, is poorly motivated?

But Macfarlane is no dupe of all these risks. His words and wordlists can promise nothing other than 'glimpses through other eyes, [...] brief access to distant habits of perception';[38] he is 'wary of the dangers of fetishizing dialect and archaism — all that *mollocking* and *sukebinding* Stella Gibbons spoofed so brilliantly in *Cold Comfort Farm* (1932)';[39] he is wary, too, 'of being seen to advocate a tyranny of the nominal — a taxonomic need to point and name, with the intent of citing and owning —

when in fact I perceive no opposition between precision and mystery, or between naming and not-knowing';[40] and he calls us to new determinations, not to the lure of a plaintive nostalgia: 'We have forgotten 10,000 words for our landscapes, but we will make 10,000 more, given time'[41] and he applauds Finlay MacLeod's call for 'a new nomenclature of landscape and how we relate to it, so that conservation becomes a natural form of human awareness'.[42] These acknowledgements and exhortations do not necessarily, of course, let him off the hook. He must probably plead guilty on some counts.[43] But then none of this should be allowed to cast any doubt on the ways in which his own writing so exhilaratingly enriches our perceptual capacities.

Languages are organizations of perceptual behaviours and faculties, are activators of the metabolic operations of perceptual energy and physio-chemical reaction. A language may help us to discern the intimate topographical relationship between rivers and forests, but it may not, if defining such relationships is not urgent to us. In absolute terms, such a capacity might seem a desirable linguistic acquisition, but it is more important that language has the ability to extend itself as needs arise than that it be asked to assimilate 'orphans' without the drive of necessitation. Translation is the motor of that necessitation, and in that respect, translation must always aim to be attuned to changing ecological conditions, must be an eco-translation. But, of course, perception should also always be asking questions about its own limits, about obstructive constraints. We must regret that language does not challenge our onomatopoeic ingenuity, does not incite us to hear better; we too comfortably think of our linguistic acoustics in terms of phonological systems rather than of imitative invention and of the intricate soundscapes available in phonemic combinations.

But even where we must admit that we have much to learn from vanishing languages about reanimating language's power as an eco-relational negotiator, we must be careful not to underplay the two-way current of this exchange, which itself depends on the written language; our anthropological linguists must write down the languages they describe even if the cultures in question are oral. What I mean is that language does not just mediate unproblematically between human perception and the environment; it is itself an ecosystem inhabited by human perception; and our ability to deepen our perception of the material world may be a spin-off or side-effect of our ability to refine our inhabitation of language as much as the reverse.

In fact the relationship between language and environment is a complex, twofold one. In the situational, pragmatic orality of Scots, impelled in some senses by a Bonnefoyian aspiration to presence, language drives us into the environment, mediates our integration, continually re-negotiates our environmental dailiness. But it is no good unless that relationship is kept living and becoming by the constancy of the re-negotiation. Alternatively, language draws the environment into itself, into a writing which may maintain its contact with an orality by incorporating performance or the performative, exploring the paralinguistic in the linguistic, but which in principle pursues another protocol, a protocol which suspends signifying momentum so that language can, over the whole range of an utterance, weave itself into intricate patterns at different levels of sense-making, acoustic, rhythmic, graphemic, etymological, intertextual. In this manner environmental values are recycled by language, drawn into the eco-system that language itself is, an ecosystem which we no less thoroughly inhabit, through the practice of reading. Thus it is likely that, here, our focus will be bifocal: we might define literature as that version of language in which the linguistic eco-system itself most absorbs our perceptual experience, becomes, as it were, a truly alternative environment, ousting all others; on other hand, we may read as if reading were the way in which the referential environment might recover itself in linguistic consciousness, invest itself with that consciousness, in order to reaffirm the colourful immediacy of its perceptibility. This is how, for many, the business of referring becomes the business of creatively naming. So either language is seen to push into environment, insisting that the linguistic exercises itself in pragmatics and paralinguisticity, or it assimilates environment, in turn either to incorporate it into its own eco-system, or to subject it to a process of sensory renewal and re-projection.

All this of course tacitly accepts that words are intimately and inescapably necessary to our perceptual capacity; without the word, the ability to name, we will perhaps register a phenomenon but it will not enter the discourse of our affective and experiential lives. So, let us be clear, the recovery of ecological awareness is all about literature, about a language which does not denote phenomena but names them: 'Language is fundamental to the possibility of re-wonderment, for language does not just register experience, it produces it'.[44]This literature, though often described as 'utterance',[45] is, make no mistake, a writing; reality is a source of, a trigger of, poetic writing: 'I began to collect stone-words as well as stones: the axe-knock syllables of *quartz*, *jet*, *chert*, *onyx* and *agate*, the classical complexities of *carnelian* and *citrine*. [Clarence] Ellis clearly loved language for its capacity to grade and sort perception, but also for the poetry it carried'.[46] It is then the gift of language that writing hands back to the environment so that it may come to consciousness, and come to a consciousness of itself.

But the notion of naming may still strike too lexicographic a note. Naming is to be understood as a much more complex process, the capture of phenomena in a total rhythmo-acoustic and syntactic meshwork, where language sheds the business of meaning, of standing for a concept or referent, and is, instead, diversely and experientially indwelt by its subject. Of the writing of Peter Davidson, and particularly of the sentence 'A little stone jetty in still water: water like pewter, extraordinary water', Macfarlane writes: 'The extreme stillness of the sentence is in part a function of its verblessness, but is due also to the reflection of water within itself ('water: water'), an effect doubled again as the word *pewter* catches and supplely returns — with a ripple — the word *water*'.[47] We might add that the chiastic arrangement of the second phrase ('water like pewter, extraordinary water') endorses the structure of reflection, and that in the rhythm of the two phrases, which I read as [× / × / / ×] [× / / ×]: [/ × × / ×] [× × / × × / ×], that is, as two antispasts (× / / ×), the first with an iambic lead-in, followed by two adonics (/ × × / ×), the second preceded by two weak syllables, the antispasts hold stillness in their stressed centres, while the adonics, with the added weaks, create a gently shimmering, slightly disturbed surface. The magic of naming is less in the word than in the weave of words, in the writing; language is made of a depth, an expressive inspissatedness and interpenetration that far exceeds the inherent 'semantic worth' of any individual word. As McClure points out in relation to McDiarmid's 'dictionary-dredging' and free appropriation of obsolete Scots lexis: 'The essential reason for the success, as it clearly is, of McDiarmid's experiments in the poetic use of rare Scots words is the almost unerring skill with which he chooses a word with the appropriate phonetic, phonaesthetic or semantic value, and often a pointedly relevant overtone from its previous use, for the immediate context: or alternatively, devises the perfect context in which an unusual word can display its intriguing and enticing qualities of sound and meaning to the full'.[48]

So what vision of translation are we anxious to establish? Not a translation devoted to the conversion of one text into another, at the expense, as it were, of the source text and for the benefit of the monoglot reader, the reader, that is, who, by the very act of translation is being reassured that he/she need not bother to become familiar with the source language. This particular version of 'post-agricultural' or 'monocultural' translation draws in its wake all the ills of colonial translation, linguistic hegemonies, cultural no-go areas (untranslatability). Translation differently conceived is, rather, the bringing of languages into contact with each other, so that each of them continues to express itself in the mind of the multilingual reader, to be active and in dialogue. Translation is not a technical affair about the transmission of particular texts: it is about those texts acting as our motivations for rethinking ourselves in relation to other languages, it is about what linguistic thinking is activated in us, and about the quality of that thinking. Language here is not thought about conversionally, but proliferatively and metamorphically. Everything is translatable but nothing is equivalent or equal. We must live Babel as thoroughly as we can, into every linguistic corner.

Notes

1. 'À Arsène Houssaye', in Charles Baudelaire, *Œuvres complètes I*, ed. by Claude Pichois (Paris: Gallimard, 1975), pp. 275–76.
2. *Scottish Spleen*, ed. by Tom Hubbard, James W. Underhill and Stewart Sanderson (Alford: Tapsalteerie, 2015).
3. Michael Sheringham, *Traversées du quotidien: des surréalistes aux postmodernes*, trans. by Maryline Heck and Jeanne-Marie Hostiou (Paris: PUF, 2013).
4. My principal sources here are: Daniel Nettle and Suzanne Romaine, *Vanishing Voices: The Extinction of the World's Languages* (New York: Oxford University Press, 2000); K. David Harrison, *When Languages Die: The Extinction of the World's Languages and the Erosion of Human Knowledge* (New York: Oxford University Press, 2007).
5. Robert Macfarlane, *Landmarks* (London: Hamish Hamilton/Penguin, 2015).
6. Baudelaire, *Œuvres complètes I*, p. 337.
7. The translations of both Perrie and Williamson appear in Hubbard, Underhill and Sanderson, *Scottish Spleen*, unpaginated.
8. See Manfred Görlach, *A Textual History of Scots* (Heidelberg: Universitätsverlag C. Winter, 2002), pp. 162–63.
9. John Corbett, J. Derrick McClure and Jane Stuart-Smith, 'A Brief History of Scots', in John Corbett, J. Derrick McClure and Jane Stuart-Smith (eds), *The Edinburgh Companion to Scots* (Edinburgh: Edinburgh University Press, 2003), pp. 1–16 (p. 15).

Companion to Scots (Edinburgh: Edinburgh University Press, 2003), pp. 1–16 (p. 15).

10. Robert Louis Stevenson, *Collected Poems*, ed. by Janet Adam Smith (London: Rupert Hart-Davis, 1950), p. 486.
11. Quoted in John Corbett, *Written in the Language of the Scottish Nation: A History of Literary Translation into Scots* (Clevedon: Multilingual Matters, 1999), p. 152.
12. Corbett, McClure and Stuart-Smith, 'A Brief History of Scots', p. 1.
13. See Michael Sheringham, *Everyday Life: Theories and Practices from Surrealism to the Present* (Oxford: Oxford University Press, 2006), p. 164.
14. Michel de Certeau, *L'Invention du quotidien* I: *Arts de faire* (Paris: Union Générale d'Éditions, 1980), p. 183.
15. J. Derrick McClure, *Language, Poetry and Nationhood: Scots as a Poetic Language from 1878 to the Present* (East Linton: Tuckwell Press, 2000), pp. 84–100.
16. McClure, *Language, Poetry and Nationhood*, pp. 24, 97. We might add, anent this point and in support of our argument as a whole, a comment made by the editors of Hugh MacDiarmid's *Selected Poems* (Harmondsworth: Penguin, 1970): 'We, the editors, were brought up in the north of Scotland and one of us spoke Scots from his childhood, yet there are a good many lines in which each of the two or three key-words was unknown to us from print, let alone from speech. In this respect, in the range of his borrowing from older literatures, dictionaries, and specialized or technical sources (all reinforcing his own dialect, south-west Border Scots), MacDiarmid was in line with the other three important innovators of the Twenties and Thirties, Pound, Joyce and Eliot. He exacts like efforts from his readers and yields like fruits, in the way of multiple associations fused in the one phrase and perception never before caught in language' (pp. 10–11).
17. Quoted in McClure, *Language, Poetry and Nationhood*, p. 103.
18. Quoted in McClure, *Language, Poetry and Nationhood*, p. 112.
19. Édouard Glissant, *Poétique de la relation: Poétique III* (Paris: Gallimard, 1990), p. 231.
20. Édouard Glissant, *Introduction à une poétique du divers* (Paris: Gallimard, 1996), p. 123.
21. Glissant, *Introduction*, p. 142.
22. Tim Ingold, *Lines: A Brief History* (Abingdon: Routledge, 2007), pp. 80–82. Ingold has the term 'meshwork' from Henri Lefebvre.
23. Édouard Glissant, *L'Imaginaire des langues: entretiens avec Lise Gauvin (1991–2009)* (Paris: Gallimard, 2010), p. 99.
24. Glissant, *L'Imaginaire*, p. 99.
25. Glissant, *L'Imaginaire*, p. 27.
26. Harrison reminds us not only that, by his calculation, something under 25% of the world's languages — say *c.* 1700 out of *c.* 7000 — have written forms (*When Languages Die*, p. 145), but also that while Rotokas (Bougainville Island, Papua New Guinea) has only six consonants, Ingush (Caucasus) has forty (p. 210); Nettle and Romaine report that Ubykh (Caucasus) had eighty-one consonants but only three vowels (*Vanishing Voices*, p. 10).
27. Görlach, *A Textual History*, p. 186. A defiant retort is provided by William Neill: '"Scots was dying at the time of Robert Burns", says yin. No it wesna. It wes gey an vieve whan I wes a bit laddie in Ayrshire an tis no deid nou tae onybodie wi lugs tae hear' (*Tales frae the Odyssey o Homer Owreset intil Scots bi William Neill*, illus. by Barbara Robertson (Edinburgh: Saltire Society, 1992), pp. 9–10).
28. Glissant, *L'Imaginaire*, p. 54.
29. Nettle and Romaine, *Vanishing Voices*, p. 22.
30. Nettle and Romaine, *Vanishing Voices*, p. 12.
31. Nettle and Romaine, *Vanishing Voices*, p. 194. It is an unjustified preoccupation with linguistic identity and self-assertion that regrettably leads James Underhill, in his introduction to *Scottish Spleen*, to launch a sustained, and equally unjustified, attack on English as a translating language, with remarks such as: 'Scots offers us a great chance to get round the pernicious prejudices that tend to pervert Baudelaire translations into English' (n.p), particularly in view of the fact that his own Scots is coloured by 'more than a hint of Geordie that comes from my Mum and Dad, from South Shields in Tyneside' (n.p.). God forbid that a translation-practice designed to put

languages at each other's throats ever be espoused.

32. Nettle and Romaine, *Vanishing Voices*, p. 196. Or, as they put it elsewhere: 'Restoration of full monolingualism where it once may have existed is not a realistic goal, because modern life makes it impossible and indeed undesirable to be entirely independent of outside influences' (p. 191).
33. But this does not mean that Nettle and Romaine would argue for the preservation of a language at any cost: 'We would not therefore support measures to preserve a language which consigned its people to economic disadvantage and political marginality' (*Vanishing Voices*, p. 156).
34. Harrison, *When Languages Die*, p. 134. Harrison earlier observes: 'Folk taxonomies may limit themselves by what is relevant to human survival in a given eco-system' (p. 39).
35. Nettle and Romaine, *Vanishing Voices*, p. 12.
36. Macfarlane, *Landmarks*, p. 9.
37. Macfarlane's glossaries themselves tacitly accept that this last distinction is not possible to maintain and indeed imply that it is undesirable that it should be maintained: alongside major source languages, dialects and sub-dialects, there are words pertaining to specialist vocabularies (e.g. 'archaeological', 'geographical', 'mountaineering', 'speleological') (*Landmarks*, p. 338).
38. Macfarlane, *Landmarks*, p. 5.
39. Macfarlane, *Landmarks*, p. 10.
40. Macfarlane, *Landmarks*, p. 10.
41. Macfarlane, *Landmarks*, p. 14.
42. Macfarlane, *Landmarks*, p. 31.
43. Macfarlane is the first to admit that his glossaries are without cross-references between languages and dialects, and without dates of usage, and that there is something 'mongrel' about the way they have been put together which might leave 'a serious-minded linguist' discontented (*Landmarks*, p. 338).
44. Macfarlane, *Landmarks*, p. 25.
45. 'All [Macfarlane's chosen models and mentors] have written with committing intensity about their chosen territories. And for all of them, to use language well is to use it particularly: precision of utterance as both a form of lyricism and a species of attention' (*Landmarks*, p. 11).
46. Macfarlane, *Landmarks*, p. 264.
47. Macfarlane, *Landmarks*, p. 214.
48. McClure, *Language, Poetry and Nationhood*, p. 93.

— 15 —

Le Quotidien sans Michael

François Bon

Les derniers peut-être à avoir été élevés dans la 'grande histoire'. En tout cas elle fondait le récit familial, et ce qui la rythmait de guerres se traduisait par la présence d'objets soit menaçants (une baïonnette ramassée sur les champs de bataille de Verdun par mes grands-parents), soit incongrus (le sabre d'un vague cousin parti en Afrique), soit déplacés (l'insigne des FFI de la Résistance que mon père a laissé des années, je ne sais pas pourquoi, dans le tiroir de la salle de bain). La guerre d'Algérie, en même temps que la télévision, pour signifier que les mêmes lois continuaient. Et puis la rupture s'est faite, par les objets notamment, bien avant qu'on comprenne ce qui en résultait pour une notion de culture qui n'avait plus rien à voir avec celles de l'art — le statut même des livres dans l'armoire à porte vitrée où ils étaient gardés, bouleversé aussi. Les livres qui sont les outils pour analyser et comprendre cette 'invention du quotidien' datent de cette même période, mais je les ai découverts bien plus tard. Alors qu'il n'y avait plus aucun moyen d'en constituer l'archive, ni comment soi-même on s'était pris au jeu des couleurs, des nouveautés, d'une croyance un peu naïve que les ombres inhérentes à l'histoire humaine s'éloignaient. Il aura fallu s'aventurer dans ce qui n'avait pas de trace préalable — même si, chez Proust par exemple, ou Ponge, ou Étienne Binet — on en trouvait rétrospectivement les outils. Et, à mesure que se décryptait cette mutation, qu'on en fabriquait l'écorché et qu'on le dressait face à ces épouvantails fades de la culture normalisée, voilà que le quotidien lui-même était ravalé par d'autres flux, écroulements, poussières. Des objets qui s'éteignaient (plus besoin d'appareil spécifique pour écouter de la musique, prendre des photographies), les chaussures et les voitures et tout le reste fabriquées tout pareil sur la surface du monde, passe encore. Mais voilà que les noms mêmes s'évanouissent, sont remplacés par des noms de marque et quand la marque s'en va on prend un autre mot. Le mot 'mp3', deux consonnes un chiffre, n'a plus besoin de rien désigner. Notre attention au concret, ce que nous avons appris à penser par constellation, le défi aux idées trop générales et synthétiques que représente l'analyse d'un morceau minuscule du temps — mais justement: assez minuscule pour être devenu poreux au dehors, à la ville, aux postures et aux gestes — sont notre bagage même maintenant que nous avons les mains vides: ce qui nous environne n'a plus promesse de continuité, encore moins promesse de marche en avant, le temps même de la pensée ne laisse jamais liberté de s'y livrer sans la pleine conscience de ce qu'il y a de norme, de politique, d'écologie (la fragmentation des terres rares dans l'ordinateur, les combats de titan derrière le navigateur ou le moteur de recherche, et l'idée même du livre jamais indépendante de l'économie qui le produit, du support qui en conditionne la page). Nous sommes dans ce nouveau désarroi, et pourtant nous y sommes agrandis: par ce que nous avons pu apprendre, ces deux dernières décennies, à revenir sur la 'traversée' du quotidien. Il fait sombre derrière la porte, nous écarquillons les yeux, et c'est peut-être la faiblesse même du quotidien qui a été le plus difficile à apprendre. Est-ce qu'elle peut être aussi notre arme? En tout cas, s'il y a nommer une dette et un hommage à Michael Sheringham, c'est là.

— 16 —

Bonnefoy, Barthes, Valéry: la poétique au Collège de France

Dominique Combe

'Et je n'ai jamais cessé, quant à moi, de penser que je me comprendrais mieux, et comprendrais mieux la poésie, si je fréquentais quelques sciences — ou tout au moins en pressentais mieux les aspects'.[1] Bonnefoy oppose l'érudition de Dante, Pétrarque ou Leopardi au mythe d'une poésie 'à l'état sauvage'. Car la poésie se nourrit de la connaissance, fruit de recherches personnelles, puisque 'les plus grands de ces successives époques, hommes pourtant d'intense culture et foncièrement des intellectuels, ainsi Nerval, Baudelaire, Verlaine, Mallarmé, Laforgue, Apollinaire, et Breton lui-même, et Paul Valéry ou Pierre Jean Jouve, se sont formés au dehors de l'Université, dont il faut bien reconnaître qu'elle traversait alors en France une assez mauvaise passe pour ce qui est des études littéraires et de la réflexion sur la poésie'.[2] Mais, à la différence de ses grands aînés Breton, Jouve, Michaux, Char ou Saint-John Perse, qui se méfient de l'Université, ou parfois l'utilisent pour ériger leur propre statue, Bonnefoy, plus que tout autre poète de sa génération, se tient proche des universitaires, avec qui il collabore régulièrement pour des séminaires, des colloques, des conférences. Bonnefoy, pourtant entré en poésie avec le surréalisme, rompt ainsi avec la 'mode post-romantique' qui, observe-t-il, 'méprisa l'université': 'les meilleurs jeunes poètes identifiaient, avec raison d'ailleurs, poésie et révolte, écriture poétique et transgressions des préjugés intellectuels ou moraux, et ils considéraient que les professeurs, prisonniers de leur projet de connaissance abstrait et spécialisé, sacrifiaient trop dans leur existence personnelle ce désir de 'vraie vie', de 'liberté libre' que rien, selon eux, ne doit contraindre'.[3] Bonnefoy, qui a fréquenté les cours de Gaston Bachelard et de Jean Wahl à la Sorbonne, d'André Chastel à l'Ecole pratique des Hautes Etudes, ou encore d'Henri-Charles Puech au Collège de France, a la nostalgie d'un Age d'or des poètes-étudiants — Hölderlin à Tübingen, Shelley à Oxford, Coleridge et Wordsworth à Cambridge. Peut-être Bonnefoy n'est-il pas non plus indifférent au rôle majeur donné au poète dans de prestigieuses chaires, comme celle de 'Professor of Poetry' à l'Université d'Oxford, dont il a lui-même reçu le doctorat *honoris causa* en 2008.

La 'communauté des critiques'

L'œuvre poétique, depuis *Du Mouvement et de l'immobilité de Douve* en 1953, s'est construite dans un dialogue étroit avec les critiques Jean Starobinski, Georges Poulet, Jean-Pierre Richard, Paul de Man, et bien d'autres à travers le monde, qui ont souvent été ses collègues à l'université. Depuis les années cinquante, Bonnefoy a ainsi scellé un pacte de confiance et d'amitié avec ce qu'il appelle la 'communauté des critiques'. La poésie 'se doit d'éprouver pour le travail universitaire un *a priori* de confiance, et lui porter grande attention, si elle veut être digne du plus sérieux de sa propre vocation, qui n'est pas de dire ce que le poète éprouve, mais d'instituer, un lieu sur terre qui aurait sens'.[4] 'L'acte et le lieu de la poésie'[5] apparaissent donc comme inséparables du geste critique, qui revêt également une signification éthique, puisqu'il engage la relation au monde et le dialogue avec les autres.

'Poète professeur', selon la formule de son maître Jean Wahl, Bonnefoy est lui-même devenu un critique qui réfléchit aux relations entre 'l'Université et la poésie', comme à l'occasion de la réception du doctorat *honoris causa* de l'Université de Sienne, en 2004. Son abondante production critique au sujet de la littérature aussi bien que de la peinture, sous la forme d'articles ou de conférences réunis en recueils, suffirait à elle seule à valoir à Bonnefoy un rôle majeur dans l'histoire des lettres et de la 'poétique', aux côtés de Sartre, qu'il n'apprécie guère, de Jouve, Breton, Gracq ou Blanchot, avec qui il entretient des rapports complexes et ambivalents. Les textes repris dans *L'Improbable* (1959), *Le Nuage rouge* (1977), *Sous l'horizon du langage* (2002), ou plus récemment *Notre besoin de Rimbaud* (2009) et *Sous le signe de Baudelaire* (2011), qui rassemblent ses écrits sur les deux poètes, entrent ainsi en résonance avec la 'critique d'écrivain', dans le genre instable de l''essai' littéraire. Par l'érudition, Bonnefoy peut dialoguer d'égal à égal avec les spécialistes de littérature ou d'histoire de l'art. Il a d'ailleurs entrepris à la fin de ses études une carrière universitaire, avec un projet de thèse dirigé par Jean Wahl sur la philosophie du langage: 'Le signe et la signification', dans la critique anglaise et la critique française, dont est issu un article intitulé 'La critique anglo-saxonne et la critique française', en 1959.[6] Il a ensuite déposé un projet de thèse complémentaire, sur la peinture cette fois: 'La signification des formes chez Piero della Francesca', sous la direction conjointe de Jean Wahl et d'André Chastel. De ces projets universitaires inaboutis témoignent articles et essais qui supposent des recherches érudites, comme *Rome 1630, l'horizon du premier baroque*, en 1970, ou encore l'impressionnante 'autobiographie d'une œuvre' consacrée à Alberto Giacometti, en 1991.

En 1981, l'élection au Collège de France à une chaire intitulée 'Etudes comparées de la fonction poétique',[7] à l'initiative de Georges Blin, dont les travaux sur Baudelaire et sur Stendhal font alors autorité, et avec le soutien d'André Chastel et de Michel Foucault, est venue couronner tardivement le parcours de l'essayiste. Depuis les tout premiers articles parus dans les *Lettres nouvelles*, Bonnefoy compte parmi les meilleurs spécialistes de Baudelaire, de Rimbaud, de Mallarmé, aussi bien que de Shakespeare. Il s'inscrit à son tour dans une lignée qui l'unit, bon gré mal gré, à Barthes et à Valéry, sous le signe de la 'poétique', dont le mot figure d'emblée dans le programme de ses cours: 'La poétique de Giacometti' (1981–83), 'La poétique de Shakespeare' (1983–84), 'La poétique de Mallarmé' (1991–93).[8] En 1982, ce n'est pas seulement un poète qui entre au Collège de France, comme Valéry en 1937, mais également un universitaire, comme Barthes en 1977.

De Barthes à Bonnefoy

Au Collège de France, Bonnefoy a en quelque sorte 'succédé' à Roland Barthes, disparu prématurément en 1980. Certes, une telle 'succession' — à la lettre impossible puisque chaque chaire est définie par et pour le candidat — tient au 'hasard'. *La Présence et l'Image*, la leçon inaugurale de 1981, ne manque pas de rappeler cette succession imprévue, un an après la mort de Barthes. Car l'étude comparée de la fonction poétique' à laquelle Bonnefoy entend se consacrer n'a guère de rapports avec la 'sémiologie littéraire', dont le projet avait été défendu par Michel Foucault. Barthes, dès 1975, place son projet sous le signe d'une nouvelle 'science des signes', d'une 'seconde sémiologie' consacrée au 'texte littéraire', dont il faut 'décrire dans toute son ampleur l'éventail des formes discursives', et analyser les 'effets de sens'. Le postulat théorique explicitement assumé est de ne prendre en considération que le sujet de l'énonciation, 'par la contrainte structurale qui oblige le sujet à n'exister point en dehors de sa parole et à se constituer ou se défaire au fur et à mesure qu'il parle'.[9] Parmi les objets d'étude figurent 'les rapports du signe avec le pouvoir et la jouissance', déjà abordés, notamment, dans *Le Plaisir du texte*, en 1973, et placés au centre de la *Leçon* inaugurale, en 1977.

De la langue 'fasciste' au 'Texte' comme 'dépouvoir',[10] le parcours de 'sémiologie littéraire' esquissé par la leçon inaugurale ne laisse aucune place à la poésie. Barthes cite Valéry, mais pour l'enseignement de la Poétique, justement, et Mallarmé pour l'expression 'changer la langue'[11] et, *in fine*, par allusion, Dante, pour l'idée d'une *vita nuova*, d'ailleurs appliquée à Michelet. La poésie apparaît bien comme 'l'objet manquant' du livre de Barthes qui, tout comme Sartre, réduit la littérature à la prose.[12]

Tout au contraire, la 'fonction poétique' est au centre du projet de Bonnefoy, qui consacre ses premiers enseignements à des poètes, au sens large (Shakespeare, Mallarmé, Laforgue, Baudelaire, Etienne Durand...), et à des peintres (Giacometti). Dans *La Présence et l'Image*, Rimbaud est cité pour 'Voyelles' et *Illuminations*, Mallarmé pour le 'Sonnet en yx', Baudelaire pour les 'Tableaux parisiens', Shakespeare pour *Hamlet*. Sur le conseil de Georges Blin, le mot valéryen de 'poétique' a été évité, mais l'expression 'fonction poétique' prête néanmoins aussi à confusion, alors qu'elle ne renvoie en aucune façon aux fonctions du langage de Jakobson. Il s'agit d'étudier la création artistique comme telle. L'expression 'fonction poétique' permet d'étendre l'idée de poésie aux arts, et en particulier à la peinture, pour un dialogue fécond non seulement avec Georges Blin, mais surtout avec le maître et ami André Chastel. C'est tout naturellement la tradition humaniste de la République des Lettres que Bonnefoy invoque lorsque, à son tour, il présente avec l'historien Jean Delumeau la candidature de Marc Fumaroli à la chaire 'Rhétorique et société en

Europe (XVIe-XVIIe siècles', avec qui il crée l' 'Institut littéraire' du Collège de France. Ainsi, loin de s'inscrire dans les traces de l'auteur du *Degré zéro de l'écriture*, et sans pour autant renouer avec l'histoire littéraire positiviste, Bonnefoy fait entrer l'étude la création poétique au Collège de France, comme Valéry un demi-siècle plus tôt.

'Bonnefoy contre Barthes'[13]

Paradoxalement, c'est devant Foucault, promoteur de la candidature de Barthes et soutien à la sienne propre, que Bonnefoy se livre à une critique en règle du 'structuralisme' et du 'textualisme'. Dès les années cinquante, étudiant la critique anglo-saxonne, Bonnefoy avait dénoncé le 'formalisme' de I. A. Richards et de W. Empson, qui s'arrêtent au 'comment' de la signification en poésie, sans jamais poser la question de ce que celle-ci signifie. 'Aucun formalisme ne saurait rendre compte de l'acte poétique', concluait-il.[14] Au New Criticism, il opposait la critique thématique française, représentée par Georges Poulet ou Jean-Pierre Richard, dans la filiation de Bachelard. Bonnefoy reproche donc à Barthes, soucieux de 'l'exploration formaliste de l'écriture' et des 'fonctionnements du langage', de s'être 'détourné de l'étude directe des poètes'.[15] Après l'adresse à l'Administrateur et aux Professeurs, il fait en direction du public une déclaration en faveur de la poésie, à la manière de Vigny dans 'La maison du berger', un poème qu'il admire depuis ses années de lycée. La 'défense de la poésie', toujours menacée par le monde moderne, se fait non seulement *après*, mais bien *contre* Barthes, à qui ramènent les expressions prêtées au 'poéticien' ou au 'sémiologue': 'le travail du signifiant', 'l'autonomie du signifiant', 'ces galaxies qu'on nomme le texte' ou le 'froissement léger des structures'.

Dans un article d'abord publié en Italie en 2001, puis repris dans *Le siècle où la parole a été victime* en 2010, '*Le Degré zéro de l'écriture* et la question de la poésie', Bonnefoy rassemble et affûte ses arguments contre cette 'critique structuraliste', tout en reconnaissant combien le débat entre l'ancienne et la nouvelle critique pouvait paraître biaisé par la 'tradition positiviste française'. Sans 'la moindre dépréciation de la pensée combattue'[16] (p. 169), à laquelle il s'estime plus 'étranger' qu''opposé', Bonnefoy récuse au nom des déterminations inconscientes la distinction, au fond très sartrienne, entre le 'style' et 'l'écriture', acte conscient par lequel l'écrivain 's'engage'. Le fond du problème tient à ce que '*Le Degré zéro de l'écriture* est un parti pris du langage' (p. 174), une 'allégeance au langage' (p. 174) qui exclut la 'donnée personnelle', la 'profondeur du psychisme' où se joue la création. En privilégiant l' 'écriture' sur le 'style', Barthes ne fait que 'recueillir les aspects de l'œuvre qui la rabattent sur le rapport social et le devenir de la société', au mépris de 'l'exploration du rapport à soi de l'auteur'. Barthes réduit la littérature à 'l'articulation des effets de langue' (p. 171) dans l' 'écriture', et voue donc irrémédiablement sa réflexion à la *prose*, c'est-à-dire au 'filet de la signification' (p. 179) qui, pour Bonnefoy, ne saurait être que 'conceptuelle'. Or, objecte-t-il, 'il y a des actes de parole qui ne sont pas simplement des événements de la signification, de simples emplois du langage' (p.

176). Et ces moment qualifiés d' 'épiphaniques' (p. 183) constituent la poésie, qui 'cherche à porter la phrase *au degré zéro de la signification conceptuelle*' (p. 185) pour faire advenir la 'présence', expérience de 'l'indéfait du monde' (p. 188).

Quand Barthes entreprend de décrire les effets de sens dans le langage voué à la polysémie et de dénoncer l' 'illusion référentielle', Bonnefoy tente de déjouer les pièges et les 'mensonges' du discours conceptuel, qui empêchent l'émergence d'une 'vérité de parole', expression sous le signe de laquelle il place un recueil d'essais en 1988.[17] La poésie, qui a une portée éthique, a ainsi vocation à rechercher la 'vérité de parole', opposée par le poète à 'l'ère du soupçon': 'Le temps n'est plus des paroles de vérité. Nous avons appris à tout soupçonner, nous savons percevoir, dans des livres devenus textes, le dire du mythe [...] là où l'on supposait autrefois que se manifestait la Présence.'[18]

De Valéry à Bonnefoy

L'élection au Collège de France a également fait de Bonnefoy, bien malgré lui, un lointain héritier de Valéry, par une ironie de la destinée qui établit une filiation entre Valéry, Barthes et Bonnefoy. A la fin de la guerre, Barthes et Bonnefoy avaient suivi les derniers cours de Valéry au Collège de France, sans imaginer qu'un jour ils prendraient le relais de l'enseignement de la 'poétique' dans la salle 8. Comme d'autres auditeurs, Bonnefoy conserve un souvenir mitigé du poète académicien vieillissant, couronné d'honneurs, mais déjà malade.[19] N'ayant semble-t-il présenté sa candidature que pour améliorer sa situation matérielle, pourtant confortable, Valéry ne manifestait pas un grand enthousiasme dans son enseignement, qu'il préparait de moins en moins, se contentant de faire part de son expérience personnelle à un public clairsemé de quelques fidèles, parmi lesquels Emil Cioran et le jeune Roland Barthes. Barthes, quant à lui, aurait sans doute plus volontiers assumé cet héritage, bien qu'il ait défini sa chaire par la 'sémiologie littéraire'. Dans 'Le retour du poéticien', en 1972, il reconnaît (et se reconnaît) en effet 'trois patrons': Aristote, Valéry et Jakobson.[20] Devenu à son tour, par la force des choses et à son corps défendant, un poète consacré, Bonnefoy critique Valéry, le poète mondain invité dans la haute société — par Noémie Révelin, la grand-mère de Barthes, place du Panthéon. Valéry 'aurait dû savoir que lorsque dans les cérémonies, la place du poète n'est pas vide, celui qui l'occupe ne sert pas la cause de la poésie, si du moins il semble satisfait d'être là'.[21]

La leçon inaugurale de 1981, publiée sous la titre *La Présence et l'Image* en 1983,[22] ne manque pas de rappeler cette filiation paradoxale et inattendue, pour se démarquer de son illustre prédécesseur: 'Mes chers collègues, je n'oublie pas que c'est dans cette salle que fut inaugurée, il n'y a pas cinquante ans, et avec quelle autorité, et que redoublait l'évidence d'un sacrifice, cette idée que la poésie ne porte pas en ce qu'elle a de plus spécifique la capacité de la connaissance de soi; et qu'on ne peut en traiter qu'au prix d'une mise entre parenthèses, où ce que l'auteur prend au sérieux, si ce n'est parfois au tragique, disons le sentiment, les valeurs, est rendu sous les yeux d'un témoin algébriste et presque ironiste au statut de simple variable dans l'équation de l'esprit...'[23]

En 2006, dans un entretien avec Serge Bourjea, spécialiste de Valéry, Bonnefoy est néanmoins revenu sur la relation pour le moins ambivalente qu'il entretient avec Valéry depuis son adolescence. Indifférent aux 'diamants extrêmes' de *La Jeune Parque*, mais admirateur sincère du 'Cimetière marin', d''Aurore', d''Ebauche du serpent', du 'Cantique des colonnes' et du 'Rameur', l'étudiant, à peine arrivé à Paris, s'est précipité au Collège de France pour écouter le cours de Poétique. Mais, vingt ans après les cours du Collège, le jeune poète de *Du mouvement et de l'immobilité de Douve*, paru en 1953, et de *Hier régnant désert* en 1958, a publié dans *Les Lettres nouvelles* un article polémique sur 'Valéry l'apostat', repris dans *L'Improbable* en 1959. En raison de leur portée philosophique, Maurice Saillet et les critiques de l'époque avaient rapproché les poèmes de *Du mouvement et de l'immobilité de Douve* de ceux de Valéry. Comme pour se protéger de la fascination que Valéry exerce encore sur lui, Bonnefoy prononce un jugement sans appel sur l'auteur de *La Jeune Parque*, à qui il reproche de 'ne pas savoir qu'on a inventé la mort' et d''[avoir] écrit sur Pascal, sur Baudelaire les pages les plus butées'. 'Nous avons à oublier Valéry', conclut-il.[24] L'argument éthique fait écho à la phrase de 'L'Acte et le lieu de la poésie', dans *L'Improbable:* 'Baudelaire invente la mort'.[25] Dans une conférence publiée dans *Variété* en 1929, Valéry considère que le poète des *Fleurs du mal* 'peut quelquefois faire figure d'un classique' par 'l'ordre' qu'il introduit dans la 'composition' et la 'pureté' qu'il donne à la 'forme'.[26] A 'Situation de Baudelaire', Bonnefoy oppose le *Tombeau de Baudelaire* de Jouve réédité en 1958, et placé, lui, sous le signe de Kierkegaard, de Jean Wahl et de la pensée existentielle. La dédicace manuscrite de l'exemplaire de *Douve* envoyé à Jouve — dont les noms sont phonétiquement si proches — fait du poète de *Sueur de sang* un héritier de Baudelaire: 'A Pierre Jean Jouve qui a maintenu, lui seul, la source vive de Baudelaire et des grands morts'.[27] Bonnefoy affirme que 'ce furent [s]es lectures de Kierkegaard, de Jean Wahl — de Jean Wahl lisant Kierkegaard — , puis de Bataille, de Chestov, de Dostoïevski' qui, dit-il, lui firent 'oublier Valéry'.[28]

'Bonnefoy contre Valéry'

'Il avait décidé que le contenu du poème, que l'on disait trop facilement, c'est sûr, le cri véridique de la souffrance ou le pressentiment de secrets de l'être, n'est qu'un élément en somme formel dans une combinatoire, et ne vaut qu'à s'effacer presque dans la loi des mots révélée.'[29] La poétique de Valéry pèche selon Bonnefoy par une abstraction d''algébriste' qui, recluse dans 'la maison de l'Idée', 'méconnaît le mystère de la présence' et oublie la 'finitude'.

Certes, dans le cours et la conférence d'Oxford 'Poésie et pensée abstraite', le lecteur de *La Soirée avec M.Teste* retrouve le rêve de découvrir les lois de la 'composition' artistique, par 'l'application du principe de causalité' à la 'production de la valeur'.[30] Mais, à la différence de l'histoire littéraire ou de la critique positiviste, dont Proust analyse les rouages dans des pages célèbres de *Contre Sainte-Beuve*, la poétique ne vise pas à dégager les mécanismes de la 'causalité' externe, du 'milieu', supposés présider à l'écriture de tel ou tel chef-d'œuvre. Habilement, le candidat Valéry fait l'éloge du travail accompli par les historiens au Collège de France, comme Lucien Febvre. Il doit aussi ménager les disciples de Gustave Lanson, comme Abel Lefranc: 'l'objet d'un enseignement éventuel de la Poétique au Collège de France, loin de se substituer ou de s'opposer à l'Histoire littéraire serait de donner à celle-ci à la fois une introduction, un sens et un but'.[31] Mais, une fois élu, Valéry fait de la Poétique une machine de guerre contre l'histoire et la critique littéraires positivistes. A partir de sa propre exéprience, éminemment subjective, il déclare vouloir plonger au cœur du processus créateur et 'conjecturer ce qui a pu se passer dans l'intime de ceux qui ont fait ce qu'il a fallu pour obtenir d'être inscrits dans les fastes de l'Histoire des Lettres'.[32] Selon un bergsonisme proche de celui de Proust, pour qui 'un livre est le produit d'un autre moi que celui que nous manifestons dans nos habitudes, dans la société, dans nos vies', Valéry est à la recherche des lois 'internes' de cet 'autre moi' qui donnent naissance à l'œuvre. Il s'intéresse en outre à l'effet que l'œuvre produit à son tour sur le lecteur, en qui elle doit susciter un état 'analogue' à celui éprouvé par l'auteur. Valéry, en cela, s'inspire non pas de Taine ou de Sainte-Beuve, mais de Poe, dont Baudelaire a traduit 'Genèse d'un poème', et de Mallarmé.

Pour décrire la création artistique, et singulièrement la littérature, Valéry recourt au modèle économique de la production et de la consommation et, du côté du lecteur, de la 'valeur'. Il envisage toujours l'œuvre dans le processus concret de sa réalisation et de son effet sur le lecteur, '*l'action qui fait*', bien plus que '*la chose faite*':[33] 'J'ai pris soin de spécifier qu'il ne fallait considérer les œuvres qu'en acte ou de production ou de consommation'.[34] Plutôt que les œuvres finies, Valéry entend donc analyser le processus de leur 'production', c'est-à-dire le *poïein*, la fabrication, le 'faire', dans une perspective explicitement aristotélicienne: 'L'œuvre de l'esprit n'existe qu'en acte',[35] qu'il faut entendre en relation avec la puissance, mais aussi, sur un plan éthique, avec l'action.

Valéry appelle donc à l'étude empirique du matériau concret de l'œuvre, le langage lui-même, dans ses effets sur la réalité et son action sur le 'consommateur'. Cette 'poïétique' — mot que Valéry aurait préféré à celui de 'poétique' — est donc une pragmatique avant la lettre, c'est-à-dire une rhétorique élargie qui envisage, outre les ressorts intellectuels de la persuasion, l'ensemble des effets produits sur le lecteur, y compris les émotions. L''état poétique' est ainsi 'produit' par le 'mécanisme [...] de l'acte de l'écrivain'.[36]

Aristotélicien, Valéry l'est déjà, et de manière ostensible. Nul besoin, donc, de 'se vouloir aristotélicien contre lui', ainsi que l'exige Bonnefoy dans l'essai de *L'Improbable*.[37] Lorsque, dans le projet de chaire, il affirme que 'la Littérature est, et ne peut être autre chose qu'une sorte d'extension et d'application de certaines propriétés du Langage',[38] Valéry conçoit ces 'propriétés' d'une manière qu'on pourrait qualifier de 'pragmatique'. Là encore, il emprunte au modèle rhétorique l'idée d'une efficace de la parole, ou plutôt de la 'voix', susceptible de faire naître chez le lecteur un 'état' ou une émotion qu'il qualifie de 'poétique' par la force des sons et des rythmes.

Certes, Bonnefoy ne peut accepter que la poésie réside seulement dans le langage, et non dans le rapport de la conscience à 'l'indéfait du monde', qu'il appelle la 'présence'. Pourtant, Valéry privilégie la dimension phonique du langage qui, justement, affranchit le langage du discours conceptuel. La poétique s'intéresse d'abord au poème comme 'intonation' et comme 'voix'. Par les sons, la poésie suscite l'émotion et fait naître du 'sens', et pas seulement de la 'signification', toujours suspecte au yeux de Bonnefoy de se porter vers le 'concept'. Ainsi, à ce stade, le cours de Poétique ne peut guère être présenté comme la réduction 'algébriste' de la poésie à une 'combinatoire' abstraite de mots sur laquelle le poéticien spéculerait, comme sur un 'objet'.[39] Dans l'*Introduction à la poétique*,[40] la tentation de l'abstraction dénoncée par Bonnefoy n'apparaît pas de manière aussi évidente, et encore moins l'idéalisme.

Il se peut que Bonnefoy garde en mémoire d'autres textes de *La Soirée avec M.Teste* ou de *Tel Quel*, qui inscrivent la poésie dans le cadre de spéculations plus abstraites sur les pouvoirs de l'esprit. Mais surtout, dans les années soixante, Philippe Sollers, Roland Barthes et les membres du groupe Tel Quel, se réclament de Valéry. Influencé par cette réception 'structuraliste', encore répandue au moment où il prépare sa leçon inaugurale, Bonnefoy lit Valéry au prisme d'une interprétation 'formaliste' de la Poétique, d'une 'Théorie de la littérature' inspirée des Formalistes russes, à travers les traductions de Todorov et de Kristeva.

* * * * *

L'âge d'une 'Théorie d'ensemble' est depuis longtemps révolu. En outre, depuis la publication *in extenso* des *Cahiers*[41] et le développement des études génétiques, l'image de Valéry a profondément changé. Il n'est plus possible aujourd'hui de réduire la pensée de Valéry au modèle textualiste.[42] Tout en qualifiant les idées de Valéry sur la poésie de 'condescendantes', Bonnefoy peut désormais reconnaître que la poétique enseignée au Collège de France, et développée dans les essais de *Variété*, dont il avait suivi régulièrement la publication, 'n'était que le plus sophistiqué de ces masques' derrière lesquels le poète s'avançait. Avec le recul, il interprète cette 'mainmise de l'intellect', contre laquelle il fallait assurément 'se rebeller', non pas comme un oubli de la présence, et donc de la poésie, mais au contraire comme une tentative pour la protéger.

Passé le temps des polémiques (qui sont d'abord des polémiques avec soi-même), dont l'article de *L'Improbable* porte encore la trace, Bonnefoy peut donc louer Valéry et Barthes d'avoir contribué à une réflexion approfondie sur la poésie comme telle. Autant qu'un poète, Valéry est pour lui 'un penseur, un essayiste' dans la filiation de Coleridge, de Poe, de Mallarmé, éloigné des manifestes et des proclamations, mais sincèrement attaché 'à mieux comprendre', et par là, à 'mieux se comprendre'.[43] En ce sens, c'est une lecture éthique du projet de Valéry que Bonnefoy propose. En effet, la poésie, comme la 'littérature' pour Barthes, s'accomplit comme un 'acte de parole'[44] qui suppose une responsabilité personnelle. Simplement, à la différence de Barthes, également lecteur de Valéry, Bonnefoy oppose 'l'acte et le lieu de la poésie' au texte: 'En d'autres mots, la poésie est un *acte*, alors que le texte qu'elle produit n'est précisément que cela, un *texte*, ce poème où la signification foisonne autant sinon plus encore que dans tout texte de prose. Et le texte entrave l'acte, le paralyse'.[45] Comme 'penseur', le poéticien Valéry, tout comme le sémiologue Barthes, se révèle en définitive un soutien pour la 'réflexion sur la poésie', sous le signe de laquelle Bonnefoy place sa leçon inaugurale. Valéry permet en effet de lutter contre l'oubli, voire le déni contemporain de la poésie, illustré par des 'maîtres à penser aussi butés qu'arrogants, ainsi Jean-Paul Sartre'.[46] A l'Université de Sienne, en 2004, Bonnefoy s'en est pris à ces mêmes maîtres: 'ni Auguste Comte ni Taine ni Sartre ni Merleau-Ponty, ces maîtres que notre enseignement s'est donné, ne se sont intéressés à la poésie',[47] pour les opposer aux philosophes qui, en Italie, se réfèrent à la lignée de Dante, Pétrarque ou Leopardi, dans laquelle Valéry pourrait s'inscrire.

Bonnefoy est donc en définitive plus proche de Valéry et de Barthes qu'il ne paraît. Malgré de profondes divergences, d'ordre philosophique, sur la nature de la poésie, il reconnaît d'ailleurs être 'fasciné' par un esprit pour lequel il éprouve 'autant d'admiration que de sympathie'.[48] N'ayant pu échanger avec le sémiologue comme il aurait aimé le faire, Bonnefoy imagine ce qui aurait pu les rapprocher. Outre la générosité et la présence 'chaleureuse' de Barthes au Collège, qui 'suscita, unanimement, l'affection',[49] Bonnefoy met en avant la complémentarité de la critique et de la poésie: 'entre la critique qui se propose d'être un discours scientifiquement rigoureux et les attestations dont se sent obscurément responsable le souci de la poésie, il n'y a nullement matière à conflit, mais au contraire un terrain de rencontre, d'échanges loyaux, de collaboration fructueuse'.[50] Et surtout, célébrant en Barthes un authentique 'écrivain', Bonnefoy reconnaît en lui une vocation de poète, authentique quoique tardive. *La Chambre claire*, 'un des livres de notre temps' qui selon lui 'orientent le mieux vers l'horizon de la poésie', efface les frontières entre critique et poésie par la 'fusion progressive de l'intellect et du sentiment', et même du 'cœur'.[51] Aussi rappelle-t-il fraternellement au public le souvenir de Barthes, dans sa propre leçon inaugurale: 'C'est un écrivain qui avait pris la parole devant vous en 1977, un écrivain pénétré du sentiment que la littérature est une conscience; et son dernier livre, *La Chambre claire*, montrait bientôt — et cela m'émeut, en la circonstance présente — qu'il se rapprochait de la poésie'.[52]

Et ainsi, malgré tout ce qui les sépare ou même les oppose, Bonnefoy reconnaît chez Barthes comme chez Valéry ce qui lui importe par-dessus tout — le 'souci de la poésie'. Ils tous trois ont en commun une réflexion critique sur la 'poétique' où la production littéraire et la théorie s'enrichissent mutuellement. Loin d' 'enlev[er] à la poésie, comme un romantisme, un surréalisme attardés le redouteraient peut-être encore', le Collège de France 'par[aît] un des lieux de vérité dont elle a le plus besoin'.[53]

Bonnefoy associe 'l'acte de poésie', qui doit être 'transitif', à l'échange, au dialogue du poète comme personne avec l'Autre. Malgré l'idée profondément anti-barthésienne d'une 'vérité de parole' apportée par le poète, Bonnefoy peut tout de même s'accorder avec Barthes, comme d'ailleurs avec Valéry, sur l''éthique du langage littéraire' invoquée par Barthes dans *Leçon*. Bonnefoy reconnaît que, en 1953, '*Le Degré zéro de l'écriture* engageait l'avenir des rapports humains autant que celui de la littérature et risquait donc de changer le cours de la civilisation elle-même' (p. 167).[54] En relisant *Le Degré zéro de l'écriture* à partir de *La Chambre claire*,

Bonnefoy replace Barthes dans la filiation de Valéry, avec qui il s'est lui-même largement réconcilié.

Notes

1. *Lieux et Destins de l'image: un cours de poétique au Collège de France 1981–1993* (Paris: Seuil, 1999), p. 274.
2. *La Communauté des critiques* (Strasbourg: Presses Universitaires de Strasbourg, 2010), p. 27.
3. Ibid., p. 26.
4. Ibid., p. 8.
5. Selon le titre de la conférence de 1958, reprise dans *L'Improbable* en 1959.
6. D'abord traduit en anglais, l'article 'Critics, English and French, and the Distance between Them', *Encounter*, 58 (July 1958), a paru en version originale dans la revue *Preuves*, 95 (janvier 1959) et a fait l'objet d'un texte inédit commandé par la Fondation Rockefeller. Sur cet article, voir les précieuses analyses de Daniel Lançon dans *Yves Bonnefoy, Histoire des œuvres et naissance de l'auteur* (Paris: Hermann, 2015), pp. 195–201.
7. Dont le projet et l'intitulé, comme on sait, sont définis par le candidat, et présentés par le professeur qui parraine la candidature — Georges Blin, en l'occurrence, qui craignait d'ailleurs que le mot 'poétique' ne rappelle le nom de Paul Valéry, qui n'avait pas laissé un très bon souvenir au Collège de France.
8. *Lieux et Destins de l'image.*
9. R. Barthes, 'Travaux et projets, 1975' in *Roland Barthes au Collège de France 1977–1980*, textes réunis par Nathalie Léger (Paris: IMEC, 2002), pp. 98–99.
10. R. Barthes, *Leçon* (Paris: Seuil, 1978), 'Points', pp. 14 et 34.
11. Ibid., p. 23.
12. Y. Bonnefoy, 'Le Degré zéro de l'écriture et la question de la poésie', in *Le Siècle où la parole a été victime* (Paris: Seuil, 2010), pp. 175–76. Toutes les références renvoient à cette édition.
13. *Le Nuage rouge*, en 1977, s'ouvre sur un essai magistral intitulé 'Baudelaire contre Rubens', dont une première version avait été esquissée pour la revue *L'Ephémère*, en 1970.
14. Cité par Daniel Lançon, *Yves Bonnefoy*, p. 198.
15. *La Présence et l'Image* (Paris: Mercure de France, 1983), p. 11
16. '*Le Degré zéro de l'écriture* et la question de la poésie'.
17. *La Vérité de parole* (Paris: Mercure de France, 1988), repris dans *La Vérité de parole et autres essais* (Paris: Gallimard, Folio essais, 1995).
18. Note de présentation de l'ouvrage par l'éditeur, le Mercure de France.
19. M. Jarrety, *Paul Valéry* (Paris: Fayard, 2008), p. 1008.
20. R. Barthes, *Œuvres complètes* IV (Paris: Seuil, 2002), p. 144.
21. *L'Inachevable, entretiens sur la poésie 1990–2010* (Paris: Livre de poche, 2010), p. 108.
22. *La Présence et l'Image* (Paris: Mercure de France, 1983). Toutes les citations renvoient à cette édition.
23. Ibid., pp. 9–10.
24. 'Paul Valéry', *L'Improbable* et autres essais (Paris: Gallimard, Folio essais, 1992), p. 101.
25. 'L'Acte et le lieu de la poésie', in *L'Improbable*, p. 116.
26. P. Valéry, 'Situation de Baudelaire', *Œuvres I* (Paris: Gallimard, Pléiade, 1957), p. 604.
27. *L'Inachevable*, p. 136.
28. *L'Inachevable*, p. 107.
29. *La Présence et l'Image*, p. 10.
30. Valéry, op.cit., p. 1347.
31. Ibid., p. 1443.
32. Ibid., p. 1343.
33. Ibid., p. 1343.
34. Ibid., p. 1354.
35. Ibid., p. 1349.

36. Ibid., p. 1442.
37. *L'Improbable*, p. 100.
38. Valéry, op.cit., p. 1440. Cette formule figurait déjà dans un hommage ancien à Mallarmé.
39. Ibid., p. 1349.
40. *Introduction à la poétique*, en 1938, réunit la leçon inaugurale prononcée par Valéry en 1937, et le projet de création de la chaire qui l'a précédée, 'De l'enseignement de la Poétique'.
41. Qui s'est achevée chez Gallimard en 2015 avec la parution du tome 13, qui couvre la période de mars 1914 à janvier 2015.
42. Les travaux de Michel Jarrety, fondés sur une abondante documentation et des archives inédites, montrent bien toute la richesse et la complexité de l'œuvre et de la pensée de Valéry sur la poésie et la Poétique (*Paul Valéry* (Paris: Fayard, 2008); *Valéry devant la littérature: mesure de la limite* (Paris: Hermann, 2015).
43. *L'Inachevable*, pp. 102 sq.
44. 'Le Degré zéro...', p. 176.
45. Ibid., p. 185.
46. *L'Inachevable*, p. 106.
47. *La Communauté des critiques*, p. 20.
48. *Roland Barthes au Collège de France*, p. 9.
49. Ibid.
50. Ibid., p. 10.
51. Ibid., p. 11.
52. Ibid., p. 13.
53. *Lieux et Destins de l'image*, p. 278.
54. 'Le Degré zéro...'.

— 17 —

Paul de Roux between Made and Found

Patrick McGuinness

Reading poets like Paul de Roux, Georges Perros, Jacques Réda and Gilles Ortlieb, I wondered about that ambition we have of looking at things in such a way as to capture them in their full unlooked-at-ness, and yet to do so without denaturing them. It's more than a paradox, and less than one too, because it is at once the most complex and the most basic problem. It's not a sophisticated poetic question, but it can take the poet into some pretty contorted postures. It's also a form of deliberate self-defeat, and something a certain sort of writer specializes in. Some things are meant to be seen, some things are meant to be looked at, and some things are meant to be noticed — and to *remain* noticed. To see them is to push it too far. Noticing is, in its way, much harder, requiring a certain tact in the face of the thing noticed, a respect for its modesty that can perhaps only be met with modesty of one's own — a modesty to which poetry, with its back-catalogue of visionaries, Orphists and unacknowledged legislators, is ill-suited to practising. The noticer needs to know when to stop, when to resist the temptation to see, and perhaps even to have a slight aversion to the very idea of seeing. It is in the holding back that the noticing process might catch the things that mere seeing misses.

Seeing has ambitions to definitiveness, exhaustiveness and totality, and this explains why I often have the sense, in the face of a poem I admire, of its leaving its subject emptied and bled out in its wake, a husk or shell of what it was before the poet decided to shine his torch onto it. The *Voyant* tradition in poetry deals in encompassing perspective, in piercing insight or flash revelation. This is the sort of poetry we associate with Hugo and his prodigal nephew Rimbaud, and further down the line with certain strands of surrealism. But the noticing process is different. Some of this is bound up with the 'carnet' as a form, and with the *carnet*'s paradoxical status as, at once, finished product — published and read in its own right — and resource, dry-run, laboratory or workshop for material that terminates in or as something else. The in-between-ness of the *carnet* is further complicated by its differing status across cultures, a difference that is difficult to translate: in France, or Germany or Italy, it has the prestige of being a genre; in English-speaking cultures, it's seen as more of an archival thing, or a place where raw material composts until it finds, or doesn't find, its way into the light.

I wrote 'mere' seeing, aware that in poetic terms at least *seeing* is the jackpot, the 'gros lot'. The poet sees more, sees further, sees deeper, sees for longer, and sees into more spheres, than the rest of us. But perhaps there's something vulgar and grasping and appropriative about seeing, and perhaps the poetry of vision itself suffers from a sort of overweening 'suffisance' that deserves occasionally to be taken down.

One of the great clichés of poetry marketing is that it makes the 'ordinary' 'extraordinary'. This is the inheritance of a poetic tradition that has for centuries defined itself using the language of promotion. By 'promotion' here I mean turning a base thing into a higher thing (alchemy, classically) rather than commercial promotion, though since the two met long ago on dust-jacket blurbs, in reviewing culture, and in the world of literary marketing, they have more in common than we think. But imagine a blurb that said 'This poetry takes the world and... well... to be honest... leaves it pretty much as it found it'. Speaking for myself, because I've spent so long reading and writing about the Romantics and the Symbolists, that's a book I've been waiting for. But would most of us — commercially, aesthetically or ideologically — *buy* it? Probably not, not just because we'd only be spending our money buying back what we already owned (the way we do anyway with the privatized utilities or the rail system, paid for at both ends by us: first as subsidy and second at point of sale), but because we expect poetry to be a process of transformation of the ordinary, or at the very least an addition to it; of what they call in universities today, 'value added'.

But what if the blurb went like this: 'This poetry takes the world and leaves it as it found it — *only more so*'? This is a rather different and more enticing proposition. Here I imagine a magnifying glass that for a moment hovers over the ordinary and the everyday, blows up the graininess beneath the flat surface presented to the naked eye, shows the bumps and ridges and the variations under what we thought was all smooth and even, and then goes, leaving everything — except perhaps us — exactly as it found it. Simultaneously, I imagine a different sort of movement: that of a metal detector as it swings across the sand, and whose beep sounds just as urgent regardless of whether it's found a Roman coin or a shred of tinfoil left over from a barbecue.

Something of what this 'only more so' might mean in literary practice is found in the work of a number of French poets who can be considered, for all their differences, as part of a lineage. It can be said to begin, for our purposes, with Henri Thomas, and to draw in Georges Perros, Jacques Réda, Paul de Roux and Gilles Ortlieb, all of whom work in and between the poem and the 'carnet', and whose terrain can be described loosely as the ordinary and the everyday.

As Michael Sheringham writes in *Everyday Life*, 'the everyday is all around us, yet we cannot "arise and go there", in Yeats's phrase; it is where we already are, though we do not see it.' That allusion to Yeats nicely captures the way the everyday both provokes and thwarts the lyric instinct. Poetry crashes against it. The everyday is perhaps the only area, subject, fact, state, mode of seeing and feeling, that is both oxymoron and tautology. It's an oxymoron because to see it is to take away (as Blanchot knew) its key, defining facet of unseen-ness; tautology because of the 'already-ness' Sheringham notes in that untaken journey we make into where we *already* are. Poetry may well be the worst possible means of approaching it. And for this reason poetry may be the most rewarding means.

For convenience here I'll differentiate the two words in ways that Micky Sheringham would find too simplistic, but which will help me move along with my thesis. I use the term 'everyday' here not just to designate subject matter, but something larger: a state of receptiveness that does not, as it were, over-receive. In this respect we could perhaps distinguish between the ordinary as a matter of events and things, and generally the realm of what, however faintly, 'happens'; and the 'everyday' as the state in which we, or the writer or the artist, perceive it, as well as the general temporal category in which the ordinary takes place. I know this is a version of the content versus form pseudo-opposition, and that the harder one looks at them the less one can tell them apart. But I think in this case that isn't an obstacle to my larger thesis but an endorsement of it.

To explain what I mean, here is an extract from de Roux's most recent and last book of 'carnets', *Au jour le jour 5: 2000–2005*:

> Un ciel brumeux, une douceur humide, quelques traces de pluie ici et là: une sente à la lisière invisible qui vous conduit à percevoir la délicatesse d'un gris (dans les nuées) et l'honnête sobriété de la lumière qui ne donne rien de trop: juste cela que nous n'épuiserons pas, que nous ne ferons qu'entrevoir et qui est le monde autour de la main traçant des lettres sur le papier quadrillé d'un calepin. — Rajoutons la livrée de ce pigeon qui s'est posé sur le faîte du grand mur et dont les nuances s'accordent si bien à la palette délicate du jour.

The lines, 'juste cela que nous l'épuiserons pas' and the 'lumière qui ne donne rien de trop', between them express a way of writing about the world that is calibrated around a mixture of intense observation and something slacker and more glancing in its focus — *glancing* in both senses: visual but also (and more so) in the sense of a *glancing* blow. The slackness and the intensity act as each other's correctives, as if each knew that perceptually it could bring something to the experience that the other couldn't.

The passage's interest is to do with its modesty, with its resistance to extremes of articulation, feeling, and vision; in short, its resistance to 'interest'. Importantly, the 'honest sobriety' of the light gives us just enough not to exhaust either it or what it shows us — light having a role, compositionally in painting and metaphorically in language, as both a quality in itself and a revealer of qualities in other things. It is like Falstaff, who is himself the light of Henry IV Part II, and who reminds us: 'I am not only witty in myself, but the cause that wit is in other men'. In de Roux's *carnet* entry, and by a sort of disabused repurposing of the pathetic fallacy, the surrounding meteorological conditions conspire to mute both the scene and the poet's response to it, rather than to intensify them.

It is nondescript but not undescribed. It then begs the question: can something remain nondescript if it has been described? Can something be seen, and then restored to unseen-ness?

Besides, this is hardly an innocent *carnet* entry, since it refers quite explicitly to the passage from looking and noticing to writing. There's no pretence, either, that the scene hasn't been — *isn't being* — attended to. If this were a painting, the painter would be in the frame; but as it's writing, the hand with the pen is on the notebook's page. It is not quite self-referential, like the famous Escher drawing of the hand drawing a hand drawing a hand — a circle of making that is giddying in its infinity and stifling its closedness, and which speaks of eternity as constraint and repetition rather than spaciousness and elevation — but there is a hand on the page writing, which shadows our hand on the page reading. The seeming afterthought about the pigeon's livery matching this variegation of delicate greys and unemphatic light — all of it unemphatically seen — draws on the language of painting as well as writing. By invoking a 'palette', quietly underlining how this banal scene has somehow 'been through' a process of attention that is far more sophisticated than it lets on, de Roux also suggests something of the method of a Dutch interior, that artistic shorthand for the everyday surprised in its natural and most intimate habitat: the scullery, the courtyard, the kitchen.

But isn't this is part of the problem? We're back to seeing rather than noticing, back to promoting the everyday and the ordinary by prising it out and putting it, conceptually, into italics or inverted commas. The Dutch interior takes the ordinary out of its flow, fishes the moment from its river of time, and makes a public frame around a private instant. It is a form of interference all the more effective for pretending it doesn't exist — hence that feeling of discomfort, even prurience, that we have before the paintings. These paintings ask what for me is the big question of art: what would things look like if we weren't looking at them? I am not sure the question gets an answer, but I think de Roux's poems and *carnets* show us what it is like to ask that question in literary (rather than, say, philosophical) practice (there's no Schrödinger's cat here). De Roux's writing takes the world and leaves it as it is — only more so. In which case, where, exactly, does the *only more so* come in?

There is nothing faux-naïf about de Roux, though many of his poems and notes are about people and things seen in courtyards or in flats, seen through office windows or train carriages. 'Chronique de la petite cour' is what he calls one of his last *carnet* entries, and that word 'chronique' is all the more playful as there's nothing to note. But because, from the moment one is paying attention, there's no such thing as nothing, the entry is rather a long one. His bird life is pigeons and sparrows, his plant life is the curtailed range of weeds and climbers that prosper in neglect, and the droopy pot plants of the big city balcony with their dusty leaves. No strutting peacocks, exotic fruit and hanging gardens here, but nor is there the exemplary parchedness and inscrutability we find in Guillevic, or the vacancy/plenitude counterpoint we find in Bonnefoy. This is a resolutely unextreme world, that no more lends itself to meaning than it retreats from it.

What strikes me in de Roux is this notion of 'épuisement'. If Perec shows that the only things to be *épuisé(e)s* in our quest to exhaust an ordinary place are ourselves, de Roux suggests something rather different: that writing *can* exhaust the world and has a duty not to. Look just long and hard enough not to exhaust what you're looking at, he seems to say. And he implies something else that is very attractive in its modesty and its tact: leave some behind for others, or for yourself to come back to. He comes back to his courtyard, his pigeon, his never-quite-empty grey sky, each time the same and each time different, and makes a large and deceptively varied *oeuvre* out of it.

Towards the end of his *carnet* for 2005, a familiar scene returns:

> Au lever, la pluie, petite pluie fine sous un ciel qui reste ensuite nébuleux. Il est neuf heures et la lumière est réduite à l'essentiel: la clarté qui me permet de voir les mots que je trace sur ce carnet. Un pigeon.

Here, de Roux registers even what gives him very little. In this case, just enough light to write by (the *carnet* again, its materiality, the hand, the words), and a pigeon. There is an aesthetic here of the 'juste assez' — the 'just enough-ness' of things — that is at least as interesting as lyric poetry's more traditional attachment to extremes of excess and lack.

At other times, the same scene, the same view, give de Roux a larger and lusher sense of themselves, and by extension of his own response to them. The entry for 14 July 2002 is comparatively long, in that it is made up of a number of separate paragraphs, through which we can trace a series of thoughts modulating, shifting, changing subject, wide-angling out, zooming back in, to the extent where — in Bergsonian terms — they aren't separate thoughts at all, but a sequence of mutually-infusing, backward-forward-moving intellectual-affective rovings. It's a fascinating set of shifts, and at the same time totally ordinary and 'everyday'. It's what happens inside all of us all the time. The day's 'cahier' starts with a contemplation of the timbre of the sky which we realize a sentence later is not that of his Parisian courtyard but of a painting of the port of Genoa 'vers 1627–1629'. It then segues (a new sub-entry) into a fascinating disquisition on the dynamic, organic, forms of fauvism being replaced by the squares and cubes of the architect ('Le monde semblait fait de cubes. La fête était finie.'), and followed, again after a break, by this lapidary and thought-provoking paragraph:

> Est-ce un paradoxe que l'époque du plus grand matérialisme soit celle du plus grand détachement quant à la terre, au monde physique, à tous les travaux manuels? Que le matérialisme conduise à la dématérialisation?

All of these ratiocinations are connected but also free-standing, and constitute a compelling insight into the mind's movements — all of which are quite ordinary in their shifts (rather necessarily than their content): something seen and noted, triggering something more abstractly thought, then a grand statement (persuasive as it happens, though even if it weren't it wouldn't matter to the shape of the movement, the intellectual-affective gesture of the day's internal events), and then finally this:

> Un ciel du plus beau gris. Car le gris peut être beau, superbe, énigmatique — éclatant. A sept heures du matin, il brille de toute sa matité, si je puis risquer le paradoxe. Plus je regarde, plus je le trouve exaltant.

To shine with mattness is a beautiful line, and it is what de Roux's writing does. That spectrum of greys is as deep and varied as any rainbow. And as for the paradox he 'risks', it may even be an oxymoron — when I reviewed de Roux for the *Times Literary Supplement* the poetry editor took the line 'shines with mattness' out of my article on the grounds that it was 'impossible'. It isn't, and it expresses something which may well be the elusive *only more so* that we're after.

But let's look again at the order of the notes, because this rich, prism-of-greys vision of the early morning sky is in fact retrospective. Part of what has happened (I imagine) is that the day's meditations on art, either in a book or an art gallery visit (it can't be at work, because 14 July 2002 was a Sunday, and Sundays are when our hours hang most loosely on their day, which in de Roux makes us all the more receptive), have in some way 'primed' the consciousness to revisit one or more 'sept heures du matin(s)' and lay them one on top of the other; or even — and this idea is attractive too — to refine and reduce them all, in the manner of a stock or a *bouillon*, down to the essential or exemplary one. To the ultimate grey, the ultimate in-between-ness of grey.

Either way, de Roux is not pretending to any sort of naïve vision here: observation is a muscle, and it needs exercise. In the course of the day it limbers up and stretches, primes itself, becomes more attentive, but also more retentive, sharper and more copious. It does so by looking at paintings, reading books, thinking about globalization, mulling over the relationship between organic and abstract forms, and generally using what there is to extend itself. These thoughts separate out from each then rejoin each other, like all thoughts, having their own porosities, their own arcs, their own shifts and modulations. They trigger each other, melt into each other, emerge from each other; they rise up and fall away. From the Genoese port sky of the seventeenth-century painting to the courtyard sky of the Parisian apartment, the *carnet* has tracked a mind going out and returning home, and though we are back where we started, we are not there in the same way as we started. As William Empson wrote: 'The wheel has come full circle, but in the meantime it has travelled along the ground'.

I want the image of poetry exhausting its subject, strip-mining it, draining its well — *é-puising* it —, to stay in our minds here. I referred rather vaguely earlier to an ecology of noticing, of looking and of seeing. Of course that's a metaphor, but there's a principle at work here — in de Roux's poetry and in that of others who approach the world as he does — which can be likened to ecology. This is very precisely in the sense that de Roux looks and writes and perceives in a way we might call 'sustainable' (another metaphor): that he does not want to exhaust, strip bare, parcel up and generally mine, experience, but wants just enough for there to be something to return to. Those unpromising scenes of courtyards and pigeons, rain-lacquered streets and grey apartment blocks, are treated as sustainable resources for writing, looked at for long enough to draw on but not so long and as to drain them of interest. He does not overfish the seas of the everyday, we might say, he does not over-log its rainforest... These scenes are returned to over and over, with often minute changes of weather and mood, as well as changes of pigeon. Perception is the spirit-level that registers the counterpoint between the still, centred bubble and the trembling, skittering, crossings of the line.

One of the most remarkable statements de Roux makes comes in the second volume of his *Carnets, Les Intermittences du jour*, covering the years 1984 to 1985: 'En fait, à chaque instant, la vie nous pétrit. Il faudrait percevoir ce travail dans l'instant le moins dramatique'. The verb 'pétrir' here is powerfully expressive: life, he says, 'kneads' us, moulds us, like clay or dough — the key is to perceive this process at its truest, most level and least 'dramatic' moment. If we recall that de Roux has been observing this 'pétrissement' for decades, then we begin to see his work not just as a matter of perception but of tenacity, and as a kind of restless 'pétrissement', or counter-*pétrissement*, in language, of life's malaxations.

Those words I used earlier — tact, delicacy, modesty — explain, more personally speaking, why I find his poetry so rewarding and so profound. In using those words I was responding to something in him that I found humane and likeable. But to balance that out, and in the light of his total and unrelenting attention to life's barely perceptible work of 'pétrissement', I'd also want to focus on his rigour and endurance. De Roux shows us what happens when, instead of promoting and transforming the ordinary, poetry curated the ordinary — became, in a way, its custodian in language.

In his 2000 volume, his slimmest book, *Paysages en cours*, De Roux writes of the 'sentiment de ne pas être plus que ce que je peux entrevoir'. To identify oneself not just with what one sees but with the amount that one sees and the obliqueness of the angle at which one sees it, is de Roux's great gift to that tired and overpoeticized relationship between seeing and writing. So many of his titles evoke the provisionality and partiality of vision. *Entrevoir* is the title of his first book of poems, published by Gallimard in 1980, and the verb suggests something not just partly-seen, but something seen among or in between other things — working, eating, sleeping, travelling, meeting friends, meeting nobody. These are the 'intermittences' of the day. This is not the Symbolist 'entrevoir' of great secrets and big revelations, rich words with capital letters, but something more modest, a more 'honnête lumière'. There is also the sense of its being the visual equivalent of overhearing: something caught through a mix of ocular eavesdropping and partial vision. 'Intervision' would be the word in English, if it existed: as if the experience were not addressed to us, yet was somehow ours by detour. This is also the everyday, the *quotidien* itself: a partially-inhabited commonality, ours yet not ours because it is also everyone else's. There is a sense in de Roux there that to understand the everyday, you also have to let go of the concept of ownership, even as you treasure the privacy and the intimacy of it. It's yours and not yours.

His 1987 book, *Le Front contre la vitre*, forehead pressed against the glass, gives a different timbre to the act of seeing: from an office, from a train, from the window of one's own boundedness, the *vitre* that is oneself. Another, *Le Soleil dans l'œil* (1998) suggests a different sort of vision, a vision holed by too much light, and makes us think of those motes of shadow that look like melting filmreel that float across our field of vision after catching an eyeful of bright sun. There's a curious paradox about de Roux: on the one hand he approaches the world sidelong, with a sort of dilated, dissipated attentiveness, and on the other he sees it with utter focus and concentration. On the one hand he is open to the unusual, on the other he always calculating the 'undramatic' average of the days.

De Roux is interested in the everyday not for its capacity to soar off into epiphanic moments but for its heft, its drag. We see this in a poem called 'Poids':

> Parfois peu de chose, moins de chose
> que d'infimes déplacements d'air: juste ce qu'il faut
> à une onde sonore pour traverser un champ
> et c'est comme un déplacement de fléau sur l'épaule:
> les poids ne sont pas moins lourds, certes
> mais disposés ainsi, la chair les accepte
> — balbutiant peut-être, celui qui déplace les poids
> et qui n'en sait rien, oiseau
> qu'une seule note pose dans la chambre.

Those carefully-disposed 'poids', unexcessive weights that build up on the scales, are a good image of routine, whether of body or mind, with its incremental dulling of our responsiveness. But for de Roux this is part of the richness too: his poems and *carnets* are about both the 'poids' and 'ce qui déplace les poids'. Here too we find that sense of economy in the 'juste ce qu'il faut': this is a delicate, even-tenored, proportionate world, which is precisely why it registers change, displacement, alteration.

The days — *au jour le jour* — are part of the weight; they *are* the weights and they are also what displace the weights. De Roux's *carnets* often read like as-yet-unwritten poems, but also often contain more-or-less finished ones. He disturbs our sense of the raw and the cooked — the note and the poem — by interjecting finished poems into the *carnets* and even, in 2004, keeping the whole year's *carnet* in poems. Meanwhile, many poems have titles that sound like diary entries: like 'Le 26 janvier' or 'Le 15 septembre', 'Le 15 octobre'. His editor and friend Gilles Ortlieb, himself a prodigious *carnet*-writer (his revealingly-titled *Sous le crible* announces his commitment to the everyday as what passes 'through' the colander or the sieve) writes: 'La frontière qu'on savait poreuse peut se trouver abolie pendant de longues périodes'.

This 'porosité' is a two-way process that insists on the shared means and the shared subject matter of the two modes. But it also challenges our sense of what is finished, or complete, and what is in process. It even challenges our sense of what *process* itself is or might be, because de Roux's notebooks are so closely imbricated in the poetry that he writes that it is hard to tell, sometimes, where the one ends and the other begins. It is like the weights that constitute one weight, the thoughts that constitute one thought; the greys that make one grey and the pigeons that make one pigeon. The process of seeing and writing, as he practises it, is individuating and full of minute discriminations, but also cumulative and layering, a 'calquage'.

We are used to thinking of a poet's notes and notebooks as the source material, and the poems that emerge from them as the refined, edited, publishable product. In painting we might find the analogy of the studio — with its quotidian mess of sketches, splattered paint and coffee-cups, full ashtrays and crumpled paper — as the notebook, and the poem as the canvas that sets out to be shown in the art gallery that is the volume. The studio is not such a fanciful metaphor, since de Roux himself, a considerable art critic, in his penultimate collection (evocatively titled *Allers et Retours*) has a poem called 'L'Atelier':

J'ai rouvert mon petit atelier
je n'y fais pas grand-chose
je regarde la pluie tomber ou le soleil
et le pigeons et les moineaux et les ombres
si belles des hautes cheminées —
passent les saisons, se polissent les outils
entre les doigts au fil des jours,
s'y brisent enfins, épaves des années,
des gestes révolus, recommencés.

The studio or workshop may or may not be metaphorical, but what is interesting about it is the way it has become a theatre for a certain kind of not-quite-nothing to happen. A side-art, a sidelong art of looking and noticing. That slackness, that bagginess of perception I referred to earlier has something more overtly sad to it than we find in de Roux's earlier books. Here we have the burdensome, enchained continuities of time and of time running out, of the 'fil des jours', the 'poids' of the hours, the rolling stock of days that chunters by emptily as the hand polishes the tools, its work constantly ended and constantly rebegun.

Our sense of the primacy of the poem over the note comes from our sense — inculcated over centuries of artistic taste — that the sole ambition and the proper duty of the formless is to become form. This is how we see things, and of course we're not wrong to do so: all narratives of making are chronological as well as structural — the move from raw material to finished product is a story of time as well as form. And like all stories, the beginning and the ends are much easier to see and locate than the middle. But de Roux's territory is the middle, and his work disrupts the hierarchy between form and formlessness as well as that sense of a fixed chronological order between the note and the poem. Each contains the other, and is made up of it. With him, the porousness is not just between the raw and cooked (poetic sushi might be the culinary version) as material, but between the raw and the cooked as states. Form can be nostalgic for the formless, just as the formless can aspire (we assume) to form. The relationship, as de Roux exemplifies it, between poem and note, is unusual in the way it respects both the note's ambition to be a poem, and the poem's nostalgia for its notehood — and for the quiet anonymity that things enjoyed before poet arrived; for the mattness of things before poetry came along with its pot of varnish.

I have, in this essay, described the modesty and the tact of de Roux's writing, and for that reason have placed looking and noticing higher on my ladder of perception that 'seeing'. I don't, however, want to leave the reader with a sense that these categories — which are mine, and which are critical categories, and heuristic too — would mean very much to de Roux. 'Regarde et ne te lasse pas', he writes, and in one of his *carnet* entries we find this: 'Faute d'inspiration, soyez attentifs, voire minutieux. [...] L'inspiration est peut-être une forme supérieure de l'attention.' De Roux is the poet of attentiveness, of minuteness, rather than of that romantic category we call inspiration. And when he does decide to propose a definition of 'inspiration' he does not look to the 'voyant' tradition or the great romantic-symbolist-surrealist inheritance, but rather defines it as a heightened form of attention. The difference is not one of substance but of degree; it is not a matter of absolutes, but of dosage, we might say.

More generally, the everyday is indeed a question of dosage, and perhaps that is the way to think about it: a sort of 'posologie' which is almost — perhaps completely — distinct from what exactly the dosage is *of*. What makes de Roux such a rewarding and humane writer is that he expertly handles both the question of dosage and the over- or under-dosage that gives life its moments of surfeit or of loss.

The poem that for me captures what poetry should do — and which does it with so comparatively little that it seems all the more powerful and spacious in its vision — is 'Copie':

> Parfois le jour comme une copie du jour
> et nos vies comme des copies de la vie.
> Quand il ne reste que très peu de choses à faire
> apparemment très peu: regarder une fenêtre
> dans les vitres d'une autre fenêtre, et le ciel
> si gris et si terne sur les toits — et regarder encore
> comme si tu allais découvrir le tout petit détail
> qui montrerait que la feuille a glissé, que c'est l'original
> qui se trouve maintenant devant toi.

— 18 —

Traversée de *La Nuit de Londres*

Dominique Rabaté

La Nuit de Londres[1] est peut-être des livres écrits par Henri Thomas le plus énigmatique, l'un des plus résistants dans une œuvre qui n'est pourtant pas avare en énigmes ou en secrets. Je voudrais commencer en citant un passage qui traduit bien, je crois, l'étrangeté du propos de ce récit. Il se situe au début du récit, dans le chapitre 3, lorsque le narrateur encore anonyme se promène dans les rues de Londres, en rêvant à la vie de Mr Smith, dont il fait le représentant parfait de l'homme des foules. Voilà ce qu'il note:

> Exclu, rejeté, mais comme celui qui rêve est exclu du sommeil, — et bien mieux que cela car ce n'est pas un rêve, — je veux dire que pour celui qui est perdu dans la foule, il n'existe pas deux mondes, — celui dont il serait chassé, et l'autre. Rien ne manque. Tout ce qu'un pauvre, élevé dans notre civilisation, désire voir, peut surgir à ses yeux, amené du fond de la nuit par le mouvement continuel qui fait qu'un visage est presque aussitôt remplacé par un autre, alors que dans la vie quotidienne, les mêmes visages vous entourent, et que leur disparition s'appelle la mort. Le dernier des hommes, plongeant dans la foule, entre dans un monde où la disparition n'est pas une cause d'inquiétude, où elle n'est plus la mort, ni même l'absence; elle est ressentie comme un battement de cil dans la vision; elle est chaque fois comme l'enlèvement d'un obstacle, à peine aurait-il surgi: ce visage, ce regard une seconde rencontré, ces façades où toutes les ombres basculent au passage... (pp. 41–42).

Étrange passage à la syntaxe hésitante, entre tirets et virgules qui relancent une phrase à la recherche d'une affirmation paradoxale et peut-être choquante. Le cœur de la révélation que tente de cerner le narrateur réside bien dans cet évanouissement heureux de la mort: ce moment où 'le dernier des hommes, plongeant dans la foule, entre dans un monde où la disparition n'est pas une cause d'inquiétude, où elle n'est plus la mort, ni même l'absence'. Et cette trace fugace de disparition est 'comme un battement de cil dans la vision'. L'anonymat indifférencié de la nuit urbaine égalise les apparitions, substitue à chaque visage un autre, à peine visage sans doute, présence fantomatique qui semble congédier le pathétique de la mort. Cette curieuse méditation sur 'l'homme qui marche à travers la foule' se poursuit par l'idée qu'il doit errer en but, aller 'à la dérive' (p. 42).

C'est cette errance, cette dérive que je souhaite accompagner et éclairer, en revenant sur ce livre fascinant, qui me semble moins un 'roman' qu'un *récit*, tant il rompt avec les usages romanesques. L'analyse de *La Nuit de Londres* me donnera ainsi l'occasion de prolonger les remarques que j'avais faites sur les différences entre *roman* et *récit* chez Thomas, du *Précepteur* aux textes des années 60.[2] Ma lecture cherchera à saisir, sinon à circonscrire, ce qui fait l'étrangeté profonde de ce texte, qui m'apparaît comme une tentative limite dans l'œuvre de Thomas. Et je remarque d'emblée que la publication de ce livre en 1956 est suivie d'un assez long moment de silence éditorial, peut-être avant que l'écrivain ne retrouve une veine précisément plus romanesque dans ce que l'on peut appeler son cycle américain.[3] Il me semble possible d'imaginer que Thomas a dû laisser passer un peu de temps pour que la puissance d'envoûtement de cette Nuit de Londres s'estompe et que s'amortisse l'extraordinaire résonance de son récit anglais.

(1) Du Il au Je — au Il

Qu'on me pardonne l'étrange titre que je viens d'écrire, et qui voudrait synthétiser la formule, non moins étrange, de la narration de *La Nuit de Londres.* Ce qui en fait le trajet singulier. Avant d'en expliciter les modes de passage, je dois dire que cette équation est à entendre dans la recherche plus globale qu'Henri Thomas mène depuis le début de son parcours d'écrivain, parcours que Pierre Lecœur a bien décrit dans son article: 'Un petit bruit de sable gratté'.[4] Car les premières fictions de Thomas sont des récits à la première personne, comme on le voit exemplairement avec *Le Précepteur,* mais c'est un Je qui se fuit, qui voudrait se métamorphoser en puissance d'affirmation moins solipsiste ou subjective. Pour Lecœur, *La Nuit de Londres* et *John Perkins* sont deux tentatives pour capter un vertige du sujet, quand les livres suivants (*Le Parjure*, *La Relique*, *Le Poison des images*) déploient une 'voix qui se cherche' dans le déplacement nécessaire d'une troisième personne vers une narration assumée en première personne par un narrateur témoin plus ou moins incertain de ce qu'il raconte. Dans ce trajet d'ensemble que l'on peut penser comme la logique de l'œuvre toute entière, il me semble donc que *La Nuit de Londres* occupe une place stratégique et cruciale, peut-être même de pivot. J'aurais envie de dire que Thomas y a poussé au plus loin l'une de ses tentations, comme pour l'exorciser. Mais ce texte témoigne peut-être aussi d'un moment de crise dans la vie de l'écrivain, annonçant la fin de son long séjour londonien.

Résumer *La Nuit de Londres* comme le passage d'un Il à Je, relayé à son tour par l'apparition d'un autre Il, c'est bien sûr aussi faire écho aux thèses — si je risque le mot — de Maurice Blanchot sur la nature même de l'écriture. On sait que pour Blanchot, écrire, c'est précisément passer du Je au Il, comme semble le montrer l'exemple paradigmatique de Kafka. Et c'est bien dans les mêmes années, au tournant des années 40 et 50 que Blanchot publie ses chroniques dans la *NRF*, et les livres où il ne cesse d'affirmer cet étrange pouvoir de métamorphose du récit. L'originalité du livre de Thomas, qui ne pouvait que retenir le critique,[5] est peut-être dans l'hésitation maintenue entre les instances subjectives et impersonnelles. Là où Blanchot semble édicter une loi d'impersonnalisation, Henri Thomas laisse place à un aller-retour qui déroute, selon une façon de vertige irrésolu qui est à la fois la réussite et l'échec de ce récit.

Présentons donc le récit selon ce jeu de passages. L'ouverture du livre se fait sur le 'personnage', si un tel mot peut convenir, de Mr. Smith, homme ordinaire des foules, nom donné à l'anonyme même, sorte de M. Dupont en version anglaise. Le narrateur nous le présente saisi par les provocations (même érotiques) des publicités urbaines, dans la démultiplication immédiate de ses figures. Il faut une bonne dizaine de pages avant que ne surgisse un 'Je', à la page 18. Et cette première mention n'intervient que parce que le narrateur, jusqu'alors impersonnel plutôt qu'omniscient, se sent tenu d'effectuer une correction par rapport à ce qu'il a dit précédemment. Cette correction fait apparaître une première occurrence subjective des plus discrètes puisqu'il écrit sur le mode quasi ironique d'un 'si j'étais Mr. Smith ou Mr. Gordon'. On lit en effet page 18: 'En disant qu'ils sont l'objet d'une provocation que personne ne mène, je suis tombé dans un piège dont je ne pourrais sortir qu'en devenant semblable à Mr. Smith'. Mr. Smith est ainsi l'impossible incarnation de ce qui ne peut avoir de visage, ni de nom, dans un monde déserté par Dieu, et voué aux fausses images. Selon le tour curieusement religieux que prend sa méditation, le narrateur note en effet:

> si Mr. Smith ne lit plus la Bible, il n'est pas indifférent que ses père et grand-père n'aient lu que la Bible, quand les rues étaient sans images. L'Éternel s'est retiré, la mécanique des images avec leurs légendes s'est mise en mouvement, mais il n'y a pas eu de rupture: Mr. Smith n'est en révolte ni contre ses pères, ni contre l'Éternel, ni contre les images. Il est celui qui est, et qui ne dit pas Je suis. Il est, il est, il est — plusieurs millions dans cette ville (p. 19).

Parodiant la formule biblique qu'il inverse, le narrateur fait de l'homme de la foule une sorte de messager athée qui est sans avoir besoin d'affirmer son être. 'Il est' — de façon neutre et trois fois répétée — ce qui apparaît sans véritablement accéder au statut plénier de l'être. Sans besoin de révolte ou d'opposition, sans donc sentir le besoin de se poser contre, l'homme de la foule existe sur un mode amoindri ou mineur, qui rend son statut d'actant ou de personnage très problématique. C'est la raison pour laquelle le premier chapitre se conclut sur un échec ou une aporie indépassable, puisque Mr. Smith est devenu plus radicalement Mr. X, 'l'inconnu d'une équation qui est la foule' (p. 20).

L'échec de la narration impersonnelle, à la troisième personne, s'explique par cette impossibilité de maintenir une relation entre un personnage et quelqu'un qui le raconterait. Mr. Smith contamine, pour ainsi dire, celui qui voudrait le décrire de l'extérieur. Le narrateur devient à son tour celui qu'il voulait caractériser et qui ne peut que lui échapper. C'est pourquoi ce même narrateur est comme forcé de sortir du bois, de parler en son nom, mais dans un 'Je' qui ne s'assure d'aucune identité stable. L'écrivain qui a tenté d'inventer une figure à l'anonyme surgit donc par nécessité, mais emporté lui aussi par l'anonymat puisqu'il n'a aucun nom, puisqu'il ne peut se nommer dès lors que c'est l'homme des foules qu'il cherche à dire. Revenant sur l'inadéquation des formules qu'il a employées, le narrateur apparaît incertain, écrivain sans domination sur un langage inadéquat, personnage à son tour radicalement solitaire.

Le personnage que *La Nuit de Londres* construit progressivement (mais en première personne), personnage que nous apprendrons à nommer tardivement Paul

Souvrault, est la figure à la fois modeste et hyperbolique de l'étranger. Français vivant à Londres, solitaire comme tout un chacun dans la multitude de la foule, 'il est', mais sans détermination. Sans doute Thomas a-t-il réussi à communiquer quelque chose du sentiment d'étrangeté que l'on peut éprouver quand on vit précisément *à l'étranger*, du sentiment qu'il a dû éprouver dans ses années londoniennes. Relisant le livre, je pensais aux quelques moments de déréalisation que j'avais pu connaître aussi quand je vivais aux Etats-Unis, et que je sortais, après des heures solitaires chez moi, avec l'impression que tout langage était devenu impossible à parler ou à comprendre.

Sorte de penseur cartésien parodique, le héros de *La Nuit de Londres* n'a plus aucun Cogito pour le rassurer. Il erre dans la nuit de la ville, dans le sentiment paradoxal d'une solitude qui n'est pas la sienne, qui ne peut pas être pleinement la sienne. C'est bien ce qu'il affirme dans cette phrase qui sonne comme un aveu: 'J'étais la foule à moi seul' (p. 27). Ne pouvant s'assurer d'une pure réflexion, le narrateur ne peut pas plus se construire dans une durée, puisque toute son errance nocturne est vouée à la répétition du même, mais d'un même sans cesse altéré et dérangé de soi. Cette double aporie explique le ton très singulier du début du livre, qui oscille entre un style très abstrait, quasi philosophique et un récit qui maintient la tension dramatique d'une errance pourtant sans but. Le texte est donc tout à la fois narratif (nommant les lieux, disant les visages rencontrés) et conceptuel (tentant de dire l'essence de la foule, le secret impossible à dire d'un singulier qui n'a plus rien d'unique).

Le paradoxe (ou l'impossibilité) culmine avec cette nouvelle contradiction: pour Souvrault, il s'agit bien de dire, de raconter et même d'élucider les 'circonstances d'un changement personnel' (p. 28), quelque chose qui aurait donc la forme d'une aventure personnelle. Mais il ajoute étonnamment dans la même page que ce changement touche aussi à ce qui 'ne me concernait pas personnellement'. Écartelé entre la nécessité de singulariser son expérience et celle de laisser être l'anonymat qui est la forme vraie de cette expérience, l'écrivain est voué à une aporie qu'il continue pourtant de creuser.

C'est ainsi que le chapitre 3, qui, selon le narrateur, aurait 'dû commencer d'une façon plus raisonnée, oui, plus abstraite' (p. 31), reprend avec l'évocation d'un collègue de bureau disparu, Florian La Barre, antithèse et confirmation de Mr. Smith. Doté d'un nom, La Barre est cependant à peine une figure, auteur lui aussi d'un carnet intime, dont la seule citation est dépourvue de toute intimité. La réflexion se poursuit autour de ce qui constituerait le 'Kha' de la foule sans essence, où s'abolit la conscience de la mort en même temps que le sentiment de l'individualité. La foule est pensée — en des termes qui évoquent les paradoxes de Maurice Blanchot — comme un centre sans centre, moins un lieu qu'un point de vue évanescent.

Le chapitre 4 prend ensuite un tour plus narratif, en essayant un nouveau départ fictionnel, avec le 'personnage' (il faudrait dire: la silhouette) de Mr. Y dont la lettre dit tout le schématisme. Là encore l'échec tient à une contradiction insoluble: pour dire l'être énigmatique de la foule, il faudrait adopter le point de vue de la mort, alors que le narrateur note évidemment, mais comme à regret: 'je restais vivant' (p. 58). L'ensemble du texte que nous lisons est ainsi frappé d'une constante ironie puisque rien ne peut coïncider avec rien, et que le sujet qui dit 'Je' est obligé de sentir la limitation irritante d'un point de vue qui ne peut suffire. Au lieu de s'enfoncer dans cette nouvelle aporie, Souvrault commence à raconter une nuit particulière, une errance sans doute récente, mais passée, où il a suivi la 'ligne blanche', dans ce qu'il décrit comme une 'glissade accélérée'.[6]

C'est donc dans ce chapitre que nous est racontée l'étrange rencontre nocturne avec les trois jeunes filles, qu'est évoqué le moment où Souvrault aperçoit Patrick Danaham, puis retrouve, de façon très invraisemblable, l'ami écrivain qui lui prête cinq livres en le ramenant chez lui en taxi. La suite des événements reste assez énigmatique, chaque rencontre semblant surgir du néant, sans lien réel de causalité, sans être jamais vraiment voulue par Souvrault, qui ne se soucie pas du tout de rendre son récit crédible. Dans cette nuit singulière, a-t-on affaire à un moment crucial? Les trois jeunes filles sont-elles l'allégorie de quelque épiphanie joycienne, où elles figureraient la version triviale des Trois Grâces? Ou n'est-ce là qu'une nouvelle dérision, une rencontre sans suite ni raison? Le point de vue du récit continue de poser problème et explique en partie l'obscurité de la narration — *obscurité*, on en conviendra, appropriée à cette nuit de Londres. À la page 91, le narrateur note en effet: 'Quelqu'un — est-ce encore moi?'. On voit bien l'espèce de dédoublement permanent qui clive le sujet, qui l'écarte de lui, qui l'impersonnalise, en irréalisant tout ce qu'il vit à mesure. Le sujet qui parle et raconte, l'écrivain qui tente d'ordonner la suite erratique d'actions nocturnes est le héros paradoxal d'un évanouissement et d'une dépossession que le livre doit précisément figurer. Chaque détail est dès lors tendu entre l'insignifiance d'un accident et le sens symbolique que l'on peut lui attribuer. C'est ainsi que l'on peut lire l'épisode de la clé égarée (perdue pour quelques heures seulement par un narrateur de plus en plus dépossédé): sa disparition marque bien que le narrateur n'a plus de chez soi, que son errance, à la différence de celle d'Ulysse, ne le ramène vers aucune Ithaque (pas même celle, modernisée, de Joyce).

Au terme de ce nouveau récit, à la fin de cette nuit initiatique et décevante, Souvrault note qu'il a 'cherché quelque chose d'impossible à atteindre' (p. 124). Et le dernier chapitre s'interrompt assez abruptement sur un verbe au futur: 'si je rencontre Peggy, je lui parlerai' (p. 138), en une sorte d'hommage à la façon de Gide dans *Les Faux-Monnayeurs*. Le narrateur imagine déjà une prochaine nuit, une autre expérience de la foule qui ne sera sans doute jamais que la même toujours altérée. On conclura volontiers que le texte de Souvrault (qui n'a pas encore de nom, qui ne le recevra que l'extérieur) ne peut se terminer de lui-même, qu'il est par nature voué à l'inachèvement de l'errance.

Il faut donc un épilogue pour nous faire sortir de la 'nuit de Londres'. Il faut l'intervention d'un autre narrateur, qui parle à son tour à la première personne, mais surtout qui constitue le narrateur anonyme de tout le livre en troisième personne, en Il. Si je reprends les termes de l'équation que je cherche à déplier, il faut donc un Je pour délimiter in extremis un Il. Il faut un nouveau passage, un changement de point de vue. Dans les pages publiées en italiques à la fin du livre, c'est maintenant l'écrivain rencontré par Souvrault qui s'exprime. C'est lui qui donne sa version du mystère qu'a poursuivi Souvrault.

On se doute que cet épilogue n'aura rien de véritablement conclusif et que l'énigme ne sera pas dissipée. Mais nous apprenons le passé commun des deux hommes, leurs relations à Paris, avec l'évocation des soirées rue Cujas. Nous apprenons surtout l'accident de Souvrault dont on ne peut connaître exactement la raison, et qui peut être tenu pour un suicide sans que cela soit dit. L'épilogue constitue donc la vie de Souvrault en un échec indécidable, car il le fait de manière ambiguë, en dissociant stratégiquement les rôles entre l'écrivain reconnu (l'homme qui publie avec une certaine fatuité comme Gilbert Delorme dans *Le Promontoire*) et celui que Bernard Pingaud nomme 'l'écriveur'.[7] La forme même du récit que nous venons de lire incombe à l'ami (au témoin lacunaire) de Souvrault qui a peut-être fabriqué un livre là où aucune forme de publication ne convenait. Ce dernier narrateur n'hésite pas à dire la profondeur du désaccord entre lui et Paul Souvrault, mais il maintient une part d'ombre et de secret, reconnaissant par exemple qu'il 'renonce à comprendre' (p. 153).

Dans ce dernier passage de relais, le JE qui parle ne dissipe pas l'énigme d'un IL sorti in extremis de l'anonymat. Éditeur posthume des notes de son ami, dont il est devenu le légataire, il est sans doute, par une nécessité que *Le Promontoire* ou *Le Parjure* explorent aussi, celui qui fait de la fondamentale absence d'œuvre une œuvre malgré tout; il est celui qui donne forme à l'informe d'une écriture inachevable; il transforme en projet ce qui échappe à tout vouloir, à toute décision subjective.

(2) L'Homme des foules

On mesure combien il est difficile de raconter ou d'exposer la matière, éminemment paradoxale, de *La Nuit de Londres*. L'équation que j'en ai proposée, le trop long rappel des différents moments du livre témoignent sans doute de l'effort que je fais à mon tour pour mettre la main sur un texte fuyant et déconcertant. Je crois que le pouvoir du récit d'Henri Thomas tient à ce mélange très particulier d'intensité dramatique, qui fait que, à l'instar du narrateur, le lecteur cherche quelque chose, attend une révélation toujours suspendue. Il est tenu en haleine par une recherche pourtant très abstraite et comme désincarnée. Menés par le désir de toucher au point de butée, au moment d'un dépassement soudain, narrateur et lecteur sont confrontés en même temps à l'immobilité foncière du récit, au caractère à la fois répétitif et heurté, presque incohérent, de tous les événements.

En vérité, *La Nuit de Londres* est un récit impossible, un récit de l'impossible. Et l'on se souvient du mot de l'écrivain répondant à Marcel Bisiaux, disant qu'il faut précisément être tenu à l'impossible.[8] Tel est le mouvement du *récit* qui va en spirale dans une suite de paradoxes où se défont tous les appuis du roman traditionnel. En un certain sens, *La Nuit de Londres* est tout à fait représentatif du courant de contestation radicale des pouvoirs du roman qui anime les années 1950. Que l'on pense à Beckett, Blanchot ou des Forêts. Tout un courant que l'éclairage polémique porté sur le Nouveau Roman a contribué à occulter, et qu'il est urgent de remettre en lumière.

Les paradoxes se disent de multiples façons, dont je veux donner d'autres exemples frappants. On lit ainsi page 53: 'N'être personne, à la place où n'est plus personne'. Voilà l'étrange vœu que le narrateur qualifie de 'cette espèce de rêve qui me ventousait l'esprit'. Dans le même développement, le narrateur sans nom confie qu'il voudrait prendre le point de vue d'un 'disparu de la foule' (p. 55). Il s'agit toujours de se mettre personnellement au lieu de l'abolition ou de l'évanouissement de tout sujet. Mais cette quête n'est pas ici du domaine de la poésie mais bien du récit, c'est-à-dire d'un effort pour raconter ce qui pourtant échappe par nature.

Avec *La Nuit de Londres*, Henri Thomas radicalise le mouvement d'une certaine modernité littéraire, dont il est consciemment l'héritier. Et cette longue méditation sur les foules est évidemment redevable à deux intertextes féconds et liés ensemble: celui de Baudelaire et celui de Poe. Le conte d'Edgar Poe, intitulé en français 'The Man of the Crowd' paraît dans le *Graham's Magazine* en 1840. Il est traduit par Baudelaire sous le titre 'L'Homme des foules' en 1855.[9] Cet étrange récit a déjà pour cadre Londres, paradigme de la ville tentaculaire du dix-neuvième siècle, lieu des rencontres bizarres et des énigmes urbaines. Le narrateur mis en scène par Poe suit, à travers la capitale anglaise, un étonnant personnage qui a piqué sa curiosité, sans réussir à savoir ce qui motive le comportement irrationnel et erratique de cet homme. Certains critiques ont vu dans l'homme âgé une sorte de double du narrateur lui-même. Mais si la piste est tentante, elle n'offre en aucune façon une résolution de l'énigme laissée ouverte par le conte.

Baudelaire, on le sait, reprend à son tour le thème de l'homme des foules, figure du flâneur urbain que Walter Benjamin a bien identifié. Dans les *Petits poèmes en prose*, le texte intitulé 'Les Foules' se propose comme une rêverie paradoxale et provocante sur les pouvoirs d'empathie du poète moderne. Baudelaire s'y livre à un éloge de la capacité à se confondre avec la foule, faisant rimer de façon aujourd'hui célèbre 'solitude' et 'multitude'. Cette faculté de passer instantanément en chacun est même, à ses yeux, une sorte de prostitution sacrée du poète, saisi par la 'singulière ivresse de cette universelle communion'.

L'homme des foules est ainsi l'incarnation paradoxale d'un nouveau régime de la subjectivité, où la multitude des semblables produit l'anonymat de chacun. À la fois le même que tous et l'autre de chacun, l'homme des foules est ironiquement soumis à la loi de la démultiplication. Le récit de Thomas opère une sorte de passage à la limite de ce motif, selon un mécanisme double de dramatisation (qui réussit à faire de cette figure le sujet de tout un livre) et une dédramatisation (puisque le héros ordinaire incarné par Mr. Smith n'a plus rien de grandiose ni même de bizarre). Le récit de 1956 semble prendre acte de la condition actuelle faite à l'homme des villes, ce marcheur urbain nocturne qui dérive sans but. J'ai déjà noté que cette activité (si le mot convient pour ce que décrit Thomas, qui laisse toute sa place à la passivité du flâneur) pouvait évoquer les pratiques des Surréalistes, relayées de façon encore plus théorisée par les Situationnistes. Quelque chose d'un automatisme de la marche entraîne l'écriture dans des chemins inattendus, dans des sentiers de traverse.

Mais plus rien ne semble devoir relever maintenant du projet, et tel est le paradoxe central que met en œuvre (et en déroute) Paul Souvrault: sa quête n'obéit à aucune direction possible. Son errance nocturne est faite de virevoltes et de moments de basculement, sans qu'aucun sens — même allégorique — ne puisse se dégager. Car, au centre toujours décentré de la foule, réside un vide qui est en même temps le vide du sujet et de la multitude. Et la seule position que devrait adopter celui qui cherche à dire le secret sans secret de 'la nuit de Londres' est ce que le narrateur nomme 'le point de vue de l'absence sur moi-même' (p. 58).

Pour l'écrivain accompli et reconnu qui se charge de l'épilogue du récit, l'échec de Souvrault prend le sens d'une leçon malheureuse. Méditant sur l'étrange destin de son camarade de jeunesse, de son compatriote exilé à Londres, il note que Souvrault éprouve une fondamentale 'hostilité' envers le langage (p. 145), dont il n'est, dans les notes de son ami, que l'une des figures de substitution. Contrairement au dernier narrateur du récit, Souvrault a décidé de refuser la poésie, et les références à Baudelaire lors de leur conversation nocturne prennent dans le premier récit un tour plutôt grotesque. Cette 'hostilité', il faut reconnaître cependant qu'elle est celle de 'tout auteur moderne', qu'elle 'suit le langage comme son ombre' (p. 145) et qu'elle est donc le lot fatal de notre temps. Mais Souvrault radicalise cette position et en fait une force d'erreur sans réparation. L'auteur de l'épilogue esquisse un débat fondamental sur les pouvoirs de la littérature et du langage, mais il préfère en revenir à une explication plus circonstanciée en mettant cette incapacité de Souvrault à faire confiance aux mots sur le compte d'une blessure personnelle ancienne, dont il ne peut dire la nature exacte.

Le jugement porté sur Souvrault à la fin du livre est un jugement à la fois sévère et amical, catégorique et modéré. Mais il contribue, dans le même mouvement que le changement de point de vue, à nous mettre à distance du narrateur anonyme qui avait dominé jusque-là tout le récit. Sans doute faut-il comprendre ce temps de recul final comme la distanciation qu'Henri thomas opère vis-à-vis de son double, dont il se désolidarise partiellement. En ce sens, on peut affirmer que Thomas est et n'est pas Souvrault. Ce 'personnage' récurrent dans son œuvre lui sert à dire une limite de lui-même, peut-être une tentation extrême, à laquelle Thomas ne doit pas succomber pour rester, lui, écrivain. Dans cette perspective, la conclusion de *La Nuit de Londres* est une façon de prendre congé de la fascination et de la menace que constitue le désir d'anonymat et de disparition.

Faisant à la toute fin du livre du narrateur anonyme un personnage (muni d'un nom, de fragments de passé) qu'un autre peut juger, Thomas donne un tour plus évidemment romanesque à son récit, comme s'il voulait reprendre le contrôle d'un mouvement de désœuvrement ruineux. C'est peut-être ce recul final que Blanchot juge avec sévérité, comme si l'écrivain s'était dérobé au mouvement neutre de sa narration première.

(3) La Passion de l'impersonnel

Est-ce là la conclusion de ce récit? Qu'est-ce que *La Nuit de Londres* réussit à mettre à distance et à cristalliser dans le même geste paradoxal? Je viens de suggérer que la figure de Souvrault — qui devient dans le récit final un peu plus un personnage, avec une certaine épaisseur psychologique et des épisodes de son passé — pourrait être comprise comme le double sacrificiel que Thomas fait mourir pour éloigner de lui un vœu qu'il partage intimement. J'ai parlé plus haut de crise personnelle, et je crois en effet que ce livre traduit une épreuve intime pour l'écrivain exilé en Angleterre. Ce serait cette épreuve qu'il représente et écarte de lui en la mettant au compte de Paul. Seul ce sacrifice final (la mort accidentelle ou le suicide logique) de Souvrault permet de sortir du paradoxe d'un Je qui n'est jamais personnel, d'un Je anonyme et voué à désirer se voir comme mort, ou absent, ou autre que lui. La logique du double basculement du Il au Je puis au Il marque donc une forme d'ordalie du récit.

Mais le motif de la disparition reste profondément ambigu. Car il reste pathétique, comme la mort prématurée de Florian La Barre, ou celle de Paul. Quelque chose ne sera pas accompli. Une promesse demeure en souffrance. Et même dans le monde paradoxal de la foule, cette forme de disparition qui échappait au pathos de la mort ne laisse advenir aucun visage, aucun autre véritablement constitué. Mais inversement, une force joue contre ce pathétique et le texte sait faire entendre un autre mouvement: celui d'une égalisation absolue des moments, des affects, des sensations. Peut-être est-ce là la fonction de cette feuille morte de platane que le narrateur veut absolument aller voir sur la grille près de chez lui. En elle, insiste encore une sorte de figure poétique, moins allégorique que témoignant d'un être-là irrécusable, d'une persistance de l'éphémère.

Faut-il voir en Paul Souvrault le héros d'une ère nouvelle de la subjectivité moderne? Son sacrifice — si c'en est un — l'élèverait-il à la hauteur du martyr? On sait que Thomas insiste, dans l'entretien avec Marcel Bisiaux, sur la qualité 'héroïque' de ses personnages, héroïsme de la déflation et du dégagement, mais héroïsme encore parce qu'ils continuent à chercher quelque chose au-delà d'eux-mêmes. Même dans l'errance, quelque chose d'un absolu guide les pas de Souvrault, quelque chose qui dérange les certitudes, déplace les codes sociaux. Mais cet absolu, un peu à la façon de ce que Georges Bataille a appelé 'l'expérience intérieure', déjoue essentiellement toute possibilité d'en faire un projet. Il ne dépend d'aucune volonté, au sens où elle émanerait d'un sujet constitué et plus ou moins maître de lui.

Énigmatique, *La Nuit de Londres* participe donc de ce que j'appelle à la suite de Maurice Blanchot, le *récit*, contre les pouvoirs du roman, dans leur défaut. Quelque chose doit encore se raconter, et emprunte donc la forme de la narration, mais l'objet du récit ne cesse de s'échapper. Le livre d'Henri Thomas pose sans doute plus de questions qu'il ne peut apporter de réponses. Et il compte, pour moi, parmi les grands textes aporétiques de l'après-guerre, au côté de *La Folie du jour* de Maurice Blanchot, du *Bavard* de Louis-René des Forêts et de *L'Innommable* de Samuel Beckett. Il témoigne donc d'un moment capital de l'histoire littéraire comme recherche de l'impossible.

Dans ce récit, je vois pour ma part une sorte de folie de l'impersonnel, menée jusqu'à la mort fictive de Paul Souvrault. En lui s'est incarnée problématiquement une passion de l'impersonnel. Par cette dernière formule, j'entends maintenir le jeu difficile et complexe entre une subjectivité et ce qui la fait défaillir. Dire: 'passion de l'impersonnel', c'est en effet une manière pour moi de ne pas parler d'une passion du *neutre*. Je retrouve en fin de parcours les réflexions que j'ai déjà proposées dans l'épilogue du *Roman et le sens de la vie*.[10] L'engagement de l'écrivain relève d'un mouvement vers l'impersonnel, ou plus exactement il se traduit par une négociation, à chaque fois singulière, entre le personnel et l'impersonnel. Et ce mouvement d'aller et venue, d'oscillation n'est pas ce que Blanchot désigne comme 'le neutre' dans *L'Entretien infini*. Ni ce que Deleuze, à sa suite, appelle du même terme.

Car il en va de l'engagement le plus personnel (entre passivité subie et décision héroïque) dans un processus de dépersonnalisation. Tel serait le sens de la quête mystérieuse, accomplie et ratée par Paul Souvrault. Tel serait le message ambigu que Thomas nous laisse avec ce récit. Tout le livre est ainsi tendu par le désir d'atteindre enfin une sorte de ligne de partage ou de passage, où règnerait l'impersonnel même. Et ce point, on le devine, serait celui d'un allègement absolu et heureux. Il offrirait le moment paradoxal d'une dépossession, que rien ne pourrait cependant consigner. Mais ce terme, toute *La Nuit de Londres* nous dit qu'il reste hors de portée. C'est la raison pour laquelle il requiert plutôt le tourniquet inévitable des personnes (du Il au Je et réciproquement). Et l'épreuve — ardue mais ravissante — de ces renversements, nous comprenons que nous devons, à notre tour, la vivre de la façon la plus intime, la plus personnelle.

Notes

1. Paru en 1956 aux éditions Gallimard. Je le citerai dans l'édition courante 'L'Imaginaire' (Paris: Gallimard, 1980). Je donnerai directement dans le cours du texte les références de pages. Je reprends, sous une forme écrite modifiée, le propos que j'avais tenu oralement lors de la journée d'étude pour le centenaire de la naissance de Henri Thomas, organisée à l'Université Paris Diderot le 7 décembre 2012 par Patrice Bougon.
2. Je me permets donc de renvoyer à mon étude 'Henri Thomas et le récit', in *Henri Thomas, l'écriture du secret*, dirigé par Patrice Bougon et Marc Dambre (Seyssel: Champ Vallon Essais, 2007), pp. 17–33.
3. Voir la belle contribution de Pierre Brunet: 'Thomas en Amérique' dans le *Cahier Henri Thomas* (Cognac: Le Temps qu'il fait, 1998).
4. On trouve son étude dans *Henri Thomas, l'écriture du secret* (*op. cit.*). Le sous-titre précise justement qu'elle porte sur les 'romans de l'écriture' entre 1942 et 1975. Voir pp. 147–63.
5. Blanchot commente en effet assez longuement *La Nuit de Londres* dans un article de mars 1957 intitulé 'D'un art sans avenir', qui paraît dans le numéro 51 de *La Nouvelle Revue Française*. On en trouve le texte aux pages 228–38 de *La Condition critique. Articles, 1945–1998*, édité par Christophe Bident (Paris: Gallimard, 'les Cahiers de la NRF', 2010). C'est dans la fin de cette chronique qu'on voit apparaître la distance que Blanchot prend quant à la fin du récit de Thomas, notamment quand il note: 'Il se peut que Henri Thomas ait eu le tort d'obéir ici à la tradition romanesque. Mais il se peut aussi qu'il ait voulu se protéger lui-même en mettant fin à un mouvement qui ne pouvait finir' (pp. 237–38). D'une certaine manière, Blanchot reproche à Thomas cette faiblesse finale. Et c'est sans doute la raison pour laquelle il n'a pas repris cette critique en livre, ni même ensuite jamais plus commenté les livres de Thomas.

6. La formule peut faire penser à Breton. Le texte de Thomas n'est pas sans rapport avec les errances surréalistes aux marges des grandes capitales, qui seront théorisées comme 'dérives urbaines' par les Situationnistes. Mais le livre ne présente aucune méthode. Il est sans commandement ni leçon.
7. Voir *Les Anneaux du manège. Écriture et littérature* (Paris: Gallimard, Folio Essais, 1992). On lira aussi avec profit son compte rendu de *La Nuit de Londres*, paru en 1957 et repris dans 'L'honnête courtier' aux pages 155–56 de *L'Occupation des oisifs* (Paris: Classiques Garnier, 'Études de littérature des XX° et XXI° siècles', numéro 36, 2013).
8. Voir page 271 de ce bel entretien pour 'Les Hommes-Livres', publié dans le *Cahier Henri Thomas*, *op. cit.*
9. Voir les notes (pp. 1362–64) de l'édition des œuvres de Poe réalisée par Claude Richard pour 'Bouquins'. Edgar Allan Poe: *Contes — essais — poèmes* (Paris: Laffont, 1989).
10. Pages 103–12 de mon essai, paru dans la collection 'Les Essais' (Paris: Corti, 2010).

— 19 —

Pereciana

Anthony Rudolf

(for my friend and fellow endotic anthropologist, Micky Sheringham, on his retirement from teaching)

> There is the enchantment of accuracy, which seems more imperative than the personal
> — Marianne Moore (*letter to Wallace Stevens*)
>
> Figures of the everyday
> — Michael Sheringham (*Everyday Life*)

In December 2005, ten years ago to the month at the time of writing, I embarked on some research for a project which did not take off. My research notes "languished" in a computer folder, until this excellent opportunity arose to resuscitate one of the topics, an exercise in what Georges Perec called "endotic anthropology". I wrote to — or, more likely, received answers from — 75 persons (writers, painters etc) in my address book, asking them the following three questions:

1) Do you listen to music while working?

The answers ranged from more than one indignant "never" to several enthusiastic "always".

2) Are the rooms in your present house/flat named differently from when you were a child?

The answers revealed that only the lounge and the WC had changed their names over the years.

3) How many places have you lived in?

This was the most interesting question in terms of endotic anthropology and I shall pursue it now.

I circulated the following group email:

> How many places have you lived in? Please exclude holiday hotels etc, unless you return or returned to the same one for many years. Please include college residences if you stayed there for at least an academic year.
>
> Please exclude any residences where you have lived for a very short time —

use your judgment.

Your reply can be one word — i.e. the number -- or a list or even a more detailed inventory, as in mine below. How typical is my experience? We shall find out.

I then listed the following residences but without the detailed locations:

Parental house 1942–66 (41 Middleway, Hampstead Garden Suburb, London NW11 6SH);

[including break to countryside near High Wycombe during the war, but length of stay now unknowable: probably very short because I recall being told that we returned to London soon enough: it was too quiet in the country]

Jewish Student hostel in France, 1961 (Le Toit familial, 9 rue Guy Patin, 75010 Paris);

Three rooms in Cambridge while at Trinity College, 1961–64 (K7, New Court, Trinity; 25 Jesus Lane; and E4, Angel Court, Trinity);

Flat in USA, 1966 (Apartment 311, 5465 South Everett, Chicago, Illinois 60615)

Two bed-sitters in London, 1967–68 (2 Powis Square, Notting Hill, London W11 2AY and 26 Granville Park, Lewisham, London SE13 7EA)

Flat in London, 1968–74 (1 Primrose Gardens, London NW3 4UJ)

House in London, 1974–81 (23 Fitzwarren Gardens, London N19 3TR)

Flat in London, 1981- (8 The Oaks, Woodside Avenue, London N12 8AR)

Excluding the wartime evacuation, my personal total is 11. The 75 replies I received averaged 17 and ranged from 7 to 37. A detailed analysis must await another occasion, if ever. Among the respondents, Julian Barnes numbered 11 residences, John Forrester 17, Lisa Appignanesi 25, Marina Warner 25, Stephen Romer 14 and Hattie Gordon 9.

— 20 —

Proust's *Bifurs*

Michael Lucey

> Tout mot nouveau introduit dans la langue y cause une perturbation analogue à celle d'un être nouveau introduit dans le monde physique ou social.
>
> MICHEL BRÉAL, *Essai de sémantique*

The momentous evening is winding down. The miraculous Vinteuil Septet has been performed and a few of the people in the audience have understood what an astonishing piece of music they have just had the good fortune to hear. Many of them, of course, have understood nothing. In any case, the performance, led by the dashing, sexually fluid, young violinist, Morel, and the evening of which it is a part have become an event to be talked about. The Baron de Charlus, Morel's protector (or at least he was when the evening began), had agreed to collaborate with the social-climbing Verdurins to organize this musical evening, which they have hosted. Aiming to further Morel's prospects, both socially and musically, Charlus encouraged his most notable connections from the Faubourg Saint-Germain to attend. Even the semi-mythical Queen of Naples made an appearance. As Proust's narrator notes, however, Charlus has not been the most diplomatic of collaborators. Collectors of artists and the artistically inclined, the Verdurins have been angling for some time to draw Morel into their ambit. Avid for social capital, they also covet the connections the guest list, as curated by Charlus, might bring them. Charlus haughtily neglects to introduce to the evening's hosts any of the titled crowd who attend mainly because he invited them and insisted on their presence. The major drama of the evening comes after the majority of the titled guests have left, most of them rudely ignoring the Verdurins. At this point, the Verdurins put into motion a scheme they have been cogitating for some time: to suggest disingenuously to Morel that the backing of Charlus (sexually dubious, they inform Morel, who has to pretend they are telling him something he does not already know much better than they do) is morally compromising for him, damaging to his reputation and his career prospects, and that their own backing would serve him better. Having among his attributes neither loyalty nor a particularly astute sense of where social advantage might lie, Morel dramatically renounces his protector in the presence of the few remaining guests. The Queen of Naples, having returned unnoticed to collect a valuable fan she has accidentally left behind, witnesses this shameful scene of betrayal, and she rescues Charlus from the painful position in which he has unexpectedly found himself, disdaining to notice either the Verdurins or Morel as she and the Baron make their exit together. The evening is thus, when all is said and done, an odd mix of success and catastrophe for all concerned.

It is perhaps especially catastrophic for Saniette, whose status as the Verdurin's whipping boy has been repeatedly exhibited to us. A socially awkward fellow, he has served as the object of sport at many a dinner or evening party. Always one to put his foot wrong, Saniette dares to suggest to Monsieur Verdurin and a few others that perhaps Morel's displays of virtuosity during the performance of the Septet had been a bit more extreme than necessary. As a result, Verdurin loudly and publicly shows Saniette the door. Saniette promptly has some kind of an attack in the courtyard, and has to be conveyed home in an unconscious state. 'Il vécut encore quelques semaines, mais sans reprendre que passagèrement connaissance'.[1]

Saniette suffers a bit at the hands of the novelist as well. In this he is similar to the doctor Cottard, whose death is announced early on in the evening — 'il a été enlevé bien vite, le pauvre professeur!' (A III, 746) — even though Charlus somehow manages to ask him for a piece of advice a bit later on in the course of the soirée (A III, 783). To make matters more confusing, once all the guests have left and M. and Mme. Verdurin are on their own, we learn that Cottard, still alive, had been unable to attend the evening party at all because he was in fact attending to Saniette, who was also unable to attend due to the fact that, having earlier that day lost all his money and gone hugely into debt as a result of a bad gamble on the stock market, he had suffered some kind of an attack. This second attack seems not to have been quite so severe as the first. If the first carried him off after only a few weeks, he survives the second by several years, because the narrator tells us that he learns something from Cottard about the Verdurin's behaviour towards Saniette 'quelques années plus tard, à l'enterrement même de Saniette' (A III, 829).

What the narrator learns at Saniette's graveside is that the Verdurins, upon hearing of Saniette's investment losses and subsequent debilitating attack, secretly arranged to rent a small apartment for him and to pay his expenses for the few years remaining between his attack and his death. Not wanting anyone to know of their generosity to the fellow they have consistently treated so badly in person, they convince Cottard to tell Saniette and everyone else that the Princess Sherbatoff left him a small sum in her will. We might think this odd story about the surprising generosity of the Verdurins towards someone they had kept inviting to their dinners and parties apparently only in order to be able to go on treating him with alarming brutality belongs to that facet of the novel that delights in revealing the many inconsistencies that exist between patterns of behaviour that a single person might exhibit on different levels of their existence. (The paradigm case of this side of the novel is Mlle. Vinteuil, whose love for her father contrasts so sharply with the ritual desecration of his photograph, witnessed by the narrator. Her girlfriend exhibits a similar behavioural discrepancy, participating in the scene of desecration, but working lovingly and painstakingly on Vinteuil's manuscripts in order to produce the score of the Septet that has just been performed in the novel.) I recount the episode here for a different reason, however, because it provides the occasion for the narrator to go off on a tangent in order to tell us of a strange word that M. Verdurin uses in talking to his wife about Saniette, a word that fascinates the narrator even though he is unable to discover what it is.

* * * * *

> Chacun de nous possède son assortiment de locutions abrégées, intelligibles pour les seuls intimes. Supposez qu'elles soient adoptées autour de nous, qu'elles deviennent d'usage courant parmi toute une catégorie de personnes, qu'elles soient répandues par la presse, ces abréviations pourront un jour prendre place dans la langue. (Michel Bréal, *Essai de sémantique*)

If the Verdurins use the undead Cottard as an intermediary between them and the equally undead Saniette, it is, so the narrator tells us, to avoid the inconvenience of putting up with scenes in which people will feel it necessary to thank them for their unmotivated act of generosity. Verdurin has a special word for scenes of this kind which he uses in talking to his wife. But, the narrator laments, this mysterious word 'n'a pu m'être dit exactement, car ce n'était pas un mot français, mais un de ces termes comme on en a dans les familles pour désigner certaines choses, surtout les choses agaçantes, probablement parce qu'on veut pouvoir les signaler devant les intéressés sans être compris' (A iii, 829). This observation is the beginning of a reasonably long digression on the category of words to which Verdurin's unknown one belongs — a digression that has nothing to do with Saniette, Cottard, or the Verdurins, but everything to do with the forms of the narrator's (and the novel's) interest in language.

Verdurin's use of this word causes his wife to smile, the narrator informs us, because 'l'emploi de cette langue moins générale, plus personnelle, plus secrète, que la langue habituelle donne à ceux qui en usent entre eux un sentiment égoïste qui ne va jamais sans une certaine satisfaction' (A iii, 829). And yet the word is, as it turns out, an example of a part of language that, whatever intimate satisfaction it is providing the two Verdurins, is in the process of disappearing from use. Had the narrator been able to report the word to us, he could perhaps have relaunched it, given it a new lease on life, conferred on it a small amount of prestige such that someone else might have wanted to use it. As Bréal points out, 'l'adoption des mots étrangers, pour désigner des idées ou des objets venus de dehors, et donnant lieu à un échange international de relations, n'est donc pas une chose blâmable en soi, et peut parfaitement se justifier [...] La chose arrive plus fréquemment qu'on ne croit'.[2] Words from another language can be appealing and trendy (as we shall see shortly), enticing to use. Yet here, the situation is different. The word is a leftover, its meaning being slowly forgotten, as only a kind of affective aura continues to hover around it:

> Ce genre d'expressions est généralement un reliquat contemporain d'un état antérieur de la famille. Dans une famille juive, par exemple, ce sera un terme rituel détourné de son sens et peut-être le seul mot hébreu que la famille, maintenant françisée, connaisse encore. Dans une famille très fortement provinciale, ce sera un terme du patois de la province, bien que la famille ne

> parle plus et ne comprenne même plus le patois. Dans une famille venue de l'Amérique du Sud et ne parlant plus que le français, ce sera un mot espagnol. Et à la génération suivante, le mot n'existera plus qu'à titre de souvenir d'enfance. On se rappellera bien que les parents à table faisaient allusion aux domestiques qui servaient, sans être compris d'eux, en disant tel mot, mais les enfants ignorent ce que voulait dire au juste ce mot, si c'était de l'espagnol, de l'hébreu, de l'allemand, du patois, si même cela avait jamais appartenu à une langue quelconque et n'était pas un nom propre, ou un mot entièrement forgé. (A III, 829)

The strange foreign word slowly becomes meaningless, except as an index of family history, or a kind of totem whose use renews certain kinds of familial bonds on certain ritual family occasions. But it ceases, in a way, to be part of what Saussure would call *la langue* — the body of linguistic information that is widely shared across a speech community. It exists more and more only in acts of *parole* — discrete instances of speech — disconnected from any but the smallest of groups of speakers. Proust's narrator emphasizes this aspect of the word in question here by foregrounding again why it cannot even be represented on the pages of the novel. The passage just cited continues: 'Le doute ne peut être éclairci que si on a un grand-oncle, un vieux cousin encore vivant et qui a dû user du même terme. Comme je n'ai connu aucun parent des Verdurin, je n'ai pu restituer exactement le mot'. At any number of points in the novel the narrator makes little indications of moments of linguistic fieldwork that lie behind his writing, investigations he has performed in order better to understand the details of someone's manner of speaking. Here he points to a kind of failure. He had no connections, and apparently could make none, with Verdurin's family, and so the word he somehow knows Verdurin to have spoken only half enters into the novel. It remains undepicted but nonetheless enters the novel as a the example of a certain kind of word, one whose situation of use is described because it constitutes an interesting instance of what the French call a *fait de langage*, a term that has been variously translated as 'linguistic phenomenon', 'speech fact', 'fact of language', or 'linguistic fact'.

* * * * *

> Nous travaillons tous, plus ou moins, au vocabulaire de l'avenir, ignorants ou savants, écrivains ou artistes, gens du monde ou hommes du peuple. Les enfants y ont une part qui n'est pas la moindre: comme ils prennent la langue au point où les générations précédentes l'ont conduite, ils sont ordinairement en avance d'une dizaine ou d'une vingtaine d'années sur leurs parents. (Michel Bréal, *Essai de sémantique*)

Towards the end of *Biffures*, Michel Leiris discusses at some length his interest in *faits de langage* of a particular kind, the kind he tells us he called *bifurs*. 'Leiris constantly draws attention to the strange materiality of words', Michael Sheringham points out, 'the manifold receptacles in which memories come to lodge, the discrete and unpredictable locales in which traces of selfhood may be identified'.[3] There are two aspects of *bifurs* that I'd like to dwell on briefly here, the first being the one Leiris describes as follows:

> J'eus recours [...] à l'expression de *bifurs* pour désigner, dans mon jargon personnel, les matériaux si peu commodes à étiqueter que je voulais amasser et brasser: soubresauts, trébuchements ou glissements de pensée se produisant à l'occasion d'une fêlure, d'un miroitement [...] ou d'une quelconque singularité, rocailleuse ou fuyante, se manifestant dans le discours, [...] remous, rides, écumes ou autres altérations de la surface (à l'ordinaire tranquille) de la langue, qui sont les générateurs d'une poésie très spéciale [...][4]

Based on this description, we might well take the moment in Proust I have just been dwelling on to be a kind of *bifur*, a moment when there is a hiccup in language that sends Proust's novel off on a tangent, a hiccup that, in this particular case, consists of a certain word being used, a word that the narrator claims to know was said but cannot discover in order to record it — because, apparently, its slide into unrecoverability is one of its key features. The special poetry associated with this *bifur* is thus interestingly not be found, as is often the case in Leiris's examples, in the repercussions that occur immediately around and as a result of a word's utterance. Rather, what is significant in Proust's *Recherche* is that the word, having been said, is unrecoverable by the narrator, and thus becomes a blank space within the novel itself, a space around which text regarding language accrues. In the course of the novel, things get choppy for a moment; the novel pauses in the face of language; perhaps its pause could cause us to remember any number of other similar moments scattered throughout the novel where the primacy of language jumps into the foreground, and whatever else is going on in the novel seems to be side railed for a moment.

Leiris, in order to compose *Biffures* and its companion volumes, made use of his famous *fichier*, the box for the file cards on which he had noted words or other pieces of information that constituted the material of his *bifurs*. Proust had his notebooks, in which he is well-known for having consigned lists of words that could be linked to *faits de langage* of one kind or another that he was considering incorporating into his novel, lists of examples whose principle of selection is more frequently than not unmentioned by him when he writes them down.[5] Consider the following, for instance:

> St Loup
> cosmique
> pratique
> catastrophique[6]

The notebook includes no hint of the reasons why words such as these would find themselves incorporated into the speech of someone like the Marquis de Saint-Loup. The novel itself, on the other hand, would include the following:

> Ces conversations aristocratiques avaient du reste, chez Mme de Guermantes, le charme de se tenir dans un excellent français. À cause de cela elles rendaient légitime, de la part de la duchesse, son hilarité devant les mots 'vatique', 'cosmique', 'pythique', 'suréminent', qu'employait Saint-Loup, de même que devant ses meubles de chez Bing. (A II, 840)

That is to say, the novelist, the narrator, and certain characters (here the duchess

Saint-Loup's aunt) are intensely sensitive to — they stumble over, or are diverted by — the effects of register whereby individuals negotiate not only group membership, but also the manner in which that membership is enacted — manners that include questions of taste, questions of generational difference, and much more. The words Saint-Loup uses are the equivalent of wearing the wrong colour of slippers to a party, or patronizing the wrong suppliers of furniture.

Bifur is, obviously, an abbreviation of *bifurcation* or *bifurquer.* It represents the moment when something happens that causes thought or language to be diverted, to switch tracks. A word is spoken, and suddenly it stands out as participating in some kind of *fait de langage.* The occurrence of a linguistic event causes other things to take some kind of a turn. One such occurrence happens, for instance, when Leiris uses the expression 'mon travail' at one point in *Biffures*, and his train of thought jumps the tracks to a passage in Bréal's *Essai de sémantique* where Bréal mentions a possible etymology for *travail* (B 81). Bréal then crops up two pages later as well, simply because he and Leiris share a name, and the result is a Leirisian sentence typical in its incapacity to move directly forward from one point to another:

> Après avoir cité mon homonyme partial Michel Bréal, m'être référé au dictionnaire Larousse, avoir rapporté une partie des propos que m'a tenus un quidam, je ne suis pas plus avancé qu'avant: les mêmes écrans me séparent de la réalité et l'on dirait que ces phrases dans lesquelles je m'embarrasse — tantôt y ajoutant des mots, tantôt y remplaçant des mots par d'autres mots — sont l'image du difficile commerce que je m'efforce de nouer avec le réel, paralysé que je suis par les mouvements les plus contradictoires et m'attardant en maints détours, justifiés seulement par la répugnance irraisonnée que j'éprouve à aller droit au fait, quel que soit mon désir d'établir entre la réalité et moi le contact le plus direct. (B 83)

Words get in the way of moving forward. They slow things down. Sentences fork, subdivide, spread out, involute in response to the words that make them up. This seems accurate enough when it comes to describing many (though not all, as we shall see) of the metalinguistic digressions found in Proust, where the narrator suddenly steps back from the narration, pausing its forward motion to begin some kind of commentary on language use, with no guarantee that that commentary will not provoke further nested digressions of its own.

As Sheringham notes about Leiris, 'Some ambiguity surrounds [...] the way the singular word [...] is regarded: is it an end in itself, or is it part of a wider network of relationships, so that its virtues reside not in itself but in its combinatory power?' (F 252). Perhaps along with the question of the combinatory power held by the word that causes a swerve in direction, there is also a question regarding the form of the network that emerges from all the switches and swerves. For finally, Leiris seems to indicate, these accumulated ramifications end up mapping out a certain territory in a certain way: 'les recoupements multiples devaient finir par tresser [les ramifications diverses] en une sorte de réseau semblable à ceux qui mettent en communication toutes les régions distinctes composant un pays' (B 281). Leiris's writing becomes 'une méditation zigzaguant au fil de l'écriture et, 'bifur' après 'bifur', cheminant de thème en thème' (B 281–82). Across the course of this meditation, it comes to seem that there is 'une forme jusque-là ignorée mais qu'on voit émerger d'un abondant lacis de traits, ici bifurcations, méandres, digressions diverses' (B 283). And as for what that form might turn out to reveal, to capture, to cause to emerge, the first on the list of possible candidates is 'le primat du langage'.

★ ★ ★ ★ ★

> C'est par le fonctionnement des facultés réceptive et coordinative que se forment chez les sujets parlants des empreintes qui arrivent à être sensiblement les mêmes chez tous. Comment faut-il se représenter ce produit social pour que la langue apparaisse parfaitement dégagée du reste? Si nous pouvions embrasser la somme des images verbales emmagasinées chez tous les individus, nous toucherions le lien social qui constitue la langue. C'est un trésor déposé par la pratique de la parole dans les sujets appartenant à une même communauté, un système grammatical existant virtuellement dans chaque cerveau, ou plus exactement dans les cerveaux d'un ensemble d'individus; car la langue n'est complète dans aucun, elle n'existe parfaitement que dans la masse. (Ferdinand de Saussure, *Cours de linguistique générale*)

Michel Bréal was among Saussure's supporters in the 1880s, when Saussure, in his twenties, was assigned teaching at the École pratique des hautes études in Paris — several decades before he would give his famous lectures in Geneva. In Proust's own stance towards language (as in Leiris's) one can find elements that resemble those found in the work of both linguists, but also something different.[7] Proust was not just making lists in his notebooks of words and expressions that would help him differentiate his characters or individuate their speech by assigning to certain of them certain kinds of idiosyncrasies. He had actual linguistic concepts — even if he didn't explicitly theorize or name them — that he wished to investigate, and his notebooks could be thought of as the field notes of a practical or amateur linguist just as much as they could be thought of as resources for a novelist. Like Bréal, he was interested in how words come and go, how meanings of words come and go, and how those linguistic processes link up with other sociological events. Much of his linguistic interest has to do with language *use*. His particular way of being interested in language use, or language in use, puts interesting kinds of pressure on the Saussurean distinction between *langue* and *parole* so famously elaborated in Saussure's teaching in Geneva in the years during which Proust was conceptualizing his huge novel.[8] Verdurin's unrecoverable word, as we have seen, is an arrow pointing down a track leading towards rich veins of social information regarding not only his own family, but conceivably larger migration patterns important in the wider social field.[9] It is filled with the potential of socialness even if there are only a handful of speakers alive who would have had the capacity to understand it in its context of use. But this is a different kind of socialness than what Saussure is thinking of when he refers to 'le lien social qui constitue la langue'.

My epigraph from Saussure's *Cours* is taken from a subsection titled 'Place de la langue dans les faits de langage' in which Saussure wishes to demonstrate how one would analytically separate out what is *langue* from what is *parole*, what is shared in language's abstract structures from what is part of an individual speech act. For Saussure, but not for Proust or Leiris, 'en séparant la langue de la parole, on sépare du même coup: 1° ce que est social de ce qui est individuel; 2° ce qui est essentiel de ce qui est accessoire et plus ou moins accidentel'.[10] *Bifurs*, after all, are as often as not what we might call linguistic social accidents that reveal something essential about the social processes in which language use is entangled. They depend on language's capacity for social indexicality, moments in the exchange of language when forms of social engagement are discovered to be immanent in acts of language use. These indexical modes 'link speech to the wider system of social life',[11] and it is those linkages that Proust and Leiris either trace or instantiate in the networks they find ways to reveal.

★ ★ ★ ★ ★

> Quand il s'agit de notre vie morale, la présence des mots étrangers peut faire l'impression d'une dissonance. Plus les sentiments à exprimer sont intimes, plus le cercle linguistique se resserre. Il y a là pour le lecteur ou l'auditeur un plaisir intellectuel de nature très fine. Comme les ménagères d'autrefois se faisaient honneur de ne consommer que le lait de leur étable ou les fruits de leur jardin, un esprit délicat est sensible à un langage où tout vient du même terroir et où se trouve répandu sur tous les mots un air de familiarité et de parenté. (Michel Bréal, *Essai de sémantique*)

The word *mousmé* is one Proust noted down in one of his notebooks: 'mousmé etc.'.[12] Pierre Loti imported the word into French from Japanese in his 1887 novel, *Madame Chrysanthème*. As Proust's editors in the Pléiade edition helpfully remind us, Loti's novel sung the word's praises in the following terms: '*Mousmé* est un mot qui signifie jeune fille ou très jeune femme. C'est un des plus jolis de la langue nipponne; il semble qu'il y ait, dans ce mot, de la *moue* (de la petite moue gentille et drôle comme elles en font) et surtout de la *frimousse* (de la frimousse chiffonnée comme est la leur). Je l'emploierai souvent, n'en connaissant aucun en français qui le vaille' (A II, 1715–16). The word, as it is imported, is surrounded by an erotic orientalist cloud.[13]

It is precisely the kind of word our somewhat prissy narrator could be expected either to despise or to find comical — perhaps along the lines of how the duchess must have reacted upon hearing her nephew describe someone as *pythique*. Indeed, the narrator declares that ordinarily he would find the use of the word *mousmé* 'horripilant. À l'entendre on se sent le même mal de dents que si on a mis un trop gros morceau de glace dans sa bouche' (A II, 653). And yet in the context in which he actually hears the word used, he reacts rather differently. That is because the speaker who uses the word is Albertine, the young woman he met a while back in Balbec, and with whom he will now be becoming better acquainted, beginning with this encounter in his own room in his family's Parisian apartment.

Mousmé is only one bit of Albertine's speech whose social indexicality captures the narrator's attention in the scene in question. There is also her way of using the words *sélection* and *distingué*, and the phrases *à mon sens* and *j'estime*. The passage shows the narrator intensely focusing his attention on Albertine's word choices, in which one potential *bifur* after another crops up, until finally *mousmé* presents itself in all its glory. And yet the novel and the narrator seem for the most part to keep themselves on track during these pages. Indeed, for several pages running the narrator more or less refuses to be diverted. In fact, in this scene, his socio-linguistic analysis seems to run on the very same track as the events of the novel itself. That is, the analytic process is taking place in the mind of the narrator who is actually in the room with Albertine, rather than being some kind of more distanced reflection. The young narrator is deciding that based on the manner in which Albertine now speaks, she could never be a serious romantic interest for him, but she could be, to use an anachronism that would surely set his teeth on edge, a good occasional hook-up. That is, if certain aspects of her speech as he rediscovers it in this encounter (having first encountered it in Balbec during the summer of their initial acquaintance) reveal that she has been proceeding to develop as any number of young women from her respectable milieu would do, other details signal to the narrator that she has been up to no good, encountering language under all sorts of more suspicious circumstances as well, circumstances that suggest other sides to her personality. She has also been allowing strange, untoward bits of language from those mysterious circumstances to filter into her own socio-linguistic repertory and to serve there as signs of what she might be available for:

> Enfin m'apparut l'évidence de bouleversements que je ne connaissais pas, mais propres à autoriser pour moi toutes les espérances, quand Albertine me dit, avec satisfaction d'une personne dont l'opinion n'est pas indifférente:
>
> 'C'est, à mon sens, ce qui pouvait arriver de mieux.... J'estime que c'est la meilleure solution, la solution élégante.'
>
> C'était si nouveau, si visiblement une alluvion laissant soupçonner de si capricieux détours à travers des terrains jadis inconnus d'elle que, dès les mots 'à mon sens', j'attirai Albertine, et à 'j'estime' je l'assis sur mon lit. (A II, 651)

The narrator's social antennae seem decidedly odd in what they discover among all the signals in the world around him. What is there, in the use of these expressions that should mark some kind of sexual availability? An annoying but brief linguistic digression does ensue here: 'Sans doute il arrive que des femmes peu cultivées, épousant un homme fort lettré, reçoivent dans leur apport dotal de telles expressions [...].' But another kind of desire keeps drawing the text back on track:

> Comme, continuant à ajouter un nouvel anneau à la chaîne extérieure de propos sous laquelle je cachais mon désir intime, je parlais, tout en ayant maintenant Albertine au coin de mon lit, d'une des filles de la petite bande, plus menue que les autres, mais que je trouvais tout de même assez jolie: 'Oui, me répondit Albertine, elle a l'air d'une petite mousmé'. De toute évidence, quand j'avais connu Albertine, le mot de 'mousmé' lui était inconnu. Il est vraisemblable que, si les choses eussent suivi leur cours normal, elle ne l'eût jamais appris et je n'y aurais vu pour ma part aucun inconvénient, car nul n'est plus horripilant. (A II, 652–53)

Here, one might think that the tension between the two competing agendas of the novel (talk about patterns in language use vs. the possibility of engaging in some kind of intimate act with Albertine) has become so great that the novel is finally going to have to jump tracks.[14] (What kind of people would use the word *mousmé*? In what circumstances would they learn of the word's existence? What are the reasons why such people would be intrinsically so annoying to the narrator?) It will do so soon enough, but it holds itself together (so to speak) for a tiny bit longer.

> Mais chez Albertine, jolie comme elle était, même 'mousmé' ne pouvait m'être déplaisant. En revanche, il me parut révélateur sinon d'une initiation extérieure, au moins d'une évolution interne. Malheureusement, il était l'heure où il eût fallu que je lui dise au revoir si je voulais qu'elle rentrât à temps pour son dîner et aussi que je me levasse assez tôt pour le mien. C'était Françoise qui le préparait, elle n'aimait pas qu'il attendît et devait déjà trouver contraire à un des articles de son code qu'Albertine, en l'absence de mes parents, m'eût fait une visite aussi prolongée et qui allait tout mettre en retard. Mais devant 'mousmé' ces raisons tombèrent, et je me hâtai de dire:
>
> 'Imaginez-vous que je ne suis pas chatouilleux du tout, vous pourriez me chatouiller pendant une heure que je ne le sentirais même pas.
>
> — Vraiment!
>
> — Je vous assure.' (A II, 653)

Certainly the narrator's own speech oddities — the seeming non sequitur he allows himself in leaping from Albertine's *mousmé* to the possibility of her verifying the degree to which he is or is not ticklish — are as worthy of note as anything to be found in Albertine's speech, and surely she must be reading as much into his manner of speaking as he into hers, following along in this game in which the sexual availability of both parties has to be implied because it apparently cannot be stated explicitly. They both must be calculating their own speech turns in response to the moves they imagine the other to be making.[15] Françoise is about to enter the narrator's room without knocking in order to bring in a lamp, which will cause Albertine to leap from the bed to a chair, bringing their dalliance to a halt, if only temporarily. The interruption also seems to allow the novel, freed from the imperious force of the libido attached to the narrator's youthful self that had momentarily kept it on track, to resume its more typical zigzagged construction, through which forward progress, if and when it is made, happens at a pace that the word dilatory might just about capture.[16] ('Proust tries our patience so long as we expect his story to move forward', Clive Bell would write in 1928, 'that not being the direction in which it is intended to move'.[17]) A lot of ground (and nine or ten pages) will be covered before the two young people return to making out together on the bed.

Albertine, *mousmé*, and the narrator all go together then to form a complex kind of *bifur*. Who knows where things are going, except probably not where they seemed to be headed. 'Tout mot nouveau introduit dans la langue y cause une perturbation analogue à celle d'un être nouveau introduit dans le monde physique ou social', Bréal insisted (E 310). Albertine is like a word from another language for the narrator, as, perhaps, he must be for her. A bit later, Bréal adds, 'quand, pour une raison ou pour une autre, nous avons commencé d'adopter un terme nouveau, nous le gravons peu à peu dans notre mémoire, nous le rendons familier à nos organes, nous le faisons passer des régions réfléchies dans les régions spontanées de notre intelligence, de sorte qu'il en est de ce terme nouveau comme d'un geste qui, par la répétition, nous devient propre, et finit à la longue par faire partie de notre personne' (E 311). The process doesn't go so smoothly between the narrator and Albertine, of course. Indeed the fascination with *bifurs* so characteristic of both Proust's and Leiris's writing seems to go exactly in the opposite direction to the one suggested by Bréal, towards a disaggregation of the person, through a loss of both linguistic control and physical coordination. Leiris:

> En porte-à-faux entre présent et passé, entre imagination et souvenir, entre poésie et réalité, j'hésite, je louvoie, je titube, j'oscille et par moments je me sens bien près de perdre pied... Qu'est-ce à dire? Mon propos est, en lui-même, de retrouver des circonstances où toutes choses se situaient, soudain, en porte-à-faux et où je sentais que j'étais sur le point de perdre pied. (B 126)

Who knows, when Albertine said *mousmé*, how reality changed? Who knew that it was precisely the word she needed to say to make the narrator ask her to try to tickle him? He may have thought he was noticing in her speech a *fait de langage* characteristic of who she was, one that opened a door his desire was pushing him towards, and perhaps that was the case. But he is made of the same stuff, and perhaps he is caught up in a language game more than he can know or admit. In any case, what we can see is that Albertine reveals that the narrator too is *fait de langage* and that he should be, in Leiris's words, 'en état d'obscurément sentir [...] en quoi le langage articulé, tissu arachnéen de mes rapports avec les autres, me dépasse, poussant de tous côtés ses antennes mystérieuses' (B 12). That is, the narrator's analytical stance towards Albertine's speech finally cannot be understood solely as evidence of the novel's sustained attention to the social and anthropological dimensions of language use. Albertine's speech constitutes a space in which the narrator stumbles, oscillates, loses his footing, fails to be who he thinks he is, in which an analytic attitude towards language itself turns out to be unstable ground. Speaking with Albertine, for the narrator, is a sustained experience of what Leiris called *bifur*. It reveals linguistic interaction to be a space in which you are other to yourself because of the way, in language, you are with others.

Notes

1. Marcel Proust, *À la recherche du temps perdu*, 4 vols (Paris: Gallimard, Pléiade, 1987–88), III, 770. Subsequent references to this work will refer to this edition and will be given in the text, marked A.
2. Michel Bréal, *Essai de sémantique (science des significations)* (Paris: Hachette, 1897), p. 288. Subsequent references to this work will refer to this edition and will be given in the text, marked E.
3. Michael Sheringham, *French Autobiography: Devices and Desires: Rousseau to Perec* (Oxford: Clarendon Press, 1993), p. 246. Subsequent references to this work will refer to this edition and will be given in the text, marked F.
4. Michel Leiris, *Biffures* (Paris: Gallimard, 1948), p. 278. Subsequent references to this work will refer to this edition and will be given in the text, marked B.
5. See, for instance, chapter 3, 'Spoken Language', in Alison Winton, *Proust's Additions: The Making of 'A la recherche du temps perdu'* (Cambridge: Cambridge University Press, 1977). Winton comments that 'one of the most striking features of the post-1914 drafts of the novel is the extent

to which Proust added to, and discussed, peculiarities of his characters' language' (p. 126). See also Marcel Proust, *Carnets*, ed. by Florence Callu and Antoine Compagnon (Paris: Gallimard, 2002).

6. Proust, *Carnets*, p. 409.
7. Jean-Yves Tadié refers to Bréal as Proust's 'cousin'. (See Tadié, *Marcel Proust: A Life*, trans. by Euan Cameron (New York: Penguin Books, 2000), p. 300.) As best I can tell, the relation between the two was quite distant and indirect: Bréal's wife's sister's daughter had married a man who was the son of the sister of Proust's maternal grandmother. Proust's correspondence reveals both that he was a reader of Bréal and that his family and the Bréal family to a certain extent moved within the same social circles.
8. Cf. Michael Lucey, 'Proust and Language-in-Use', *Novel: A Forum on Fiction*, 48.2 (2015), 261–79.
9. 'Me référant au terme de 'bifur' [...] j'entendais mettre plutôt l'accent sur l'acte même de bifurquer, de dévier, comme fait le train qui modifie sa direction selon ce que lui commande l'aiguille et comme fait la pensée, engagée quelquefois, par les rails du langage, dans on ne sait trop quoi de vertigineux ou d'aveuglant et entraînée dans un mouvement qui pourrait être baptisé tout aussi bien biffure, car on perçoit ici une équivoque, un loup sur lequel on revient, comme cela se produit dans le cas d'un lapsus (sitôt lâché et sitôt raturé) à l'instant qu'on se dit 'c'est ma langue qui a fourché', ma langue qui s'est fourvoyée, à une fourche de routes ou croisée de chemins' (B 279).
10. Ferdinand de Saussure, *Cours de linguistique générale*, ed. by Tullio de Mauro (Paris: Payot, 1987), p. 30.
11. Michael Silverstein, 'Shifters, Linguistic Categories, and Cultural Description', in *Meaning in Anthropology*, ed. by Keith H. Basso and Henry A. Selby (Albuquerque: University of New Mexico Press, 1976), p. 53.
12. See Proust, *Carnets*, p. 403.
13. As Malcolm Bowie put it, it 'brings an exotic micro-climate with it [...]. When used by Albertine it connotes not simply the Orient but the tantalising cross-currents of homo-erotic feeling that are in play among Albertine's female friends. A woman looks at another woman, renames her, and is overheard by an excitable male' (Bowie, *Proust Among the Stars* (New York: Columbia University Press, 1998), p. 222).
14. It feels rather like one of those moments in a Looney Tunes cartoon where a character's legs are increasingly and impossibly split on two vehicles that are rapidly diverging, threatening the (fortunately) animated character with some kind of irrevocable corporeal split. Cf. 'Box Car Blues' at around 3:49: <http://looneytunes.wikia.com/wiki/Box_Car_Blues?file=Bosko_-_Box_Car_Blues.>
15. See, for instance, the way Jacqueline Rose recounts this scene from Albertine's point of view in her novel *Albertine* (London: Vintage, 2002), pp. 44–52.
16. 'Si lent est mon clopinement de piéton, à travers le maquis de phrases où il pourrait sembler que je me promène moi aussi' (B 81) observes Leiris as he prepares to introduce Michel Bréal into his labyrinth.
17. Cited in Leighton Hodson, ed., *Marcel Proust: The Critical Heritage* (London: Routledge, 1989), p. 382.

— 21 —

Bref

— des nouvelles d'aujourd'hui —

Pierre Alferi

Écartelée entre les tâches parallèles, fracassée par la multiplication des écrans, distraite par les sollicitations incessantes du commerce, morcelée par les déplacements urbains, notre attention a de plus en plus de mal à se fixer sur des objets littéraires, fussent-ils narratifs. À espionner le lectorat du métro, on croirait que seuls fonctionnent encore le *suspense* addictif et l'immersion glaciale promis par les pavés policiers anglo-saxons ou scandinaves. Ce serait ignorer les nouveaux modes de lecture, dont les supports n'alourdissent pas les sacs. Sur les ordinateurs portables, les tablettes, les liseuses, les *smartphones*, la mode est aux micro-récits, aux *flash fictions*, à la *tweeterature*. Diffusées par des sites (tel le germanophone *Kurzgeschichten*), des revues en ligne, des *newsletters*, objets de concours, échangées au sein de communautés semi-privées (par envoi quotidien aux abonnés, par exemple, pour *365tomorrows : A New Free Flash Fiction Scifi Story Every Day*), explorant tous les genres — de la fable à la science-fiction — , ces formes brèves sont adaptées aux formats nouveaux de la communication écrite, comme les cent-quarante caractères de *Twitter*, le *sms*, le *mail*, le *blog*. Certains critiques, notamment en Amérique latine, y voient même la « manifestation littéraire la plus caractéristique du XXIème siècle. » Sont-elles pour autant nouvelles *en tant que* formes narratives? Quels sont leurs modèles? Quelle est leur généalogie? Que nous dit leur succès sur ce qui est, aujourd'hui, attendu d'un récit? Sur ce qui pour nous fait événement, mérite d'être conté? Ces historiettes et leur manière de tourner court offrent-elles à l'art du récit la chance d'un renouveau à la mesure de la révolution numérique en cours? Ou ne sont-elles que la poussière en quoi tombent les formes éculées de la fiction narrative, ses pires poncifs, une littérature de gare insignifiante vouée à s'autodétruire comme les messages de *Snapchat?* Telles sont les questions sur lesquelles je voudrais, aujourd'hui, nous inviter à réfléchir.

Si la littérature devait un jour disparaître pulvérisée à force d'avoir voulu faire court, son histoire formerait une étrange boucle. Car elle a commencé aussi par le très bref : par le lapidaire, dans la pierre. Les micro-récits éphémères lancés sur les réseaux sociaux témoignent de la commodité de nos claviers de poche et de la rapidité d'une diffusion par mise en ligne sans conséquence. La brièveté des inscriptions millénaires que recueillent les épigraphistes trahit tout le contraire, à savoir la technique laborieuse du graveur sur pierre, le marteau, le ciseau, le poids sacré donné à chaque mot, la foi dans la surhumaine résistance de l'écrit au temps et à l'usure. Être bref, cela ne s'est jamais résumé à faire court. Dans la dédicace, la devise, l'épitaphe, la maxime ou l'oracle, il s'agit d'ellipse et de condensation, de vitesse et d'élégance, donc d'une économie dynamique du sens où prévaut sa tension interne. La *brevitas* latine est une vertu du discours, dont Quintilien donne une définition elle-même brève : « Ne pas en dire plus qu'il ne faut ». Elle est le pendant de la *copia*, ou « abondance », cette ressource de l'orateur à chaque instant mobilisable pour broder, enfiler les exemples et les lieux communs. Le commentaire profus des *Adages* par Érasme s'est posé en modèle savant et de l'une et de l'autre. La *brevitas* fait merveille dans le sarcasme, la charge des auteurs d'épigrammes, mais se rencontre aussi chez les meilleurs des historiens, au premier rang desquels le bien nommé Tacite. Néanmoins, même chez le conteur, elle s'exerce plutôt dans le domaine moral, dans le registre du jugement. Sentence ou oracle : le bref tranche.

De fait, les formes brèves ont dû beaucoup de leur fortune aux traditions de sagesse, puis aux moralistes. Des préceptes denses, ciselés, frappent l'imagination et se transmettent plus sûrement.

À bon chat, bon rat.
Pierre qui roule n'amasse pas mousse.

La tradition orale a une fonction conservatrice, et les proverbes qui en proviennent, ces « trous creusés par plusieurs générations de fourmis » (comme les appelle Baudelaire dans ses brèves *Fusées*), nous semblent souvent ternes comme des galets trop frottés, à peine moins plats que les dictons météorologiques. Il suffit pourtant d'en user dans une situation concrète, de les mouiller de notre salive, pour y voir briller l'un des éléments fondamentaux de ce que Jakobson nomme la « grammaire de la poésie » — le parallélisme, avec tous ses effets d'asymétrie — et pour voir chaque mot y déployer le large éventail des sens et des connotations sédimentées en lui. Longue est l'histoire des pensées brèves, qui de la *gnomè* grecque et de la *sententia* latine, par l'apophtegme du grand homme, le caractère du moraliste, va jusqu'à la maxime personnelle de Chamfort, au fragment philosophique du romantisme, à l'aphorisme nietzschéen. Longue, cette histoire est bien sûr traversée par des forces contraires. Ainsi la polysémie, la versatilité du proverbe et de la maxime, qui les rendent propres à tant d'usages, furent étouffées par les morales religieuses réactionnaires quand elles entreprirent de les amalgamer en un corps de doctrine placé sous une autorité divine. Dans le *Siracide*, *L'Imitation de Jésus-Christ*, les *Sourates* du Coran, les sentences deviennent lois, leur collection se fige, leur lecture est contrainte. On ne joue plus ; on apprend par cœur, on ânonne.

Mais le raidissement sclérotique du sens n'est pas la règle, il fait plutôt figure d'exception. Car la brièveté même des formules bien tournées et leur disparité poussent la pensée morale plutôt dans l'autre direction, celle de l'ouverture interprétative, dans les sagesses populaires comme dans l'éthique des moralistes. Au-dessus des recueils de sentences ou de pensées, c'est toujours une doctrine fantôme, aux contours incertains, qui plane. Bien avant Platon et Aristote, les Grecs s'échangeaient les formules d'une sagesse souple et prudente, attentive à l'occasion et au hasard, au *kaïros* et à la *tukè*. Et bien après l'établissement des dogmes monothéistes, les sentences des moralistes, dans leur savant désordre, faisaient appel à la sagacité de chaque lecteur/lectrice, sollicitaient son imagination. Leur dispersion faisait contrepoids à l'universalité péremptoire de chacune, comme s'il y avait autant de principes que de cas. Les recueils de ces formes brèves, ceux de La Rochefoucault, Vauvenargues ou Joubert, laissent à chacun le soin d'y tracer un parcours singulier. Leur morale est celle, adaptable, révisable, d'une conduite dans le monde. Comme dans de larges pans de la pensée aphoristique chinoise, elle engage une casuistique infinie et un art combinatoire sensible à « la nature prodigue des êtres individuellement différents » comme Chamfort nous en avertit dans l'*incipit* de ses *Maximes et pensées.* Et le même avouait : « Ce que j'ai appris, je ne le sais plus. Le peu que je sais encore, je l'ai deviné. » Dans le registre éthique et philosophique, les formes brèves semblent ainsi convenir davantage à une pensée clairsemée, comme en archipel. Leur densité, la courbe de leur trait, élancée, mémorable, se trouvent souvent précipitées de façon joueuse dans leurs derniers mots. On appelle cela une « pointe ». L'esthétique et l'éthique raffinées de la Renaissance en ont fait grand cas. Et la pointe, ce principe d'ingéniosité, où Baltasar Gracian voit l'art même du génie, relève bien d'une tension du sens, appliqué savamment mais ponctuellement au provisoire. Une certaine équivocité s'y maintient toujours.

Événement

Cette excursion loin de la fiction narrative d'aujourd'hui n'était pas un détour. Car celle-ci pratique, surtout quand elle est brève, quelque chose d'analogue à la pointe. Les « micro-fictions » de quelques lignes, voire quelques mots, s'attachent en effet, dans la très grande majorité des cas, à mettre en valeur l'événement qu'elles relatent en lui donnant un tour ironique ou paradoxal. Une pointe narrative, qui n'est plus une « figure de mots » mais une « figure de pensées » temporelles et causales, répond à la pointe rhétorique des sentences.

« Aujourd'hui, mon téléphone est foutu, ma cheville est en miettes et ma nuque est bloquée. Aujourd'hui, j'ai marché sur mon chat en descendant les escaliers. VDM (un micro-récit sur l'application Vie De Merde). »

« La lune se levait quand le monstre d'acier bleu s'ébranla, agitant ses longues pinces haut devant lui. Il détruisit plusieurs tours et immeubles. Un feu se déclara. La ville s'empourpra, belle comme sous un coucher de soleil. Encore un idéaliste qui veut attraper la lune, pensai-je. (Prix Pépin d'Or 2009.) »

Les sites et revues consacrés aux récits très brefs se réclament volontiers du Félix Fénéon des *Nouvelles en trois lignes* ou de la célèbre nouvelle en six mots d'Hemingway — *À vendre : chaussures de bébé, jamais portées.* Hélas, ni les récits de *tweeterature* ni les nouvelles en six mots qu'il ma été donné de lire sur leurs sites officiels ne se hissent jamais à la hauteur de ces modèles, pourtant modestes. À force de vouloir à tout prix tourner court ingénieusement, ces mini-nouvelles se précipitent vers leur fin, laquelle absorbe tout. Dans son peu d'espace respirable, l'écriture, squelettique, se résume à un art de la chute vite assommant. Quoi qu'en disent les promoteurs exaltés des sites dédiés à cette miniaturisation narrative, les textes qu'un bon éditeur publierait y sont rares, plus rares encore les véritables réussites. Certes, il arrive qu'un auteur expérimenté parvienne à tirer quelque chose d'une contrainte spatiale si drastique. Par exemple Bruce Sterling, pour l'anthologie de science-fiction du magazine *Wired :*

Rester humain coûtait trop cher

Mais ces « nouvelles formes brèves » m'apparaissent, pour le moment, surtout comme le refuge des fantasmes un peu puérils, des poétismes un peu niais et des blagues un peu lourdes qui ailleurs ne passeraient pas.

Les effets de la « tournure courte » dans le récit ne sont donc pas seulement comparables à ceux de la *brevitas* dans le registre moral. Ils en sont souvent la caricature. Ainsi les micro-fictions, obnubilées par la pointe, cèdent en général à l'attrait d'une chute facile, au risque de ne laisser que le souvenir d'une plaisanterie. Dans les meilleurs des cas, elles intègrent en réduction les dispositifs narratifs classiques de la nouvelle et de l'anecdote. La *short-short story*, dite aussi *flash fiction* (ou encore *smokelong story*), d'une ou deux pages, n'est d'ailleurs qu'une nouvelle brève ou une anecdote, comme il en existe au moins depuis le début du XXème siècle. Ces deux formes, en fait vénérables, ont été définies, d'un point de vue esthétique et plus récemment statistique, par leur traitement de l'événement. Nommée par Boccace, pensée par Gœthe, disséquée par Robert Petsch, la nouvelle narre un seul événement par une suite de quelques scènes. L'anecdote, justifiée à l'origine par la célébrité de son protagoniste, désigne aujourd'hui tout traitement d'un événement en une seule scène. Le défi narratif des formes brèves apparentées est de maintenir la vraisemblance d'un déroulement — sa *probabilitas* — à une échelle réduite. Les inconvénients de celle-ci, notamment pour le déploiement d'un quelconque art verbal, sont compensées, comme l'avait bien expliqué Poe, par l'unité d'attention et donc d'impression, dans une quasi-simultanéité de tous les éléments.

Mais de quel « événement unique » s'agit-il au juste? Qu'est-ce qui mérite d'être conté, fût-ce en seulement trois lignes? Nos vieilles traditions narratives, en littérature comme ailleurs, limitent considérablement le champ de l'événement : il s'agit pour elles d'une action humaine, de préférence extraordinaire, toujours édifiante en un sens ou un autre, et qui, le plus souvent, triomphe des obstacles. Dans le dispositif de base qui découle de cette restriction, le début crée l'attente que la fin seule comblera, il pose une question dont il diffère la réponse. Aux deux tiers du récit, l'épreuve ou la contradiction produisent une rupture d'équilibre, un basculement, un renversement de situation (*Wendepunkt*). Et cette péripétie centrale — l'événement décisif, unique dans le cas de la nouvelle ou de l'anecdote — aboutit à la résolution du conflit, par le succès (beaucoup plus rarement l'échec) des héros. Ce schéma, pour idiot qu'il soit — et les docteurs en *storytelling* en proposent trente-six variantes, divisées en trois, cinq ou sept étapes, déclinées en genres de conflits ou intrigues de base — se retrouve en effet partout. Quoique tous les récits littéraires dignes d'être lus s'en écartent, quand ils ne lui tournent pas le dos, il continue de structurer la grande majorité des récits publiés, longs et brefs. Plus que le détail de sa construction, qui n'intéresse guère que les scénaristes, la conception de l'événement qu'il suppose mérite d'être interrogée. Action humaine, donc, insolite, pleine d'enseignement, mais qui, pour donner lieu à péripétie et à dénouement, doit strictement obéir aux lois de la causalité, à la continuité linéaire du temps. L'événement n'est qu'un maillon de plus, un peu plus saillant que les autres, dans la chaîne d'airain des causes et des moments. La « pointe » narrative qui l'agrémente enfin est une ironie matérielle qui s'est logée en lui : un retour de bâton — tel est pris qui croyait prendre — , ou un effet pervers, une inversion des rôles ou un acte contreproductif.

Or nos *flash fictions*, nouvelles ou anecdotes, reposent dans leur immense majorité sur cette préconception de l'événement, cette surévaluation de l'action humaine, ce causalisme obtus. Le plus souvent, loin de favoriser l'expérimentation, leur brièveté expose le vieux squelette davantage que les gros romans, qui en multipliant les intrigues secondaires font un peu oublier la stéréotypie de leur logique narrative. Voilà pourquoi, sans doute, lorsqu'on lit des récits brefs en ligne sur les sites qui ont fleuri depuis une décennie, la sidération que leur chute cherche à produire a quelque chose de machinal : la pointe en est trop émoussée.

Attentat

C'était pourtant tout autre chose que les *Nouvelles en trois lignes* de Félix Fénéon laissaient espérer, entrevoir par la brèche qu'elles ouvraient dans la prose narrative. Rien de moins qu'un nouvel art du récit dont le bref serait le levier, voire, selon son ami Mallarmé, le « détonateur ». Il s'agit en effet d'un moment explosif, suivi de près par ce que j'appellerai une *césure anarchiste* dans l'histoire des proses brèves. En 1892, à la suite de banales échauffourées entre militants et policiers à Clichy, la première vague d'attentats qu'elle ait connu stupéfia l'Europe. Le poseur de bombes Ravachol fut arrêté et mis à mort en juillet de la même année. L'année suivante, ce fut le tour de Vaillant, qui en avait mis une à la Chambre des Députés. Encore un an, et un anarchiste italien de dix-neuf ans poignarda le président de la République Sadi Carnot, qui avait eu le tort de ne pas gracier Vaillant. (Le manche de son arme était rouge et noir.) On sait que de cette période, close avec les deux dynamitages de la bande à Bonnot par la police en 1913, date la naissance d'une incarnation du démon qui n'a rien perdu de son aura fantasmatique : le « terroriste ». On sait moins que l'anarchisme fut alors en vogue dans une large frange des milieux littéraires et artistiques, celle-là même où naîtraient les avant-gardes du vingtième siècle. Il y eut à son égard des sympathies publiques claironnées par des auteurs aussi divers qu'Oscar Wilde, Maurice Mæterlinck, Paul Verlaine, Octave Mirbeau, Émile Zola et même le peu progressiste Frédéric Mistral. *La Révolte*, revue anarchiste, attira des plumes prestigieuses au moment même où Laurent Tailhade commentait dans son supplément l'attentat contre la Chambre des Députés en des termes restés célèbres : « Qu'importe la victime si le geste est beau? » Sans doute cette mode littéraire fût-elle d'assez courte durée. Mais Uri Eisenzweig a montré de façon convaincante, dans le chapitre intitulé « Poétique de la bombe » de son remarquable *Fictions de l'anarchisme*, qu'elle n'a pas gagné les esprits *en dépit* de ces attentats meurtriers, mais bien *en raison* de leur survenue. Elle n'a jamais été plus forte, en effet, qu'au comble de leur violence, autour de mars 1892. Comment l'expliquer?

Quand elles étaient profondes, ces sympathies allaient de pair avec des choix esthétiques radicaux. Fénéon réinventa le récit très bref en traitant le fait divers comme un météore, une petite explosion imprévisible et sans suite. Les *Nouvelles en trois lignes* publiées dans *Le Matin* sont en effet des merveilles de « prose émaciée ».

— *L'insolent soldat Aristide Catel, du 151e, singeait les gestes du gradé Rochesani. Le Conseil de Châlons l'emprisonne deux ans!* L'exiguïté stimule son inventivité dans la ponctuation expressive et le rythme. — *Comme les Lemoine, d'Asnières, devaient des termes, leur propriétaire coupa l'escalier : chute des enfants, — plusieurs mètres.*

Le fait divers devient chez lui un hiéroglyphe social : un signe frappant, figural, et qui demeure énigmatique. — *Une jeune femme s'est jetée dans la Seine, au pont de Saint-Cloud. Elle a dit son regret d'être repêchée, et a tu son nom.*

Les symbolistes furent des passionnés de faits divers. Comme Roland Barthes un siècle plus tard, ils y lisaient des « signes dont le sens reste incertain, [...] riches de déviations causales ». De cette fascination héritèrent André Gide, pour ses chroniques judiciaires, et Robert Musil, pour l'ouverture, littéralement accidentelle, de *L'Homme sans qualités.* Mais c'est bien Mallarmé, dans ses *Grands faits divers* de 1897, qui en livre la clé. S'il y déclare scandaleusement : « Allons droit à l'attentat futur », c'est que, tout comme le fait divers, l'attentat semble survenir hors causalité, tel un événement absolu. Il arrive n'importe où et n'importe quand, arbitrairement. Sa violence meurtrière le gêne — il avoue sa pitié pour les « badauds estropiés » — , mais il loue la lumière d'épiphanie, la clarté non causale qu'une bombe répand sur la ville. Dans un renversement de perspective qu'on peut juger idéaliste, le rejet implacable des lois sociales qu'exprime l'attentat anarchiste n'est pour lui qu'une image du rejet des conventions esthétiques sur lequel se fonde sa pratique. Pour l'auteur de proses brèves qu'il fut aussi, ce rejet est précisément celui du récit causaliste, héroïque ou naturaliste, à visée morale ; rejet de la représentation, en art comme en politique, du roman et de ce qu'il appelait ses « rédactions ». Assez de la *mimésis* romanesque, de ces narrations linéaires et de ces descriptions léchées qui sentent l'Histoire-Géographie! Place à l'événement, à l'événement pur!

Pas d'histoire

Mon hypothèse est que le nouvel art du récit bref, né dans cette violente césure (ou cette césarienne) du terrorisme anarchiste, est un art du *non sequitur*, de la narration d'événements sans cause et sans finalité. L'œuvre de Fénéon n'en fut que l'embryon. S'affranchir à la fois de toute croyance étiologique et de toute visée morale sera toujours, assurément, une gageure — presque une folie. C'est s'interdire l'histoire. « Il n'y a pas d'histoire. Il n'y en a jamais eu. Il n'y a que des situations, sans début, sans milieu, et sans fin. » Ce mot de Jean Epstein, toutes les avant-gardes artistiques du XXème siècle, ou presque, l'ont pourtant fait leur. Elles ont été, toutes ou presque, anti-roman. Cela ne l'a pas beaucoup dérangé, le roman, toujours prêt qu'il est à repartir *comme en quarante.* Mais, si les avant-gardes furent pour le moins méfiantes à l'égard des longs récits continus, c'est qu'elles ont pris la mesure, mieux que l'ensemble de la société, du caractère traumatique et syncopé de l'expérience historique propre au XXème siècle dès sa deuxième décennie, où le signe du désastre fut donné par un attentat. La téléologie, lueur au bout du corridor à suivre, s'éteint quand la relation d'un événement ne se soucie plus de transmettre une expérience profitable. Or « l'expérience », remarquait Walter Benjamin en 1933, « a subi une chute de valeur, et cela s'est produit à une génération qui, entre 1914 et 1918, a fait l'une des expériences les plus monstrueuses de l'histoire universelle. »

Quoiqu'elles prennent l'air de fables, il n'est rien de moins édifiant que les nouvelles de Kafka, sinon peut-être les *prosettes* de Walser, dont Benjamin sentit sur-le-champ le caractère convalescent, voire post-traumatique. Rien de moins romanesque, sauf à les dissoudre comme il s'y efforça ensuite, que les *Épiphanies* écrites par Joyce dans les premières années du siècle pour narrer l'avènement d'une conscience dans la concaténation violente de sensations et de pensées qui affluent simultanément. L'absence de finalité devint même une revendication dans les *Nouvelles et textes pour rien*, puis les petites proses tardives de Beckett. Ces formes brèves inouïes ont, du point de vue du sens, les deux caractères apparemment contraires que Barthes a distingués dans le *haïku*, et son cousin narratif qu'il nomme l'*incident :* elles sont immédiatement claires, mais elles suspendent le « sens », au sens élevé de l'importance significative et de la finalité. En soulignant l'aspect dérisoire de leur argument, elles pratiquent une *épokhè*, une mise hors circuit du sens attendu. Ce sont, à en croire Barthes, des formes anti-allégoriques.

Pour mettre à nu l'événement, il ne suffit pas d'éteindre la finalité au-dessus de lui. Il faut encore court-circuiter la causalité — toujours partielle ou sinueuse — qui, en lui donnant l'apparence de la nécessité, nous donne l'illusion qu'il était prévisible. La dérive, la digression, voire la divagation de Charles-Albert Cingria s'y emploient, comme celles que pratiquèrent ses devanciers fantasques, adeptes de longues promenades et de discussions à bâtons rompus avec des inconnus : Dorothy Wordsworth, Thomas de Quincey. Chaque *Air du mois* de quelques pages confié par Cingria à la *Nouvelle Revue Française* prenait de vitesse la logique narrative. Il sautait — à vélo, souvent — d'une heure, d'un sujet, d'un incident à l'autre avec une grâce et une simplicité confondantes. Parfois, le véritable événement du récit avait eu lieu hors-champ, dans le hiatus entre deux phrases, et l'on y assistait rétrospectivement, après un coup de frein tournant. De façon beaucoup plus savante, acrobatique et ostensible, Antonio Pizzuto alla déloger les chevilles causales de la langue elle-même dans les très courtes proses hyper-denses auxquelles il consacra la fin de sa vie. De ses *Pagelles* et *Paginettes* d'un bloc ont progressivement disparu conjonctions, articles et verbes conjugués, faisant place nette pour une scène explosive, où objets, personnes et actions sur un pied d'égalité se percutent et se répercutent.

Ces accélérations, ces compressions, ces interruptions intrépides sont peut-être les « attentats futurs » rêvés par Mallarmé. À la différence des bombes anarchistes, elles n'ont pas fait sensation ; beaucoup encore, dans le champ littéraire, ignorent leur existence. C'est aussi qu'elles ont relaté des événements peu mémorables. Le canari est mort dans sa cage. Un garçon a offert à sa voisine un kaki. Il a plu trois jours d'affilée. Déjà, dans les « haïkus en prose » de Soseki, comme ensuite dans les *Récits de la paume de la main* de Kawabata, l'événement, sans intérêt du point de vue moral ou causal, n'était même plus paré des atours de l'extraordinaire ou de l'important.

Car il arrive dans la vie quotidienne. Il y est au secret. Il passe, comme tout ce qui s'y passe, incognito, sauf aux yeux des rares romanciers, comme Emmanuel Bove ou Henry Green, qui se montrent vraiment curieux des petits faits banals. D'un abord décevant, ils sont peut-être le secret inestimable du quotidien, ce que Georges Perec appelait l'« infra-ordinaire ». Infime, discret, dérisoire, quelque chose, inaperçu, ou bien diffus — quelque chose est arrivé. Un avènement propre à chacun et à personne — *Ereignis* — , commun à tous.

On dirait cependant que ces déflagrations muettes ont eu des retombées chez les meilleurs auteurs populaires de fictions courtes depuis les années cinquante. Chez Salinger, dans toutes ses rencontres fortuites avec des enfants. Chez Carver, dans ses scènes de ménage sans charme. Chez Brautigan, lorsqu'il agglutine de minuscules péripéties grâce au liant arbitraire et poisseux du *Sucre de pastèque.* Ces exemples sont rares, et déjà anciens. Un peu plus récemment, un livre sous-estimé de Michelle Grangaud cousait plusieurs centaines de micro-événements bouleversants, de gestes qui devenait une *Geste*, une épopée du quotidien. Mais il est resté un hapax.

La présence très minoritaire de ces récits non dénoués, non résolus, au sein de la *flash fiction* contemporaine me conduit à poser, pour finir, deux questions. La première est un peu angoissée. Où sont les nouvelles d'aujourd'hui? Où sont les textes « tournés court » qui tiennent ce pari de l'événement mis à nu, dépouillé de son vieux prestige héroïque, reproduit hors de tout enchaînement fatal et de toute leçon de morale? Il ne vous aura pas échappé qu'à mesure que l'idée de cette *nouvelle d'aujourd'hui* se précise, sa distinction d'avec le poème en prose s'amenuise. Certes, elle ne peut plus, ne doit plus être allégorique à la façon des poèmes en prose de *Gaspard de la Nuit* ou du *Spleen de Paris.* Certes, il s'agirait avant tout, et encore, d'un récit, quitte à trahir Maurice Blanchot, qui terminait le sien, le dernier, par ces mots : « Un récit? Non. Pas de récit. Plus jamais. » Mais je crois que, pour l'essentiel, et pour la poésie et pour le récit, la séparation générique entre fiction très brève et poème en prose est inopérante, voire nocive. Certaines jeunes revues, comme *Double Room*, en travaillant activement à l'effacer, suscitent des textes plus stimulants que toutes les *smokelong stories* qui peaufinent vainement leur intrigue et leur chute. Les nouvelles d'aujourd'hui se trouvent plutôt dans des formes incertaines, hybrides ou déchirées, que dans des miniatures de romans scénarisées et calibrées pour les réseaux sociaux.

Ma seconde et dernière question concerne l'enchaînement, la mise en série de ces très courts récits — leur *fix-up*, comme on dit sur les sites de *flash fiction.* Elle est évidemment moins grave. Faire un livre, composer un recueil, ce n'est en aucun cas vital. Par définition, pour le bref les supports possibles abondent. Postés, lancés sur Internet, cohabitant dans des revues, lus à haute voix en moins de temps qu'il n'en faut pour fumer une cigarette, ils peuvent revendiquer leur légèreté pour entretenir la « pensivité évanescente » caractéristique, selon une spécialiste, des lecteurs et lectrices du métro. Leur assemblage peut néanmoins produire une forme, c'est-à-dire une expérience, nouvelles. De la juxtaposition de brèves narrations autonomes résulte une complexité non systématique que sollicitent l'imagination et la pensée. Les recueils de nouvelles classiques promettent un genre d'unité symbolique ou thématique. Mais d'autres collections peuvent esquisser un paysage, fresque ou bien mosaïque, un puzzle, un tissu plus ou moins serré, une constellation, une structure fractale ou réticulaire ; la carte, enfin, d'un monde où l'événement a lieu partout sans crier gare, où le *suspense* a cédé le pas au suspens du présent. La paradoxie de telles tortueuses fantaisies, quelqu'un en a eu le pressentiment exact il y a presque cent cinquante ans. C'est Baudelaire, dans la dédicace du *Spleen de Paris :*

> Mon cher ami, je vous envoie un petit ouvrage dont on ne pourrait pas dire, sans injustice, qu'il n'a ni queue ni tête, puisque tout, au contraire, y est à la fois tête et queue, alternativement et réciproquement. Considérez, je vous prie, quelles admirables commodités cette combinaison nous offre à tous, à vous, à moi et au lecteur. Nous pouvons couper où nous voulons, moi ma rêverie, vous le manuscrit, le lecteur sa lecture ; car je ne suspends pas la volonté rétive de celui-ci au fil interminable d'une intrigue superflue. Enlevez une vertèbre, et les deux morceaux de cette tortueuse fantaisie se rejoindront sans peine. Hachez-la en nombreux fragments, et vous verrez que chacun peut exister à part. Dans l'espérance que quelques-uns de ces tronçons seront assez vivants pour vous plaire et vous amuser, j'ose vous dédier le serpent tout entier.

— 22 —

Le 'Hasard heureux' du contemporain: réflexions sur l'étude de la littérature au présent

Laurent Demanze

> C'est dire qu'il faudra un hasard heureux, une chance exceptionnelle, pour que nous notions justement, dans la réalité présente ce qui aura le plus d'intérêt pour l'historien à venir.
>
> Henri Bergson

L'étude de la littérature contemporaine à l'université est désormais pleinement institutionnalisée: colloques, essais et thèses le prouvent. Et cela, au point que l'étude du contemporain connaît aujourd'hui un tournant réflexif et méthodologique qu'il faut saluer: l'on s'occupe désormais d'en dresser l'archéologie comme peuvent le faire les travaux de Lionel Ruffel ou de Mathilde Barraband qui saisissent des inflexions dans les imaginaires du temps ou inscrivent le contemporain dans une histoire longue;[1] l'on s'attache aussi à étudier les processus de classicisation des auteurs contemporains et le vieillissement des corpus. Malgré quelques développements importants, il manque encore un véritable protocole méthodologique ou un essai réflexif pour qui s'attache à saisir ce que l'étude du contemporain bouleverse dans notre pensée de la recherche littéraire et quelles démarches élaborer pour composer avec la présence vive des écrivains et des œuvres en devenir. À la lecture des projets qui essaiment aujourd'hui, ce manque sera sans doute bientôt comblé: en attendant, les pages qui suivent voudraient esquisser quelques pistes de réflexion.

L'Université oscille, comme l'on sait, entre le conservatoire et le laboratoire, entre la transmission et l'invention. Le développement et la légitimation de l'étude du contemporain mettent sans nul doute l'accent sur les nouvelles perspectives du savoir, la constitution d'un champ inédit ou, pour emprunter le vocabulaire des sciences sociales, d'un terrain nouveau. Cependant, la proximité des auteurs, les interactions du critique et de l'écrivain, mais aussi l'instabilité d'une littérature encore en devenir ont souvent été perçues à la fois comme une aporie et un risque. Une aporie épistémologique d'abord, parce que, selon une formule récurrente, le présent rend myope: les valeurs sont encore mobiles et les arêtes des événements encore peu contrastées. En un mot, le temps n'a pas encore rendu son jugement. Mais l'on sait que ce jugement du temps ne cesse jamais d'évoluer et que ceux que nous hissons désormais dans notre panthéon ont connu des siècles d'anonymat, des périodes de latence et connaîtront des heures discrètes: c'est un jugement qui ne cesse d'être rendu d'année en année, se contestant et sapant son autorité à mesure. Un risque ensuite, parce qu'alors l'on craint de confondre l'écriture universitaire et la découverte journalistique, l'exercice d'une méthodologie ferme et la pratique d'une lecture mondaine. Car tout l'enjeu est bien celui-là: considérer les œuvres du présent avec les outils critiques, les savoirs universitaires qui ont fait leurs preuves sur les siècles précédents. Avec l'espoir que le langage universitaire se renouvelle au contact des œuvres d'aujourd'hui. Comme le rappelle Dominique Viart dans son article 'De la littérature contemporaine à l'Université: une question critique', la présence de la littérature d'aujourd'hui dans les amphithéâtres ne se fit pas sans de nombreuses réticences. Cette intégration prolonge, note-t-il, un plus ample mouvement marqué entre autres par la création d'un parcours spécifiquement consacré à l'étude des lettres modernes. Pourtant, continue le critique, '[c]ela ne signifiait pas seulement un changement de corpus, mais aussi un changement de méthode. La critique littéraire se découvrait alors de nouvelles pratiques autant que de nouveaux territoires.'[2]

La cartographie toujours à refaire de la littérature contemporaine devrait alors sans doute inviter à proposer de nouvelles expériences, à inventer de nouvelles méthodes, ou du moins et plus modestement à interroger les présupposés de notre pratique. Car travailler sur la littérature d'aujourd'hui amène à repenser les limites d'un corpus, les interactions de champ universitaire et la fabrique des valeurs. L'étude du contemporain gagnerait alors à dialoguer au plus près des autres sciences sociales pour y puiser des outils et des expériences comparables, de l'histoire du présent aux méthodologies de l'enquête et de l'entretien.

Historien du présent

La légitimation actuelle des études contemporaines doit sans doute beaucoup au goût du présent qui traverse l'époque, comme l'a montré François Hartog dans son essai, *Régimes d'historicité*:[3] il me semble important de toujours réinscrire les devenirs d'une discipline dans une histoire culturelle élargie pour saisir aussi de quoi ils sont le symptôme. L'étude de la littérature au présent n'est en effet pas sans analogie avec l'émergence presque simultanée de l'histoire du temps présent: il y a là une proximité d'objet et d'enjeux méthodologiques à approfondir. La revendication d'une histoire du présent est récente, et apparaît après l'essor des *Annales* qui privilégiait l'étude de la longue durée, pour proposer une histoire culturelle centrée sur des invariants, au détriment de l'histoire événementielle et politique. Elle date essentiellement du dernier quart du XXe siècle, et plus précisément de 1978 avec la création de l'Institut d'histoire du temps présent fondé par François Bédarida au sein du CNRS. Si cette pratique historiographique s'est développée institutionnellement depuis peu, il ne faut pourtant pas oublier qu'elle prolonge des préoccupations anciennes, puisque, dès l'émergence de l'histoire, Hérodote et Thucydide privilégiaient une historiographie du proche contre les récits colportés par la tradition.

Cette approche historiographique ne fut pas sans susciter réserves et prudences, tant elle soulève de nombreuses difficultés épistémologiques et heurte de front la passion du passé au cœur même de la démarche historienne. Car interroger le présent avec une démarche historienne invite à brouiller en permanence la distinction entre histoire et mémoire, à interroger l'inscription de l'observateur dans son champ d'étude et à poser en permanence la délimitation de son champ. En effet, l'histoire du temps présent ne dispose pas, à la différence des autres champs historiographiques, d'un territoire aux limites chronologiques fixées. La mobilité des bornes qui s'avancent en mesure en aval invitent à penser un découpage d'ordre conceptuel et problématique, davantage que chronologique.

Dans un entretien récent,[4] Henry Rousso soulignait au moins trois lieux conflictuels dans l'appréhension d'une histoire du présent: l'obstacle du délai de réserve, le changement des sources historiographiques et l'inachèvement de l'histoire. D'abord, sources et archives ne sont pas immédiatement à la disposition des chercheurs, car l'État maintient un délai de réserve avant de diffuser largement ou d'ouvrir au public les documents: il faut entre trente et soixante ans pour accéder aux documents les plus vifs de la mémoire nationale, entre protection de la vie privée et préservation de la cohésion nationale, entre secret intime et secret d'État, au point d'imposer aux historiens d'autres sources et d'autres modèles inquisitoriaux. Ensuite, à la différence de bien des périodes analysées, l'histoire du présent impose une grande hétérogénéité des sources documentaires: sans doute moins d'archives mais des témoignages audiovisuels, presse, sources informatiques et mémoire orale, qui nécessitent non seulement d'affiner les méthodologies pour maîtriser cette diversité hétérogène des sources, mais aussi de repenser en permanence l'articulation entre mémoire orale et histoire écrite, sans nécessairement penser ce passage de l'oral à l'écrit comme montée en objectivité. Enfin, et surtout, l'historien du présent se heurte essentiellement à l'inachèvement des événements historiques. Il faudrait, en effet, pour saisir l'histoire, un recul qui dépassionne les débats: parce que la signification des événements ne se donne à lire que dans l'après-coup lorsque l'oubli a accentué les arêtes des événements considérables, en jetant dans l'arrière-plan ce qui demeure secondaire. Une telle réticence manque cependant l'apparition des nombreuses sciences sociales — sociologie, science politique, économie — qui s'attachent à dire le présent, au milieu des acteurs essentiels non sans penser en permanence les interactions entre l'observateur et les objets de l'analyse, c'est-à-dire en posant la nécessité d'une réflexivité de l'acte interprétatif. Ce faisant, l'un des enjeux de l'histoire du présent, c'est de réintroduire la dimension temporelle dans les saisies du monde contemporain, en mettant en lumière les effets de rythme, les périodisations courtes ou latentes: elle rend l'observateur attentif à des durées infimes, à des phénomènes de cristallisation de l'événement comme à des résurgences du passé à travers la frénésie de l'immédiat .

Comme on le voit, les enjeux de l'histoire au présent ne sont pas sans secours pour l'étude du contemporain: on reconnaît dans ces trois lieux conflictuels, trois enjeux auxquels se confronte le chercheur sur le contemporain. D'abord, il s'agit de travailler *sur le vif*, sans délai de réserve, puisque le chercheur compose aussi avec des acteurs vivants: l'étude du contemporain incarne l'un des désirs essentiels du geste critique, comme l'a vigoureusement rappelé Jean Kaempfer, la rencontre d'une conscience et la compréhension d'une altérité.[5] Il faut du tact pour dialoguer avec cette épaisseur humaine et travailler avec la conscience des interactions entre le discours critique et la création même, d'autant plus quand un nombre important d'écrivains sont eux-mêmes enseignants et chercheurs. Ensuite, l'hétérogénéité des documents: le chercheur doit en effet apprendre à réinscrire le texte littéraire dans son champ, fait de réceptions journalistiques, d'entretiens, de festivals, de résidences, etc. L'analyse d'une parution doit de plus en plus s'ouvrir aux effets de traîne comme aux conditions de sa genèse, et pour cela le texte seul ne suffit pas: le critique sur le contemporain doit ouvrir l'œuvre sur son espace d'inscription, en constituant son terrain de recherche à partir d'une grande diversité documentaire — vidéos, sites web, correspondances, entretiens, etc. — . Enfin, l'étude du contemporain engage à saisir des œuvres en devenir, dont la réception et la légitimation sont en cours: cette saisie d'une littérature dans son devenir, et non pas académisée ou patrimonialisée invite, comme on le verra, à considérer des régimes de vérité distincts.

Des régimes de vérité différenciés

La formule, autrefois paradoxale, d'une histoire du présent conduit en effet à envisager une pluralité de vérités historiques. Soit la vérité historique est ce qui se donne dans le surgissement de l'événement, c'est-à-dire l'effraction subie ou dans l'effarement éprouvé par les témoins. Soit la vérité n'apparaît que lorsque la poussière de l'événement est retombée, que la violence des acteurs, et leur partialité, se sont apaisées et que l'on peut à loisir interroger causes profondes et déterminismes cachés. D'un côté, une vérité vécue au présent dans l'inconscience des raisons invisibles mais sous la force de ce qui arrive. De l'autre, une vérité vécue comme décantation, où le savoir ne vient que dans l'après-coup des émotions et des rivalités éteintes. Les romans de Stendhal ou de Claude Simon nous l'ont fait comprendre: la vérité d'une bataille est différente lorsqu'on la vit depuis le tumulte et la confusion du combat ou depuis le calme d'un état-major. Quelle vérité détient l'acteur, immergé dans la situation présente? La force de vérité du présent oscille en effet selon les perspectives: soit qu'on décrive le présent comme opacité de l'immédiat ou absence de recul aveuglant, soit qu'on le valorise comme participation même à l'événement et expérience vécue. Reste à décider si l'analyse d'une situation doit rendre compte du moment tel qu'il est vécu ou dans la distanciation du retrait, car ce que l'on gagne en objectivité et intelligibilité à mesure que l'on s'éloigne du présent, on le perd sans doute en capacité expressive ou en réactivité.

Sans l'expliciter clairement, celui qui travaille sur le présent a choisi un régime de vérité contre un autre: il travaille depuis une situation, avec ses aveuglements et ses revirements. Mais cette confusion avec laquelle et contre laquelle il travaille, il est faux de la croire moins vraie ou moins légitime, sauf à croire en une décantation des valeurs et des mérites, en somme en un tribunal de l'histoire, qui obéit à un modèle fort eschatologique. Car il n'est on le sait d'histoire que du présent, depuis un présent qui juge et analyse selon ses repères et ses valeurs: l'historiographie littéraire de demain ne sera qu'une historiographie élaborée depuis un autre présent, sans nécessairement détenir un savoir privilégié sur l'aujourd'hui. Étudier le contemporain, c'est, me semble-t-il, refuser de hiérarchiser ces régimes de vérité et revendiquer à l'inverse des perspectives multiples sur le présent, comme il convient d'étudier les œuvres du passé à la fois comme des moments de notre histoire littéraire et des événements qui eurent lieu dans un présent donné. La pluralité de ces régimes de vérité différenciés n'exempte pas pour autant de la recherche de la valeur, comme on le verra.

L'Œuvre en devenir, le texte à distance

Dans un article récent, Dominique Rabaté remarquait la coïncidence entre le développement des études sur la littérature contemporaine et la fin du mythe du corpus clos de l'œuvre littéraire. Si l'interdit a longtemps pesé de travailler sur la littérature vivante, c'est que l'œuvre était encore en gestation et dans un inachèvement fondamental qui battait en brèche la conception d'un corpus comme totalité organique et cohérente: 'L'idée classique qui dictait cet interdit de travailler sur un écrivain vivant était d'avoir accès à la totalité de l'œuvre [...].'[6] Le développement de la génétique textuelle, l'attention portée aux manuscrits, correspondances ou brouillons ont contribué à brouiller les limites de l'œuvre et à déplacer l'accent des études: le chercheur est habitué désormais à considérer une œuvre comme un processus en cours et en devenir, mais avec ses étapes et ses cristallisations, en somme comme un inachèvement figé.

Ce faisant, prendre en charge un texte contemporain, c'est l'inscrire dans une historicité, interne et externe, qui tend à lui restituer son étrangeté. En effet, l'un des écueils du contemporain est selon moi l'*illusion de proximité* qui efface les héritages discrets et atténue les déterminismes de champ. Le travail du chercheur consiste autant à proposer des lectures qu'à *fabriquer de l'éloignement et de l'altérité*, en brossant un contexte et en inscrivant l'œuvre dans une rythmicité plurielle. Si l'ambition des chercheurs en littérature sur les œuvres plus anciennes consiste souvent à souligner l'actualité, sinon la modernité, des textes du passé, celle du chercheur en littérature contemporaine est de travailler à dessiner des contrastes pour montrer comment une œuvre fait événement en déplaçant ses conditions de réception: il s'agit en somme de déjouer la naturalité de la réception d'une œuvre récente et de l'artificialiser. Sans doute est-ce une des différences majeures entre la critique universitaire et la critique journalistique, qui traite de ce qui nous entoure, de ce dont tout le monde parle et qui fait l'*actualité*. L'étude du contemporain peut bien alors revendiquer l'inactualité, comme le propose Giorgio Agamben,[7] mais c'est alors risquer de se retrancher derrière la posture du retrait ou le refus de l'actualité littéraire, pour mieux légitimer son discours et différencier ses méthodes du journalisme comme l'a montré Lionel Ruffel[8] dans un récent colloque. À défaut d'inactualité, la recherche sur le contemporain gagne à produire de l'étrangement pour reprendre ce vieux mot que Carlo Ginzburg a récemment remis au centre du débat historiographique[9] et à poser cette question que Jacques Derrida avait su nous faire entendre: de quoi, de qui sommes-nous les contemporains? Sommes-nous nos propres contemporains?

Valeurs et interprétations

Comme le souligne à très juste titre Dominique Vaugeois, un des fondements de l'herméneutique littéraire tient à la 'présomption de valeur'.[10] La minutie des lectures proposées ou la pertinence des outils sollicités sont garanties par l'autorité de l'écrivain, par la reconnaissance patrimoniale du texte étudié qui fondent sa richesse présumée. L'inscription de l'auteur dans un panthéon imaginaire de la littérature légitime l'hypothèse d'une herméneutique infinie ou d'un sens dernier à se tenir toujours en réserve: un reste qui résistera et relancera toujours le désir d'interprétation. En somme, la valeur présumée d'un auteur ou d'une œuvre permettrait d'asseoir la richesse des lectures: la patrimonialisation de l'œuvre permet le jeu aporétique des interprétations, l'inscription de l'œuvre dans le trésor des œuvres passées ouvre l'espace multiple des lectures présentes.

Mais cette aura de l'écrivain consacré qui fonde nos études littéraires n'est ni immédiate ni intangible: elle est pour une part importante la somme des réceptions et des lectures, le dépôt des interprétations successives que l'on a pu faire d'une œuvre. Il y a toute une histoire à écrire des processus de classicisation des auteurs,[11] selon les siècles et les écarts avec les esthétiques dominantes, en tenant compte des lieux de légitimation que sont l'université, l'école, la presse ou même les tribunaux: une histoire plurielle, différenciée et stratifiée. S'il est possible donc de fonder notre pratique de l'herméneutique littéraire sur une 'présomption de valeur', c'est que toute une durée a contribué à constituer une mémoire des œuvres et à composer une hiérarchie des auteurs. Cette sédimentation historique qui assoit la valeur des œuvres classiques a le mérite de légitimer les protocoles herméneutiques et de faire taire le doute sur les interprétations proposées, elle risque cependant de faire oublier le nécessaire soupçon sur nos pratiques, voire sur la valeur littéraire des textes étudiés: l'incertitude de la valeur d'une œuvre est peut-être un doute qui enrichit la lecture d'un texte, en rappelant que toute interprétation doit aussi être une évaluation et que la patrimonialisation d'un écrivain ne garantit pas nécessairement les lectures que nous proposons.

Je serais tenté de renverser la perspective et de considérer que c'est là l'une des forces paradoxales du travail universitaire sur la littérature d'aujourd'hui: travailler avec le soupçon permanent de l'illégitimité et de la fragilité de nos objets, de la caducité de nos méthodes. Il y a un risque du contemporain qui est aussi, il faut l'avouer, ce qui rend son étude passionnante: comme le note Dominique Viart, dans un fort article, '[e]ngager la recherche sur ce terrain, c'est entrer dans un risque que ne connaissent pas les spécialistes des siècles passés'.[12] Ce renversement des perspectives amènerait à considérer que la valeur d'un texte n'est pas un donné, stabilisé ou fixé, mais la sédimentation des interprétations successives et conflictuelles qui s'en saisissent. Étudier la littérature contemporaine à l'Université amènerait en quelque sorte à procéder à rebours, en suspendant la 'présomption de valeur' pour au contraire mettre à l'épreuve la valeur d'un texte *par* les possibles herméneutiques qu'il libère: non plus la valeur consacrée d'un texte comme caution légitimante des lectures, mais la force des lectures pour faire émerger la valeur. Un tel renversement amène évidemment à se confronter en permanence avec la fabrique de la valeur, ses enjeux et ses dispositifs. L'herméneutique littéraire a donc tout intérêt à s'adosser aux études sur la classicisation, en prenant plus fortement en charge les effets de champ: prix littéraires, présence médiatique, postures, etc. Même si une œuvre ne s'y résorbe pas, elle est aussi portée par un acteur vivant dans un champ et cela ne doit pas être minoré, au risque de reconduire des pensées de l'autonomie du texte en négligeant comment la littérature *se pratique*. Un tel renversement implique aussi l'exigence des lectures, même pour des œuvres consacrées, et l'engagement du chercheur à se risquer sur des auteurs encore peu travaillés.

Engagements littéraires

Étudier la littérature contemporaine, c'est pour l'essentiel élaborer un terrain d'étude: sélectionner un auteur, circonscrire une œuvre en cours en interrogeant sa cohérence, inscrire cette œuvre dans un devenir de l'histoire littéraire, contextualiser l'œuvre en tissant des affinités électives à travers le champ littéraire, comprendre les métamorphoses de cette œuvre et comment elle se débat avec elle-même ou à la recherche d'elle-même... Le chercheur sur le contemporain ne travaille donc pas sur un objet déjà constitué, mais sur un objet en permanence en cours d'émergence.

Il n'est pas en cela très différent des autres chercheurs sauf à considérer qu'il entre fréquemment en dialogue avec les écrivains sur lesquels il travaille et que ses travaux ne sont pas sans conséquence sur la légitimation ou la réception de ces écrivains. Il y a donc une double interaction avec le champ littéraire: une constitution dialoguée, voire dialogique, des œuvres d'une part, puisque écrivains et critiques sont le plus souvent en dialogue et il y a une légitimation des auteurs par leur présence dans un colloque ou un programme de séminaire. Le chercheur a donc pleinement conscience non seulement de *réfléchir* sur des œuvres en devenir, mais aussi d'*infléchir* par son regard même l'objet qu'il étudie. D'autres sciences se sont affrontées à ces interactions, au point de mettre en place des protocoles ou de poser les enjeux et les risques de ces interférences. La littérature contemporaine attend encore de telles réflexions: on pourrait alors s'interroger sur la place de la parole des écrivains contemporains dans le texte du critique, réfléchir au statut des entretiens ou encore attendre du critique qu'il inscrive de manière réflexive sa place dans l'étude qu'il propose, comme cela se pratique à l'intérieur de certaines sciences humaines. Ce tournant réflexif de l'étude du contemporain manque encore, et l'on aimerait qu'à défaut d'un manuel quelques articles du moins interrogent l'art de l'entretien universitaire dans ses multiples manifestations: séminaire, festival, rencontre en librairie, etc.

Le travail du critique n'est plus dès lors celui d'un observateur éloigné de son objet mais celui d'un acteur, impliqué dans les débats et plus largement dans la vie du champ littéraire. Il est peut-être juste alors que cette implication se traduise par des formes d'engagement littéraire, ou du moins avec la conscience d'une responsabilité envers son présent. Le critique est souvent amené à expliciter ses choix d'objets d'études, à être militant en faisant découvrir tel auteur encore peu connu, tel éditeur dont le travail exigeant mérite la reconnaissance. Et même si sa prise de position ne prend pas les formes d'une critique négative, défendue par exemple par Pierre Jourde,[13] le choix d'un objet suppose d'en écarter d'autres, d'en passer sous silence certains. Même si je reste souvent réservé sur la tonalité pamphlétaire de ses essais, je n'en suis pas moins convaincu que l'étude du contemporain gagnerait à être ici ou là plus sévère dans ses jugements, moins consensuelle aussi: elle est parfois trop engagée dans des enjeux institutionnels pour mettre à l'épreuve les textes qu'elle étudie. Travailler sur le contemporain, c'est en effet être au cœur de la fabrique des légitimités et des valeurs, mais ce doit aussi être l'assumer en pleine conscience: avec responsabilité.

Une légitimation problématique

Prendre acte de l'instabilité des valeurs et de la fragilité des hiérarchies, ce n'est pas pour autant renoncer au jugement esthétique, ou se retrancher derrière un relativisme sceptique. Car si les histoires littéraires connaissent des résurrections singulières et des séismes qui remodèlent les paysages, c'est d'abord parce qu'elles sont un processus en cours, jamais clos et sans cesse remis sur le métier. C'est ensuite le signe que les travaux du chercheur s'inscrivent dans cette historicité des jugements et des valorisations. Comme le remarque Dominique Rabaté, l'enseignant 'est obligé de réfléchir aux mécanismes de production de ces valeurs, aux phénomènes d'autorisation dans lesquels l'Université joue aussi un rôle.'[14]

L'historicité des procédures de légitimation engage à contextualiser le geste même du chercheur pour y déchiffrer les présupposés d'époque et les impensés culturels ou sociaux. Car les valeurs défendues par l'enseignant pourront être 'reçues comme des symptômes de l'époque où nous sommes engagés'[15] continue Dominique Rabaté. Le geste critique s'accompagne dès lors d'une critique des mécanismes de légitimation, et doit expliciter en permanence sa position, de manière réflexive et soupçonneuse envers son propre geste. Constituer en quelque sorte l'autoportrait de nos valeurs, le cadastre de nos goûts, cela n'a rien d'un repli subjectif, mais au contraire un moyen d'expliciter l'enquête littéraire menée et de mettre sa lecture en débat: il faut relire ici les développements connus sur la dialectique de la subjectivité et de l'objectivité qui ouvrent *L'Âge d'homme* de Michel Leiris. Reste à suivre la proposition récente d'Ivan Jablonka: instituer un je de méthode au sein même de nos textes critiques, c'est là un outil argumentatif plus qu'un aveu personnel.[16]

À cet égard, il est saisissant de constater combien la littérature contemporaine ne cesse de se saisir de ces légitimations problématiques pour faire trembler en permanence le grand roman de l'histoire littéraire, ou pour mettre en crise le tribunal du temps. On songe bien évidemment à Pascal Quignard qui s'attache à faire revivre les obscurs, à Pierre Michon qui de livre en livre joue du contraste concerté entre le désir de renommée des artistes et le hasard qui les élève ou les plonge dans l'oubli. Cette résurrection des oubliés et des mineurs est une ligne de force de la littérature contemporaine: songeons à Gilles Ortlieb dans *Des orphelins* ou encore à Stéphane Audeguy dans *L'Enfant du carnaval*, sans oublier les enquêtes de Didier Blonde. Tout se passe alors comme si l'époque contemporaine donnait à lire de manière réflexive par des figures détournées ses propres conditions de réception et les apories des jugements qu'elle rencontre. C'est que l'époque contemporaine a sans doute fait son deuil de la figure du grand écrivain, inoubliable et éternel, qu'on le célèbre à la façon hyperbolique et ironique de Pierre Michon,[17] ou qu'on le déplore dans une veine nostalgique.[18] Cette perte est sans doute bienheureuse, car elle engage paradoxalement à laisser ouvert le récit que l'on peut faire de la littérature actuelle, sans jamais le clore. Autant dire que la légitimation des œuvres et des écrivains doit être maintenue comme un processus critique problématique. L'on aurait tort de l'oublier maintenant que l'étude sur la littérature contemporaine est pleinement institutionnalisée. Ou pour le dire autrement, la légitimité problématique de ses objets et de sa démarche est sans doute l'une des singularités de l'étude du contemporain: elle demeure ouverte à l'incertain et au hasard, mais c'est un 'hasard heureux' pour reprendre la juste formule d'Henri Bergson.

Notes

1. Je renvoie notamment au programme de recherche que mène Lionel Ruffel au sein de l'IUF: 'Archéologie du contemporain: littérature, cultures, savoirs' et au projet de Mathilde Barraband sur les histoires littéraires du contemporain 'L'Histoire littéraire du contemporain', *Tangence*, 102 (2013), ed. by Mathilde Barraband. Voir aussi: 'L'histoire littéraire face à la création contemporaine', *RHLF*, 113 (2013).
2. Dominique Viart, 'De la littérature contemporaine à l'Université: une question critique', <http://www.fabula.org/atelier.php?De_la_litt%26eacute%3Brature_contemporaine_%26agrave%3B_l%27universit%26eacute%3B%3A_une_question_critique> [accessed October 2015].
3. François Hartog, *Régimes d'historicité: presentisme et expériences du temps* (Paris: Le Seuil, 2002).
4. Henry Rousso, *La Hantise du passé: entretien avec Philippe Petit* (Paris: Textuel, 2008).
5. Jean Kaempfer, 'Donation entre vifs: l'écrivain contemporain et le professeur de littérature', *Études de lettres*, 298 (2015), ed. by Vincent Verselle and Joël Zufferey, 'Les Échelles du texte', pp. 237–53.
6. Dominique Rabaté, 'Récit ou roman? Réflexions actuelles sur un débat français', in *Vous avez dit contemporain? Enseigner les écritures d'aujourd'hui*, ed. by Jean-Luc Bayard & Anne-Marie Mercier-Faivre (Saint-Étienne: Publications de l'Université de Saint-Étienne, 2007), p. 19.
7. Giorgio Agamben, *Qu'est-ce que le contemporain?* (Paris: Rivages, 2008).
8. Lionel Ruffel, 'Inactualité du contemporéanisme littéraire', in *L'Inactualité: la littérature est-elle de son temps?* ed. by Gilles Bonnet (Paris: Hermann, 2012), pp. 197–204.
9. Carlo Ginzburg, *À distance: neuf essais sur le point de vue en histoire* (Paris: Gallimard, 'Bibliothèque des Histoires', 2001).
10. Dominique Vaugeois, 'L'Université et l'évaluation de la littérature contemporaine', *Fabula*, *<http://www.fabula.org/atelier.php?L%27Universit%26eacute%3B_et_l%27%26eacute%3Bvaluation_de_la_litt%26eacute%3Brature_contemporaine>* [accessed October 2015].
11. On renvoie aux travaux de Marie-Odile André sur les mécanisme de classicisation et à la journée d'études organisée par Mathilde Barraband et Marie-Odile André: 'La littérature contemporaine à l'épreuve de sa réception universitaire: classicisation et vieillissement du contemporain', journée d'études à l'Université Paris 3, mars 2014, à paraître.
12. Dominique Viart, 'Au risque du contemporain: pour une critique des enjeux', *Les Temps modernes*, 672 (2013), 242–53 (p. 244).
13. Pierre Jourde, *La Littérature sans estomac* (Paris: L'Esprit des Péninsules, 2003).
14. Dominique Rabaté, p. 19.
15. Dominique Rabaté, p. 20.
16. Ivan Jablonka, *L'Histoire est une littérature contemporaine: manifeste pour les sciences sociales* (Paris: Seuil, 'La Librairie du XXIe siècle', 2014), p. 240.
17. Pierre Michon, *Trois auteurs* (Lagrasse: Verdier, 1996); *Corps du roi* (Lagrasse: Verdier, 2002).
18. Henri Raczymow, *La Mort du grand écrivain: essai sur la fin de la littérature* (Paris: Stock, 1994).

— 23 —

Prose between Stations

Patrick McGuinness

Things seen/heard from the top floor of the Brussels/Luxembourg Inter-City Express (only the train is fast — life inside and out takes place in some other zone of time, as thickly weightless as footage of an astronaut cooking breakfast between planets):

At Ciney a bull nonchalantly mounting a cow (this is outside the train) as the cow grazes on, pestling mouthfuls of grass with a slow swing of her jaw. She chews in time to his slack thrusts, each one hovering effortfully at the edges of itself, as if pulling into and out of velcro. This is the middle-distance, with neither the prestige of the faraway nor the imperiousness of foreground. The whole scene depends on the train's speed, which allows the traveller, forehead laid refreshingly against the glass, to pick it out with a distinctness and granularity that is at first disproportionate to its interest, but which quickly becomes its interest.

At Ottignies, students from Louvain-la-Neuve climb aboard with backpacks full of laundry for their mothers to wash: a journey of twenty minutes undertaken with a month of clothing. They are equipped to emigrate, but instead descend, as they always do, twenty minutes later, at Gembloux, where three workmen off the day shift at a zinc-plating factory step on and talk about their friend who hanged himself yesterday, the evening of the burial of his wife, dead last month of a pulmonary thrombosis.

At Namur three kindergarten teachers replace them seat for seat, discuss the school's Christmas decorations, affectionately mention a troublesome boy they like but whose life is in danger of going... (one of them searches for the right phrase, then with a little laugh gestures around her and says with a sort of embarrassed satisfaction:) *off the rails*, then settle down to comparing different brands of sleeping tablet with the discrimination and adjectival range of sommeliers discussing vintages.

The sky is a mild, uninsistent grey, streaked with oily-looking damp like those little cloths they put on headrests of armchairs in old people's homes.

This raw material thinks of all the contortions it would have to go through to become a poem, and decides to stay as it is: nondescript, if not undescribed.

— 24 —

Poet's Poetry

Michel Murat

On dit souvent 'poésie lyrique' sans trop savoir ce qu'on entend par là; l'habitude y pourvoit. Mais il faut s'arracher à cette paresse. J'essaierai donc de donner, au moins pour mon propre compte, et si outrecuidant que cela puisse paraître, une définition du genre lyrique en tant que tel. La perspective que j'adopte est structurale davantage qu'historique. C'est pourquoi j'entrerai en dialogue, dans les brèves remarques qui suivent, plutôt avec Jonathan Culler qu'avec Guido Mazzoni, dont l'impressionnante *Histoire de la poésie moderne* se situe sur un autre plan.[1]

Je considère comme acquis trois points préalables: que la poésie n'existe pas en soi mais qu'elle est une production culturelle et sociale, soumise à des conditions déterminantes et historiquement variables; que cependant elle présente une certaine constance dans le temps et une certaine stabilité dans ses formes, suffisantes pour qu'on puisse envisager d'en faire la théorie; qu'enfin la persistance du mot 'lyrique' dans la tradition occidentale constitue l'indice pragmatique de l'existence d'une configuration identifiable et spécifique — sous réserve d'une comparaison sérieuse, c'est-à-dire avec d'autres aires culturelles.[2]

Définir la poésie lyrique comme un genre, c'est proposer des critères la différenciant d'autres genres attestés de poésie (cette catégorie étant provisoirement conservée; il va de soi qu'elle n'a pas la même définition ni la même extension en 560 avant et en 1810 après Jésus Christ: mais c'est toujours le même nom qu'on lui donne, critère ici encore décisif). La configuration que sa récurrence impose comme environnement pertinent est celle de la grande 'triade': lyrique / épique / dramatique.[3] Les trois genres mobilisent les mêmes matériaux, savoir et fable. C'est par les modalités de la mise en œuvre qu'ils se distinguent.

Le genre de la poésie dramatique repose sur un élément distinctif, la scène en tant qu'institution sociale; sur cette scène se produisent des acteurs qui 'imitent' les actions des hommes. Aristote autonomise la *mimesis* autour de la construction du *mythos*, ce qui permet de dissocier la scène du rituel civique dont elle faisait partie. Mais quoi qu'en dise Florence Dupont,[4] il crée moins cette dissociation qu'il n'en prend acte: son geste rend la scène exportable ou transposable, il ne la supprime pas en tant que condition constitutive du genre dramatique; ce n'est pas une réduction littéraire.[5]

Le genre de la poésie épique repose sur l'institution d'une matière à transmettre. La Muse 'rappelle' un fonds d'histoires communes; la communauté est constituée par la connaissance partagée de ces histoires, que le poète actualise par son récit, en choisissant le motif autour duquel il organise les *res* (par exemple: la colère d'Achille, l'homme aux mille ruses) et en variant les détails. Le cas de la poésie didactique, d'Hésiode à Virgile, n'est pas très différent: le poète se définit dans les deux cas comme médiateur d'un savoir qu'il transmet ou d'une histoire qu'il raconte, et qui constitue à tous les sens du terme son sujet.

Qu'est-ce qui différencie la poésie lyrique? Négativement, c'est d'être un genre non mimétique, alors qu'épique et dramatique, comme l'ont affirmé aussi bien Aristote que Platon, ont en commun d'être des genres mimétiques. Positivement, c'est d'être ce que je nommerai la 'poésie du poète' (l'anglais est plus suggestif: *poet's poetry*). En d'autres termes, un genre dont l'élément définitoire est l'énonciation poétique, et non la matière qu'elle prend en charge (comme dans l'épique) ni le lieu où elle se produit (comme dans le dramatique — je dis 'lieu' pour simplifier). Apollinaire parlait d'orphisme ou de poésie orphique, et c'est bien en ce sens de 'poésie du poète' qu'il l'entendait. Il en résulte que la tâche première de ce genre est de constituer sa propre parole: je veux dire, de l'instituer et de la différencier. La parole lyrique se présuppose elle-même: plus précisément son *devoir* est de s'auto-réaliser avec une force (*enargeia*) suffisante pour être reconnue comme telle, c'est-à-dire pour que ses destinataires soient convaincus de la valeur et du bien-fondé de ses propres prétentions; cette conviction n'a rien de rationnel, elle agit sur les émotions, d'une manière qui lorsqu'elle est réussie (au sens pragmatique) est incompréhensible: en d'autres termes, comme un charme. C'est là que se trouve la fonction de la poésie lyrique: créer une communauté définie non par la co-présence au spectacle (comme le théâtre) ni par la co-possession d'un savoir et d'une mémoire que le poète actualise (comme l'épique), mais une communauté instituée par l'énonciation poétique elle-même, quelles que soient les conditions concrètes de l'interlocution (récitation ou lecture différée), et partageant un *monde*, celui que le poète 'fait' et dans lequel il nous introduit. La première utilité qui puisse être assignée à un tel acte est évidemment celle de la célébration: éloge, offrande.

Ce processus d'auto-réalisation peut s'accomplir dans le cadre d'un rituel ou constituer en soi une sorte de rituel. Dans ce cas le terme souvent employé de 'laïcisation' ne me paraît pas approprié: le rituel qu'est la poésie n'a pas à être considéré comme un 'supplément', un tenant-lieu d'une religion perdue, mais plutôt comme une religion d'un type particulier. C'était l'idée de Mallarmé, pour qui 'opérateur' ou 'desservant' ne sont pas des métaphores: la religion du Livre ne remplace rien, mais elle doit advenir.

Le poète n'est pas *moi* quand il dit *je*: tant qu'il parle, il occupe une position pleine, celle d'agent de la création continuée (à la manière du Dieu de Descartes). Mais cette action crée une position discursive qui peut être investie par la subjectivité, celle du destinateur aussi bien que du destinataire, les deux étant fonctionnellement liés et en rapport d'interdéfinition (comme le montre très bien la variation des pronoms dans 'Zone' d'Apollinaire). Il est inutile, dans ces conditions, de supposer quelque spécificité que ce soit du 'sujet lyrique'. Car ce sujet est la projection (virtuellement anthropomorphe) d'une structure: il n'en est ni le fondement ni la condition de possibilité.[6]

L'instance symbolique qui autorise le poète à revêtir sa majuscule peut varier:

elle peut être religieuse, sociale (c'est le cas des cours princières) ou purement traditionnelle (lorsque le poète s'autorise de la littérature). L'instanciation du Poète, son sacre ou son intronisation, se trouve à tous les bouts de la chaîne: présupposée par la prise de parole, alléguée par les invocations d'incipit, représentée de manière directe ou allégorique, produite comme effet par le discours poétique. Les scénarios varient en fonction des circonstances socio-historiques.

En voici un, qui me servira de transition: c'est une des *Illuminations* de Rimbaud, 'Royauté'. Je propose de lire ce texte comme une fable de l'avènement et de la destinée de la poésie lyrique dans un régime démocratique, celui de la 'place publique', c'est-à-dire de l'opinion. Comment être roi dans un régime démocratique? Le texte répond en mettant en scène une hiérogamie entre *je* (le poète) et *elle* (la poésie), qui reprend à son compte le *je*. La royauté, titre du poème, consiste dans la relation d'une pure volonté, sans détermination extérieure ('je veux qu'elle soit reine') à un effet constaté ('en effet ils furent rois'). Le poème suggère, avec l'image des 'jardins de palmes', une issue sacrificielle. On peut le lire comme une sublimation du statut de la bohême artiste, dont le livre de Nathalie Heinich sur *L'Elite artiste* expose les données sociologiques.[7]

* * * * *

Comment la parole lyrique se produit-elle en tant que monde? Comment produit-elle l'écart qui lui permet d'être ce qu'elle prétend, de *faire sa preuve?* Comment le poète peut-il bander l'arc d'Ulysse? C'est là que nous trouvons des procédés fondamentaux, ce qu'on peut appeler des structures d'auto-réalisation (je préfère ce terme à 'performativité' et à 'réflexivité', qui peuvent en être une conséquence). J'en décrirai quatre principales: l'apostrophe, la scansion, la figure, le parallélisme (au sens large de Jakobson), en m'appuyant sur les réflexions de Jonathan Culler et le livre de Northrop Frye, *Anatomy of Criticism*.[8]

L'Apostrophe

Jonathan Culler a depuis longtemps, et magnifiquement, montré la place centrale de l'apostrophe.[9] On peut y voir un procédé primordial en tant qu'elle pose par convention (*thesei*) l'espace d'interlocution, et qualifie le poète par contrecoup, comme celui qui produit une telle adresse (au 'Vent d'Ouest', par exemple, dans l'*Ode to the West Wind* de Shelley). Par rapport à la prise de parole, au *je* énonciateur, elle a la propriété de mettre en place de manière dynamique l'espace de l'interlocution en allant directement au pôle le plus éloigné, et le cas échéant en impliquant le sujet dans la structure elle-même sans qu'il apparaisse au niveau de surface. Je partage entièrement les analyses de Jonathan Culler sur l'invocation comme figure de la vocation (figure instituante ou qualifiante du poète), sur sa prétention à faire événement (qui peut être déniée ou contestée de l'intérieur).

En revanche la fictionnalité qu'il considère comme inhérente à cet acte, et qu'il exemplifie en retenant exclusivement les cas où le poète s'adresse à des 'objets inanimés' ('O Temps', 'ma douleur') et de préférence pour leur intimer de faire ce que par nature ils font ('souffle, ô vent', etc.), me semble être un usage particulier et historiquement situable de l'apostrophe, caractéristique de la poésie romantique. La capacité d'instituer l'espace de parole est sur le fond identique lorsque le poète s'adresse, plutôt qu'à la Nature, à un interlocuteur humain (théorique ou non, dans la poésie amoureuse: 'J'ai tant rêvé de toi que tu perds ta réalité'[10]), ou à un être transcendant mais objet de croyance véritable, partagée ou non (Dieu dans les Psaumes ou dans la poésie mystique, chez Claude Hopil, chez Claudel); et même à un membre de l'élite professionnelle, intellectuelle ou sociale à laquelle le poète prétend appartenir, ou appartient de fait: car ce qui compte est que celui-ci soit présenté comme le destinataire pertinent du poème: 'Tu jouis (mon Ronsard) mesmes durant ta vie / De l'immortel honneur que tu as mérité'.[11] Je dirais pour ma part que la figure de l'apostrophe exemplifie de manière maximale, démonstrative, une structure dont la portée est plus large; qu'on peut donc y voir, plutôt qu'une condition générale du lyrisme, son emblème énonciatif.

Le caractère créateur de monde du lyrisme n'entraîne pas comme conséquence que le monde créé par le poème soit fictif *en tant que tel*. Je préfère dire que la différence entre fiction et non-fiction se trouve neutralisée: elle n'a pas d'importance. Il y aurait trop à perdre à dire que le lyrisme n'est que fiction, et dans bien des cas c'est contre-intuitif. Que vaudrait le poème de Blake, 'London', des *Songs of experience*, si le *youthful Harlot's curse* et le *Marriage hearse* n'étaient que des fictions sans rapport avec la vie des hommes?[12] C'est de la réalité que le poète nous parle, une réalité plus essentielle (je ne dis pas: profonde, car elle n'est en rien dissimulée) que la réalité empirique: c'est bien à 'notre' réalité empirique qu'il donne du sens. Ce que nous devrions essayer de comprendre, c'est l'attitude épistémique induite par la poésie lyrique et appropriée à elle: ce qui correspond au 'willing suspension of disbelief' que Coleridge postule pour la fiction. Pour la poésie lyrique en effet, la notion de croyance ne convient pas. Ce qui varie me semble-t-il selon que le poète invoque un 'objet inanimé' ou au contraire 'Andromaque' — et par contraste le cygne, dans ce même poème de Baudelaire — c'est plutôt le type d'émotion sollicitée; celle que soulève le cygne est de nature allégorique, celle que suscite l'image d'une personne humaine comme Andromaque 'Auprès d'un tombeau vide en extase courbée'[13] touche les régions d'une empathie plus intime; qu'Andromaque soit une fiction (proposition qui en elle-même, n'a de sens que par rapport à une conception positiviste de l'histoire) n'y intervient nullement.

La Scansion langagière

Il y a un autre moyen de constituer l'espace et le mode de communication propres à la poésie lyrique: c'est de battre la mesure. Le vers en tant que tel représente ou emblématise cette propriété fondamentale. Plutôt qu'aux sociétés archaïques, que je ne connais que par ouï-dire, je pense au *rap* contemporain. Même s'il est souvent fruste, il montre très bien comment une scansion *langagière* — j'insiste sur ce point, une guitare ou une batterie n'ont pas le même office — suffit à structurer un espace d'énonciation, à poser dans un rapport dialogique spécifique des instances que la subjectivité investit aussitôt, et dont se dégage une euphorie ou une violence communautaires. La scansion n'institue pas le lyrisme de la même manière que l'apostrophe; mais elle a le même pouvoir fondamental d'auto-réalisation. Elle n'a pas besoin de raconter ni de transmettre, elle se passe de *mimesis* et même de scène: en se communiquant à l'auditeur, elle fait advenir la poésie du poète.

Cependant elle est limitée: la scansion langagière constitue une structure assez rudimentaire en comparaison des possibilités offertes aussi bien par la composition musicale (dans quelque style que ce soit) que par le sémantisme du langage naturel. En elle-même elle n'offre pas de possibilité de développement contrapuntique ni métalinguistique ou 'polyphonique' au sens des linguistes. Elle est par conséquent vouée à entrer en composition avec d'autres procédés qui augmentent ses possibilités de variation et lui confèrent des ressources réflexives: c'est-à-dire avec une rhétorique. Il faut cela pour passer de *Grand corps malade* à 'Amas doré d'ombres et d'abandons'[14] (on peut préférer le premier, mais dans nos métiers il était difficile de s'y tenir).

Apostrophe et scansion sont des processus véritablement constitutifs du lyrisme; ils sont la plupart du temps associés et il est difficile de les hiérarchiser. Les deux suivants, au contraire, supposent que le cadre générique soit déjà constitué.

La Figure

Le troisième moyen pour la poésie de se produire comme puissance d'auto-réalisation réside dans sa capacité de nommer: son pouvoir adamique. Laurent Jenny a mis en évidence dans *La Parole singulière* l'événementialité langagière de la figure avec autant de force que Jonathan Culler l'a fait pour l'apostrophe.[15] Ce procédé, pas plus que les précédents, n'est propre au genre lyrique; mais il y est plus nécessaire qu'ailleurs: c'est en lui que réside la magie démiurgique à quoi le lyrisme prétend.

Je ne m'y étends pas. Il suffit de dire: 'thy bed of crimson joy' (Blake), 'a grief ago' (Dylan Thomas), *Capitale de la douleur.* La métaphore n'est même pas nécessaire. Dans le poème que j'ai déjà évoqué, 'Royauté', Rimbaud écrit: 'En effet ils furent rois toute une matinée où les tentures carminées se relevèrent sur les maisons'. Remarquons que l'adjectif dans lequel se manifeste la puissance du lyrisme n'est pas métaphorique, non plus que le verbe 'se relevèrent': l'*auto*-réalisation est dite par l'absence d'agent, par ces tentures qui se meuvent d'elles-mêmes (qu'on ne parle pas ici de réflexivité!) et dont la couleur, aurait dit Pascal, 'éclate aux esprits'.

Le Parallélisme

J'aurais pu dire 'structure', mais je préfère reprendre le terme de Jakobson en lui donnant l'extension la plus large. Il s'agit en effet d'une structure *actualisée* par des procédés d'itération de niveau variable, mais tels qu'ils apparaissent comme une configuration, c'est-à-dire qu'on ne puisse plus les considérer seulement comme des faits d'itération: en d'autres termes que la séquence syntagmatique devienne le principe d'organisation d'un paradigme. Ceci est bien connu, mais ne constitue pas à mes yeux une définition alternative ou concurrente du lyrisme, puisqu'il s'agit d'un facteur évident d'auto-réalisation.

Cependant la structure nous oriente vers l'idée d'une *poésie de la poésie*, ce qui est autre chose qu'une *poésie du poète*. Elle n'est pas liée à l'établissement d'une relation de communication, ce que Jakobson formule en disant que la fonction poétique n'est pas une fonction comme une autre, mais un type particulier de 'visée'. Comme l'a vu avec perspicacité Frye, la structure ainsi entendue est l'emblème d'un objet et non d'un acte.[16] Ceci me conduit à ma conclusion.

Il y a là en effet un processus par lequel le poème lyrique tend à se détacher du poète. Cette émancipation est nécessaire dans une culture de l'écrit à la bonne transmission du message et à son appropriation par le récepteur; on la voit à l'œuvre très tôt, dès la période archaïque. Mais parfois, souvent même chez les romantiques, le poème se retourne contre le poète. Dans le second 'Spleen' de Baudelaire, la solidité cristalline des parallélismes construits autour des adjectifs dérivés en position d'épithètes antéposées, 'boiteuses journées' et 'neigeuses années', contredit avec une sorte d'ironie objective le thème initial, c'est-à-dire l'éparpillement du sujet en fouillis de vieux papiers. Le poème fait le contraire de ce qu'il dit, et le poète le laisse faire; mais c'est un poète moderne, qui sait qu'il y a une beauté saisissante et cruelle à travailler contre soi, comme l'*Héautontimorouménos*.

Lorsque le poète permet au poème de se montrer en gloire sur la page, dans l'évidence de sa différence typographique, il laisse se produire entre lui et son œuvre, qui n'est plus exactement une parole, une sorte de scission. Est-ce chez Baudelaire l'aveu d'une crise du lyrisme 'à l'apogée du capitalisme', crise dont l'ironie romantique aurait formé le prologue? Ce genre d'explication me semble banal, et peu adéquat. Il existe pourtant une tension, dont la source n'est pas la transmission au lecteur et l'itération mémorielle, en quoi on peut voir au contraire la destinée heureuse du lyrisme: mais plutôt la possibilité que le texte se referme sur lui-même et opère pour son propre compte. En ce sens la faillite du lyrisme, ou son ennemi mortel, serait le *texte* comme le voyaient les avant-gardes critiques des années 1970 — si cette idée du texte n'est pas elle-même un fantasme.

Je me bornerai donc, pour finir, à deux exemples. Le premier est celui d'une réappropriation magistrale de la structure par le poète: c'est le *Coup de dés* de Mallarmé, que l'on peut définir comme le geste par lequel la poésie du poète, sa puissance d'auto-réalisation, se projette dans une structure visible; geste où triomphe la conception la plus fondamentale, la plus radicale du lyrisme tel que je l'ai ici défini. Le second est presque au nadir: c'est le petit bonhomme de *Paysage*, le calligramme d'Apollinaire: 'Amants couchés ensemble vous vous séparerez mes membres', dont le *a* en minuscule grasse de grand corps représente le visage de profil. Au lieu de s'inscrire dans l'espace du spectateur et de s'adresser à lui, le personnage s'inscrit dans l'espace du tableau, comme un acteur de l'histoire qui nous est montrée sans que nous y soyons impliqués. Le poème se détourne du lyrisme comme le personnage se détourne de nous pour aller vers son destin. C'est toujours Orphée, mais ce qui reste d'Orphée quand son propre pouvoir le projette sur l'espace hostile d'une page 'absolument moderne', celle de l'éternel retour.

Notes

1. Jonathan Culler, *Theory of the Lyric* (Cambridge, MA: Harvard University Press, 2015). Guido Mazzoni, *Sur la poésie moderne* [Bologne: Il Mulino, 2005], trad. Céline Frigau Manning (Paris: Garnier, 2014). Ma réflexion s'est nourrie de discussions avec Jonathan Culler, puis avec Guido Mazzoni lors de leurs séjours comme professeurs invités à l'ENS. Le présent article est la version remaniée d'un exposé présenté lors d'une journée d'étude sur le lyrisme, organisée en 2008 avec Jonathan Culler et autour de son travail.
2. Voir par exemple Earl Miner, *Comparative Poetics: An Intercultural Essay on Theories of Literature* (Princeton, NJ: Princeton University Press, 1990). Pour la lyrique grecque, voir Claude Calame, *Masques d'autorité: fiction et pragmatique dans la poétique grecque* (Paris: Les Belles Lettres, 2005).
3. Je ne tiens compte ici ni de l'histoire de cette 'triade', ni des critères de définition fixés à l'époque romantique. Sur ces questions voir Gérard Genette, *Introduction à l'architexte* (Paris: éd. du Seuil, 1979).
4. Florence Dupont, *Aristote ou le vampire du théâtre occidental* (Paris: Aubier, 2007).
5. Lorsque la scène mimétique n'existe pas, le genre tend à se définir par défaut en relation avec le genre lyrique, dont il partage le caractère d'institution rituelle. C'est très bien vu dans *La Quête d'Averroès* de Borges: faute de pouvoir définir (et traduire) *tragœdia* et *comœdia* dans une culture où la scène n'existe pas, Averroès les identifie à un genre brillamment représenté dans le Coran, à savoir le 'panégyrique', le discours de célébration à la manière de Pindare.
6. Je me sépare sur ce point du courant critique qui a fait florès en France après la publication du livre édité par Dominique Rabaté, *Figures du sujet lyrique* (Paris: PUF, 1996), et qui s'est épuisé à démonter (ou à dépasser) l'opposition entre le lyrisme défini comme expérience subjective authentique et le lyrisme entendu comme discours d'une *persona* fictionnelle.
7. Nathalie Heinich, *L'Elite artiste: excellence et singularité en régime démocratique* (Paris: Gallimard, 2005).
8. Northrop Frye, *Anatomie de la critique* [Princeton, NJ: Princeton University Press, 1957], traduction par Guy Durand (Paris: Gallimard, 1969).
9. Jonathan Culler, 'Apostrophe', *Diacritics*, 7.4 (1977), 59–69.
10. Robert Desnos, 'J'ai tant rêvé de toi', *A la mystérieuse* [1928], repris dans *Corps et biens* [1930] (Paris: Gallimard/Poésie, 1968).
11. Joachim du Bellay, *Les Regrets* [1558], sonnet XX.
12. William Blake, *Songs of experience* [1794], 'London': 'But most thro' midnight streets I hear | How the youthful Harlot's curse | Blasts the new born Infant's tear | And blights with plagues the Marriage hearse' ('Mais surtout par les rues nocturnes j'entends | La malédiction de la jeune Prostituée | Dessécher les larmes de l'Enfant nouveau-né | Et frapper de pestilence le corbillard du mariage').
13. Charles Baudelaire, 'Le Cygne', *Les Fleurs du mal* [1861].
14. Paul Valéry, 'La Dormeuse', *Charmes* (Paris: Gallimard, 1922).
15. Laurent Jenny, *La Parole singulière* (Paris: Belin, 1992).
16. Il en voit une réalisation caractéristique dans l'énigme, définie comme 'réduction du langage à une forme visible', sorte de hiéroglyphe potentiellement associé à une image, dont l'équivalent rhétorique serait la désignation périphrastique, à la manière des *Kenningar* chers à Borges: 'la lune est le soleil des loups' (Northrop Frye, *op. cit.*, pp. 341–42).

— 25 —

Venise ou le Léviathan de nos jours ou humanisme & tourisme

Michel Deguy

(cette offerte à la mémoire du grand lettré notre ami Michael Sheringham trouve circonstance dans la manifestation des habitants de Venise le 13 septembre 2016 contre l'agonie touristique de leur cité devenue étape de la Croisière mondiale)

Du 14e au 21e siècle, l'Europe a été, aura été, la phase magnifique de l'humanité. Toute ici résumée, tangible: architecture, institutions, beautés espacées, ingéniosités associées, splendeur... Et 'tout' est achevé.

L'immensité de la République (de) Venise, un pays monde, est encore sous les yeux, de haut, carte-de-la-terre sous la carte du ciel, en synopsis comme la Rome 'regrettée' par Du Bellay: avec toutes les îles, le cordon du Lido, la rive terrestre.

Aujourd'hui, en plan sur mes genoux et en vaporetto, un œsophage-colon dans le réseau de ses veines, le pontage de ses vaisseaux, avalant, déjetant, vomissant, absorbant, comme une vieille ridée qui va se noyer.

Imagine un Léviathan hobbesien, le fameux dessin d'Abraham Bosse, tel que chaque tête devenue spécimen individualisé de multitude ethnique omniterrestre se presse en monstre à millions de faces spécifiques en écailles browniennes: multitude de multitudes reflétées.

La 'population mondiale' n'a pas seulement augmenté arithmétiquement: nous sommes huit milliards, dit le démographe. Mais un humain aujourd'hui, disons: consomme (ou existe, ou installe...) dix fois plus que son aïeul au 18ème siècle (considéré par Lévi-Strauss comme celui de l'équilibre terrestre). Autrement dit, nous sommes, vivants, 80 milliards, peut-être 800 milliards.

Sur le pont Rialto, de loin à ton arrivée, DIESEL en vingt mètres de hauteur, une 'marque'. Venise est une énorme boutique de luxes et de pacotilles, de 'faux'. Venise est son aéroport prolongé, étendu: croisements de groupes dans le bruit langagier de leurs usages, de leurs types, se ruant vers les *soldes*, précipitation anxieuse vers les *gates* dans le chaos du *Duty Free*. Que font les clients distincts en flux de consommateurs? Ils (se) photographient. C'est le passage: tout le passé *passe* en millions de photos par minutes, sans interruption, un gelato dans la bouche du selfiste.

Car personne — stupeur — ne visite plus. Accademia, San Rocco, Frari, Correr... ces jours de plein août, Léviathan est au dehors, millions de 'touristes'; l'amateur a disparu. Imaginez la Scuola Grande de Tintoret vide. Cinq à six Japonais *entrent* dans la Salute. Quelques contemporains à la Dogana, impeccable évidement central où les blancs se regardent, 'accrochés', où nulle 'œuvre' ne parle de la fin de l'art; de la fin de Venise. Venise est une *installation*, répliquée homothétiquement par la 'librairie' *Acqua Alta*, toute une gondole bourrée d'albums sur Venise, et dans les cours les monceaux d'in-octavo ruisselant du dernier orage. Le narrateur s'assied sous le *Condottiere* de Verrocchio, l'équestre *sublime* à dix mètres de haut.

C'est la *lagune*. Que se passait-il avant les moteurs? Peut-on même évaluer l'effet sur la mer lagunée des millions de moteurs en marche surpuissante? Il n'y a plus de Venise république, projet, aventure vers le monde, puissance, 'grandeur', *polder*... Une *réserve*, oui, mais de quoi? Etrangement le narrateur songe au Parc Kruger, entre l'Afrique du Sud et le Mozambique, où les grands animaux sont conservés vivants. Serait-ce ici que l'humanité devenue touristique est exposée?

— 26 —

Oxford

Stephen Romer

for Micky Sheringham

In the pink (salmon?) and luminous high room
the conversation is of the mot juste
and surely the mot juste must presuppose
something out there to which justice may be done?
What shade exactly of yellow really is it, say,
twines and untwines in the early autumn
(September) sunshine (sunlight)
over the head of my learned interlocutor
who is talking closely of the *pays de cocagne*
and how from wordplay the nevertheless solid artefact
may come into being without atmosphere, how indisputably
the signs agree there arose a rose — or indeed
a braid, twine, plait, mane revolving silently in the light
beyond my interlocutor through the window
uninvented, I'm inventing nothing — romantic throwback! —
this is happening in my life now (then) *because it is (was)*
a twine of lime or is it sycamore? — I cannot see from here —
(could not see from there) — is untwining against All Souls —
and knowing *which* is life or death, I cannot help feeling
(*feeling?!*) — the life or death of this poem.

— 27 —

On Turning-Points

A Sermon Preached in the Chapel of All Souls College on Sunday, 2 November 2008

Michael Sheringham

A few months ago I went to a meeting of the Humanities Divisional Board. For the first time, it was being held in the newly refurbished building that has become the headquarters of the History Faculty. This was the old City of Oxford High School for Boys in George Street, dating from the 1880s, and in the less enthralling bits of the meeting my eyes wandered round the high ceilings and mullioned windows as I tried to imagine what it would have been like full of schoolboys, and to compare it with the classrooms of my own Victorian Grammar School. Then, all of a sudden, it struck me that this was the school my father had attended in the mid-1920s, and I remembered that he had been deeply unhappy there. It was very strange to feel that in the room where I was sitting, experiencing at worst mild boredom, on another Friday afternoon eighty-five years earlier, my father may have suffered very acutely; that the same walls could have been witness to his distress and my sudden discomfiture, when the gulf between past and present suddenly narrowed.

My father's inability to cope with Oxford Boys led his parents to take an unusual step. Through family connections he was sent off to be tutored by the Reverend William Ellison, the Director of Armagh Observatory, who was also a noted Hebrew scholar. My father learnt astronomy, was taught Hebrew, and generally seems to have thrived in this unusual set-up. He went on to outstanding studies in oriental languages at Trinity College Dublin, to theology, colonial service, and broadcasting. He had a long and varied life.

In retrospect, what happened to my father at Oxford Boys was a watershed. It altered the landscape of his life. Changing the metaphor, it constituted a new start. There was a before and an after: it was a turning-point. But what do we mean when we talk of turning-points? Do they exist? Are there criteria for establishing whether an event was a turning-point, particularly where individual lives are concerned? The question can be asked in different ways. But I think it has a bearing on what we do as we mark All Souls Day, and commemorate the actions of our predecessors between these walls and outside them. Our college is a repository of lives, and to reflect on the stuff that lives are made of, and on their grammar, so to speak, is to think about what commemoration can mean.

Turning-points in individual lives are about change, and the capacity to change (or else the capacity steadfastly to refuse change) and it's reasonable to wonder if, even in the most apparently secular of contexts, there isn't always a religious dimension, and to ask if the ethical aspect of turning-points doesn't always carry with it the aura of conversion. One of the things that makes St Augustine's account of his conversion so gripping — in western autobiography this is the mother of turning-points — is the tension between psychological truth and, on the one hand, narrative truth, and on the other hand, religious truth. In the Scriptures, conversions are generally rapid; the turning-point involves responding to God's call, on the road to Damascus for example. The travails of the doubting individual may be evident, but they are seldom dwelt upon or dramatized, as they are so touchingly in the Book of Jonah. Jonah tries to hide himself from God's presence. He resists God's call to go to Nineveh and goes to Joppa instead, 'and [...] found a ship going to Tarshish [...] paid the fare thereof, and went down into it, to go with them unto Tarshish from the presence of the LORD' (Jonah 1. 3).

Augustine's great turning-point is the 'Tolle, lege' incident. The year is 386. Augustine is a Professor of Rhetoric residing in Milan. He is in a dreadful state: one by one, all his intellectual doubts, emotional reservations, and scruples about Christianity have been dispelled. No longer a Manichean, he is available, and in principle willing. But he is stuck on the brink, unable to cross the divide between his old self and a new one, seemingly incapable of giving up his old attachments and sensual appetites. He goes out into the garden in tears, and throws himself down by a fig-tree. And then it happens. He hears 'the sing-song voice of a child in a nearby house' saying, again and again, the words 'Tolle, lege', 'Tolle, lege' — 'Take it and read it, Take and read'. He wonders if it's a children's game, concludes it isn't, and assumes that this must be a 'divine command' to 'open my book of scripture and read the first words on which my eyes should fall'. He picks up the copy of Paul's *Epistles* that he'd jettisoned earlier, and reads the first passage on which his eyes alight. It is an exhortation to give up bodily appetites in favour of Christ, and it fits him like a glove, or a glass slipper: he tells us that by the time he'd reached the end of the sentence, all his doubts had been dispelled, and confidence filled his heart.

This was a turning-point.

Or was it? Certainly it makes a good story. When we read *The Confessions* this sequence pulls Augustine's life into focus. It gives what was inchoate a clear shape. But how appropriate is it to suggest that this moment gave Augustine's life its meaning, turned it into a destiny? In many ways it's obvious that the 'Tolle, lege' is symbolic rather than real. Far from coming out of the blue, the incident is the culmination of a complex process recounted in detail, and the moment of conversion is foreshadowed in numerous ways. For example, just before, a friend, Ponticianus, tells Augustine about Anthony of Egypt's conversion which had involved falling on some words from St Matthew; and then another story about a colleague whose conversion had been prompted by reading a life of Anthony. Augustine's description of this act of reading is remarkable for its account of a spirit in the throes of metamorphosis,

> [...] he turned back to the book, labouring under the pain of the new life that was taking birth in him. He read on, and in his heart, where you alone could see, a change was taking place.

Augustine acknowledges the impact *on him* of his friend's account of the effects, on one man, of reading about the conversion of another:

> While he was speaking, O Lord, you were turning me around to look at myself. For I had placed myself behind my own back, refusing to see myself. You were setting me before my own eyes [...]

If the multiple strands and mirrorings of Augustine's narrative undermine the literal truth of a chain of events, what is conveyed is an inner process working at several levels, turning on the difficulty of breaking the chain of habit, and the feeling of being 'one soul torn between conflicting wills'. We are shown someone who knows obscurely that he is changing, but is somehow frozen, unable to break out of his old self.

Too much emphasis on the 'Tolle, lege' incident can obviously seem a gross betrayal of the real meaning. And when one looks more closely, as Augustine's commentators have done, there is much to suggest that he may not have meant us to read too literally since most of the ingredients were traditional or conventional — the suddenness of the conversion, the garden, the fig-tree, the child's voice, the practice of 'sortes biblicae' where the scriptural text opened at random is considered divinatory. Moreover, not surprisingly, the substantial iconography of the 'Tolle, lege', including a famous painting by Fra Angelico, filters out the ambiguity. The way Augustine tells it, there were crucial moments of interpretation and decision, even within the incident itself: he had to decipher the child's call, open the book, decide what the words meant. But the paintings usually depict chubby cherubim bearing scrolls and little flags emblazoned with the magic words, 'tolle lege', as in a game show where the grinning compère urges: 'go on, open the box'.

It may be that turning-points answer a need for coherence, but at the risk of traducing something very valuable — the fact that to live is to change and to be changed, and that the capacity to turn can be a virtue as well as a skill. It's one thing to see turning-points as vantage points, as sites of recognition where we take stock of something that has been happening for quite a while — a fine example would be the point in the course of Newman's immensely subtle and powerful account of the intellectual and emotional currents at work in his conversion process, where he famously exclaims 'I looked in the mirror and I was a Monophysite'. But it is another thing to attribute substantial agency to what is adventitious. There is something ambivalent about the whole notion of turning that makes me feel equally ambivalent about Mrs Thatcher's 'The Lady's not for turning', and Bill Clinton shamelessly milking the motif of turning at a White House Prayer Meeting, after the Lewinski affair, where he cited at length a beautiful passage from a Yom Kippur liturgy which begins: 'Now is the time for turning. The leaves are beginning to turn from green to red to orange [...] [but] for us turning does not come so easily [...]'

In Samuel Beckett's play *That Time* the protagonist talks of a series of moments involving a loss of identity, times when 'you started not knowing who you were from Adam'. And he then invokes a turning-point. But the burden of this turn is that turning-points are bogus, that their logic of before and after, up till then, and ever since, doesn't fit with a profound sense that experience is endless discontinuity, with no events to speak of, only changes, and with the plain fact of birth, seen as expulsion from the womb into an alien universe, as the only real event:

> Never the same [Beckett's character muses] but the same as what for God's sake did you ever say I to yourself in your life come on now could you ever say I to yourself in your life turning-point that was a great word with you before they dried up altogether always having turning-points and never but the one the first and last that time curled up worm in slime when they lugged you out and wiped you off and straightened you up.

Henry James once expressed a robust scepticism when William Dean Howells put it to him that 'every man's life had had its turning-point'. And when his friend insisted that James's year at Harvard Law School, where he spurned legal studies for novel writing, 'must have' been a turning-point, James observes that he

> welcomed the suggestion — for the kindly grace of it, the element of antique charm and bedimmed romance that it placed, straight away, at the disposal of my memory; [...] I wondered whether I mightn't find, on ingenious reflection, that my youth had in fact enjoyed that amount of drama.

The fastidious doubt could hardly be more patent: 'ingenious reflection' sounds like arbitrary fabrication, 'romance' and 'drama' seem to place the turning-point squarely in the domain of fiction. Yet as he warms to the theme, James gives a fine evocation of the 'momentous junctures in question':

> Occasions of the taking of the ply that is never again to be lost, occasions of the true vocation or the right opportunity recognised more or less in a flash, determinations in short of character and purpose and above all of a sharper and finer consciousness.

James sees turning-points as the products of ratiocination and semi-fictive construction. To look for a turning-point is to examine one's life in a certain way, responding to the appeal of what he calls 'the question itself'. We could say that for him the turning-point is a cognitive device that fosters a certain kind of attention to the self, a particular sort of transaction between an individual and his or her past experience.

To play down the dramaturgy of turning-points in our sense of human lives can have the twin virtues of acknowledging the place of fiction and narrative in self-understanding, and of playing up the importance of the uneventful, the ordinary and the quotidian, the shapelessness of our everyday existence, and the value of paying attention to it without turning it into something else. And yet I think that there are reasons — spiritual reasons — for reflecting on turning-points. And one reason is that to think of a life as having a shape, as hanging together around some major articulations, is a way of bridging the gap between ourselves and others.

In W. B. Yeats's poem 'All Souls Night', written in Oxford in 1920, the poet summons up the souls of his late friends Horton, Florence Emery, and McGregor.

Encapsulating each one's life course in a couple of stanzas, Yeats draws out the tension between earthly or bodily commitments and a spiritual vocation that took his friends to wilder shores. And in each case he pitches the balance between solitude and community, which he identifies in all three lives, on a key turn — the death of Horton's wife, Florence's decision to become a missionary teacher, the 'meditations upon unknown thought' that left McGregor 'crazed' with loneliness. For his act of commemoration Yeats invokes a particular mode of thought that can wind like a 'mummy-cloth', embalming and preserving, but more importantly can emulate the wanderings of the soul; so that, 'wound in mind's wandering', the poet communes with the departed in their ethereal realm. We may legitimately prefer to come back to the firmer ground of Yeats's other great biographical poem, 'The Municipal Gallery Revisited' where, having reviewed the portraits of many of his friends, the poet asks to be judged in the company of the lives that were intertwined with his rather than alone.

There are things about living that turning-points cannot fathom. But equally there are dimensions of our lives, including that part of ourselves that exists through community with others, through fellowship for example, that the language of turns and turning-points, the language of what Kipling called 'pivot-experiences', can help us perceive. However dubious they often seem, turning-points have a significant place in collective memory. Yet here, as in the personal sphere — in Augustine for example — the process of sense-making is what counts, more than the product. Although it may be a device for shaping or quarrelling with oneself — a way of thinking — the turning-point may ultimately be above all an emblem, an *aide-mémoire*, a mnemonic. Some events have necessarily life-changing consequences. Yet even then, what will make them turning-points in the life of an individual, or a collective body, is the way they are lived through, confronted, evaded, edited. The mood of the turning-point may be imperative — 'This do in remembrance of Me' (Luke 22. 19) — but its true tense is the future perfect: this will have been a turning-point.

Insisting that we pay heed to the abject, sprawling untidiness of selfhood, the 'foul rag and bone shop of the heart', Yeats invited us to be sceptical of 'masterful images because complete', and notably of 'Character isolated by a deed | To engross the present and dominate memory'. One can see what he means. But we can also share, I think, the implication that 'masterful images', of the kind that turning-points provide, have a rightful part to play in the ways we engage with, and think about, ourselves and others.

References

SAMUEL BECKETT, *That Time*, in *Collected Shorter Plays* (New York: Grove Press, 1984)

HENRY JAMES, 'The Turning Point of My Life', in *The Complete Notebooks of Henry James*, ed. by L. Edel and Lyall H. Powers (New York: Oxford University Press, 1987)

SAINT AUGUSTINE, *Confessions*, trans. by H. Chadwick (Oxford: OUP World's Classics, 1991)

W. B. YEATS, *Collected Poems* (London: Macmillan, 1982)

RUDYARD KIPLING, *Something of Myself* (Harmondsworth: Penguin Books, 1977)

INDEX

www.ingramcontent.com/pod-product-compliance
Lightning Source LLC
Chambersburg PA
CBHW080326030726
47593CB00010B/2905

9781781883549